George Clarke Musgrave

**To Kumassi with Scott**

A Description of a Journey From Liverpool to Kumassi with the Ashanti ...

George Clarke Musgrave

**To Kumassi with Scott**
*A Description of a Journey From Liverpool to Kumassi with the Ashanti ...*

ISBN/EAN: 9783337011109

Printed in Europe, USA, Canada, Australia, Japan

Cover: Foto ©Andreas Hilbeck / pixelio.de

More available books at **www.hansebooks.com**

# TO KUMASSI WITH SCOTT.

A DESCRIPTION OF A JOURNEY FROM LIVERPOOL TO
KUMASSI WITH THE ASHANTI EXPEDITION, 1895-6.

BY

## GEORGE C. MUSGRAVE.

---

WITH ILLUSTRATIONS FROM SKETCHES BY
MR. H. C. SEPPINGS WRIGHT, ARTIST CORRESPONDENT TO THE
"ILLUSTRATED LONDON NEWS," AND OTHERS.

---

London:
WIGHTMAN & Co.,
"THE WESTMINSTER PRESS," REGENCY STREET, S.W.
1896.

*By special permission of*
H.R.H. PRINCESS HENRY OF BATTENBERG.

TO THE MEMORY
OF
COLONEL PRINCE HENRY MAURICE OF BATTENBERG,
MAJOR V. J. FERGUSON,
AND
THE OTHER OFFICERS, NON-COMMISSIONED OFFICERS AND MEN,
WHO LOST THEIR LIVES
IN THE CAUSE OF HUMANITY AND CIVILIZATION IN
ASHANTI, 1895-6,
THIS WORK IS RESPECTFULLY INSCRIBED.

# PREFACE.

The 1895-6 Expedition to Ashanti took place at a time when the British Empire was in a ferment; wars and rumours of wars abounded on all sides. Excitement ran high, and in the midst of the turmoil, the operations in West Africa were forgotten or put aside for matters of more pressing import. Newspapers were full; the international troubles caused much pressure on their space, and little beyond brief telegrams on the movements of the force, was published; therefore, a more comprehensive account of the expedition will be of interest to many.

The campaign was a bloodless one, but none the less heroic; for that march to Kumassi, through dense forest and deadly swamp, was fraught with perils more to be dreaded than the arms of the savage Ashantis.

The British force marched 140 miles through the jungle, leaving numbers on the road, sick of fever and dysentery. They invested the capital; the King and his chiefs were captured, the bloody fetish power destroyed, and the force, sadly reduced by sickness, returned to the coast, having freed a large district from the tyranny of a bloodthirsty despot and opened up a vast territory to trade and civilization.

This record of the expedition is chiefly comprised of a series of articles and letters written at different times and places on the journey from England to the Gold Coast and on the march up country, which I have endeavoured to make of general interest by touching on the habits and customs of the people, digressing somewhat from a formal account of the campaign alone. The march did not lack interesting incidents, especially as we drew near to and entered Kumassi, and I have attempted to faithfully portray these various scenes on the road.

GEORGE C. MUSGRAVE.

FOLKESTONE, *June, 1896.*

# CONTENTS.

## CHAPTER I.

Leaving England—Our Passengers—The Canary Islands—Las Palmas—Teneriffe—Orotava—The Peak . . . . . . . 1

## CHAPTER II.

The Gambia—Sierra Leone—Freetown—The West India Regiment—Sherbro Island—Secret Societies—Liberia—The Kroo Tribes—Cape Palmas—The Gold Coast Surf—Major Piggott—View of Cape Coast Castle . . . . . . . . . . 11

## CHAPTER III.

Ashanti—Kumassi Dynasty—Previous Quarrels—Sir Garnet Wolseley's Expedition—Osai Mensah—Adansi—The Last Trouble with the Ashantis—Sir Francis Scott's Force . . . . . . 28

## CHAPTER IV.

The Gold Coast—Cape Coast Castle—Filth and Neglect in the Town—The Special Service Officers—Captain Larrymore—The White Race—King Tackie— Foreign Competition — Missionaries — A Fanti Wedding—A Fetish Funeral—A Native Ball—Christmas in Fantiland—Maternity . . . . . . . . . . 43

## CHAPTER V.

Ashanti Envoys—The Palaver—West African Squadron—The White Troops—To the Front!—Bicycling in Africa—Akraful—Night in the Bush—Cowardly Niggers—African Villages—Mansu—Attempted Murder . . . . . . . . . . 67

## CHAPTER VI.

Sunday in the Wilds—Prince Henry's Donkeys—Lost Kit—The Artillery—Assin Yan Comasse—African Royalty and European Ideas—A King—Fetish Ceremonies—Prahsu—Crocodiles—New Year's Day—The Ansah Princes—The Ashanti in War—Staff Officers described—Arrival of the Troops—The Houssas—The Mohammedan Negro . . . . . . . . . .

## CHAPTER VII.

Over the Prah—Loathsome Diseases—The Native Levy — Flying Column to Bekwai—Akusirem—Fumsu — Braffu Eadru—Native Dishes—Long Pig Chop or Iguana—A Riot—The Adansis—Death of Major Ferguson—Snakes . . . . . . . . 108

## CHAPTER VIII.

Prince Henry Ill—Fomonah—An Alarm — Annexing of Bekwai and Abadoom—The Kings described—The Drink Question in Africa—News of Prince Henry—Through the Swamps—A Dash from Bekwai—Native Beauty—Darwinism—Advance in Close Column—Camped in the Forest—An Ashanti Embassy—An Unfortunate Occurrence—Near the Goal—Tornado in the Forest . . . 129

## CHAPTER IX.

Kumassi—King Prempeh—The Queen Mother—Courtiers—A State Reception in Kumassi—A Procession by Torchlight—The Golgotha—The Royal Palace—Sacrifices—Sunday in Ashanti—The Last Scene—Prempeh's Downfall—The Loot . . . . . 151

## CHAPTER X.

Bantama described—Human Sacrifices—The Fall of Fetishism—Africa for the Africans—Samory—Fetish Trees Destroyed—English Impressions—The Future of Ashanti—A Midnight Reconnaissance—Prempeh's Country House . . . . . . . . 184

## CHAPTER XI.

Coastward March—Peace Society Precepts—Death of Prince Henry—Eating Dead Bodies—A Civilised Negro—The Coast—Arrival of Prempeh—Conclusion . . . . . . . . . 202

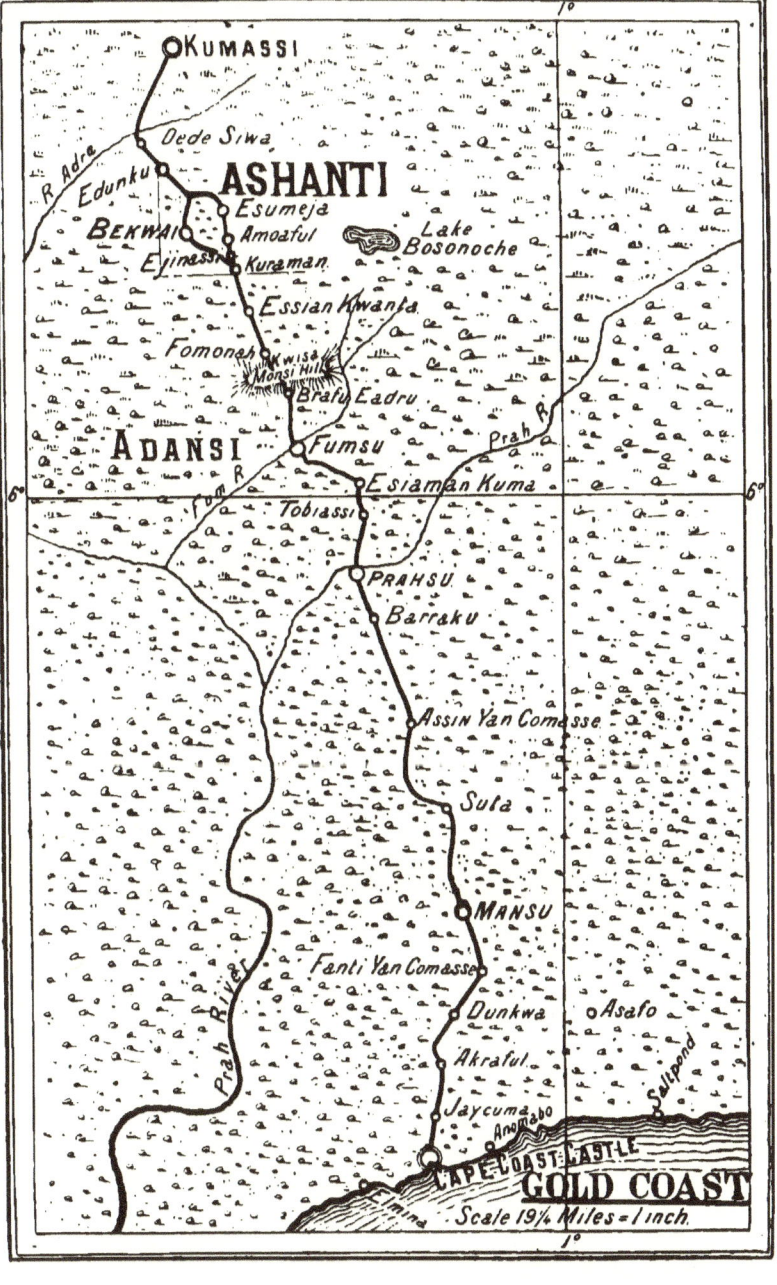

# TO KUMASSI WITH SCOTT.

## CHAPTER I.

LEAVING ENGLAND—OUR PASSENGERS—THE CANARY ISLANDS—LAS PALMAS
—TENERIFFE—OROTAVA—THE PEAK.

LIVERPOOL landing-stage in a thin slanting rain, with grimy dock labourers shifting hawsers off the bollards on a dirty wet quay, releasing the tender, and by so doing they part husband and wife, lover and sweetheart, mother and son. The outward bound ones crowd to the port side, the others cling to the chains on the edge of the wharf. Young wives, struggling to keep back the tears that will come, wave wet handkerchiefs to dear ones on board, while mother and sister say the parting words to son and brother. The tender reaches the ship, luggage is transferred and the vessel slowly steams down the river as cheer after cheer goes up from those on board and is answered by the crowd on shore. Then England, the dear old mother country, grows less distinct, till only a faint grey line is visible, and the feeble echo of a last cheer is borne across, almost drowned by the swish of the waves as the tide runs up the Mersey.

Such was the scene on November 30th, 1895, when the good ship "Loanda" started for West Africa.

We had on board officers and men to the number of 100, chiefly of the Army Service Corps and Engineers, also a detachment of Artillery for Sierra Leone. The holds were full of baggage, ammunition, filters, tanks and other stores for use in the forthcoming expedition to Ashanti for which the majority of passengers were bound.

There was a mixed company on board, among others being His Excellency Colonel Cardew, Governor of Sierra Leone, returning with his wife to resume his duties there; also his *aide de camp*, Captain Morant; Surgeon Colonel Taylor, Principal Medical Officer to the expedition; Captain Benson, commanding the Ashanti Artillery contingent; Surgeon-Captains Maher and Josling; Captain Norwood, R.A.; Captain Hall; Lieutenant Faber, R.E., and Mr. Haddon Smith, Assistant Colonial Secretary at Lagos; Mr. Bennett Burleigh of *Daily Telegraph* fame, and Mr. Seppings Wright, special Artist to the *Illustrated London News*, represented the Press, the remainder of the passengers being health-seekers for the Canaries to winter.

After passing Holyhead, we lost sight of land and everyone prepared to settle down for the voyage. The first day past, we were getting over what one may call the unsociability of the average Britisher, and officers and civilians alike were soon rubbing shoulders in the comfortable smoking room, driven in by a sweeping wind off the Channel. The ladies soon disappeared, and there were the usual melancholy faces of passengers vainly trying to ward off the remorseless *mal de mer* and appearing cheerfully at dinner, but their heroic efforts would only last through the soup, when a hasty retreat was beaten to watch the seascape from the ship's side. Many of us, more fortunate in not dreading the horrors of sea sickness, found plenty to occupy the time as we ploughed our way through the choppy outskirts of the Bay; but once passed Finisterre, the ladies emerged from their cabins, the sick ones re-appeared, and things brightened considerably on board. In the evenings we were enlivened by impromptu concerts on the troop deck, and it is marvellous what a large amount of talent can be found among British "Tommies" when opportunity arises for them to show it.

After Finisterre the temperature sensibly changes, the sun gives notice that it has come to stay, and we realised we were at last reaching the delights of a more southern latitude. Life on board became a pleasure as we steamed through a calm blue sea, and the time was passed by many diversions. Our genial skipper, Captain Jones, never let conversation flag when he was near, for he had an inexhaustible stock of anecdote ever ready. A sweep on the day's run of the vessel was instituted, and shuffle board or deck quoits freely indulged in.

A week after leaving Liverpool we reached Grand Canary, dropping anchor in the port of La Luz at 5 a.m. A glorious day was just dawning, the sun rising in almost eastern splendour.

After the usual formalities were gone through, we got a clean bill of health from the authorities, and as the yellow flag was hauled from the fore-peak, dozens of waiting bumboats closed in, our decks being swarmed by eager vendors of the various commodities that delight the eye of the traveller. The majority of these swarthy merchants dealt in tobacco, cigars, and Florida water, but there were many others with baskets of fruit, canaries in wicker cages, and native-worked fans and shawls. The collection was completed by two light-skinned Parsees with their suave salaams and stock of silks, shawls, and Benares work. One or more of these itinerant Hindoo merchants are to be found at every port of any size east or west. How they come and how they return to their own country again is a mystery, but they apparently thrive and are born traders with all their outward cringing and hypocritical cast of countenance.

From the ship, the Puerta de La Luz, and Las Palmas, which is some three miles distant, have a most picturesque appearance, the low flat-roofed white buildings looking truly oriental as they stretch away up the sides of the hills, which form a pleasing background in dark outline against a cloudless sky.

We were soon pulled ashore in one of the native boats manned by picturesque-looking ruffians who crowded round the foot of the gangway. Though the distance to the breakwater is barely 100 yards, the fare is on a sliding scale, which never goes below one shilling for each person, however you may try to beat them down. There were eleven passengers in the boat I journeyed in, and we were asked two shillings a head, reduced under pressure to one shilling—not a bad four minutes' work for three men to earn eleven shillings. It is as well not to remain late on shore when your vessel is leaving, especially at night, as the tales are many, of unwary travellers who have lingered till the warning whistle has sounded, and then found, to their dismay, the boatmen in league together, requiring a large sum before any of them will row to the ship. Remonstrance is in vain, and you must either accede to their exorbitant demands or lose the vessel. I heard of one case in which a belated traveller was rowed a few yards from the landing stage when the boatmen drew in their oars and demanded £5 before they would proceed. Unfortunately his ship had signalled twice and was on the point of sailing, so he had to pay up and look pleasant, hoping to obtain redress on arrival at the ship's side. The men rapidly drew off the moment he put his foot on the ladder, and disappeared in the gloom with a derisive " A good evening, Johnny."

By the way, every Englishman in Canary is addressed by the street boys and other pests in the familiar style of "Johnny," greatly incensing a pompous fellow traveller of ours visiting Las Palmas. As he stepped on the quay he was greeted by a volley of cries from the waiting cabriolet drivers, "Hi, you Johnny, take my car," to his evident annoyance and our amusement.

The Port of La Luz has almost a natural harbour formed by a small peninsula joining Grand Canary by a narrow isthmus, and a stone breakwater, built at right angles to this, forms the three sides of a square within which the largest vessels can float in safety. The harbour is easy of access at all tides, and this fact has no doubt done much in recent years to bring Grand Canary to the front as a coaling station.

Las Palmas can be reached from the landing stage by train, or rather steam tram, or a light tartana drawn by two or three horses may be hired to go by road, the charge being one peseta = 8d. for each person.

The horses of Canary are a distinct breed, being small, well formed, and very swift, but no proper care is taken of them, and few can be found that are not more or less covered with festering sores, while the drivers use the lash mercilessly. The hotels have private carriages and horses of their own for hire, and these are necessarily kept in a better condition.

Las Palmas itself does not offer many attractions to the visitor, and a day is sufficient to make one thoroughly acquainted with all places of interest in the city itself. The Cathedral is a large edifice in the centre of the town, and its two towers make it conspicuous at a long distance. It is a fine building from an architectural point of view, and contains some large and well executed frescoes, while the wood carving inside well repays a visit. The interior is Gothic, with three large naves, four transepts and chapels at the side. An intending visitor would do well to try and be present at the regular afternoon service which is fully choral. The organ is a splendid instrument, while the excellence of the choir quite keeps up the reputation that the Spanish Church has always held for its fine music.

The Bishop of Las Palmas had returned a few days before our visit and the island was *en fête* to receive him. He had been to Madrid to try and stop the conscription, which was denuding the Canaries of men to serve in the Spanish army in Cuba. Several had evaded the order by fleeing to the interior and hiding in the mountains, but two thus captured were shot as an example, and the offer of a free pardon to all who gave themselves up at once,

SCENE NEAR LAS PALMAS.

had the desired effect. The Bishop's mission was only partially successful, and the streets were thronged with miserable weedy looking conscripts lounging about in ordinary clothes, but arrayed in white helmets many sizes too large. The few Spanish regular troops stationed in the island appeared to be a smart body of men, with none of the slovenliness of dress usually a characteristic of continental armies, but the poor conscripts just about to start for Cuba were very inferior, appearing ridiculous against the smart English "non-coms." who were allowed on shore from the "Loanda." Spain at that time had more men in her last remaining American possession than the whole of the standing army of Great Britain, exclusive of the troops serving abroad, and yet she has been unable to quell the insurgents. She has depended a great deal on these young untrained men with the obvious result, and from reports I heard in Las Palmas, if the figures are ever published, we shall find the story of France and Madagascar retold with more action and bloody detail. Yellow Jack has made fearful ravages among these unacclimatized youths; for Cuba has a worse reputation perhaps for unhealthiness than any other part of the West Indies. The little news that does leak out is carefully watched and cut down by lynx-eyed officials before it can leave the country, and no reliance can be placed on any report published. The Canaryites have been specially favoured with conscription, as they are supposed to stand the climate better than their brothers in Spain.

Las Palmas boasts of a theatre, visited by various opera companies of more or less ability. Putting the merits of the performance on one side, the building itself and the interior fittings would put many more pretentious English playhouses in the shade. Near the Cathedral is a handsome building, the lower part of which is used for the municipal offices, the upper chambers for the museum. The interior of the building is elaborately fitted, the corridors and passages being decorated in a specially fine style, and the upper galleries are filled with a miscellaneous collection containing many unique specimens. Some of the corridors resemble our Royal College of Surgeons' Museum, but less ghastly and more interesting are the Guanche remains to be viewed. The Guanches were the original inhabitants of the islands, but any exact information as to who, and what they were, is difficult to obtain. As a race they were a harmless people, almost civilized in their habits, and having a good system of government. Spain attempted to obtain possession of the Canaries in 1385, but they did not succeed in bringing the whole group into subjection till a hundred years later. Under the cruel persecution of their relentless conquerors the last of the gallant Guanche race disappeared in the sixteenth century, since which time Spain has retained almost undisputed authority over the islands, which have become a Spanish province rather than a colony.

The guide of the museum was as great a curiosity as any of the specimens under his charge, for he not only refrained from asking for a gratuity, but firmly and politely refused one when offered.

I tried to obtain an order to visit the bone-yard attached to the cemetery, but found it was too difficult and tedious a matter to get the requisite permit, for the wheels of Spanish Officialism are clogged with red tape and move but slowly. The rich in Canary rent graves in the cemetery for their deceased friends, but with the poorer classes the remains are buried for a few months, the bones then being dug up and deposited in the adjoining bone-yard. This is certainly not a practice that commends itself from a hygienic standpoint, and shows little consideration for the feelings of the relatives, who know with what scant ceremony the remains of departed friends will be treated.

Las Palmas is well supplied with hotels, the three leading ones being under English management. Of these Quiney's, the oldest established, is right in the town, but the others, the Métropole and the Santa Catalina, are built in the outskirts on the road to the port. The Métropole is the leading hotel in Las Palmas, and as a sufficient guarantee for the excellence of all the arrangements, I may mention that it is one of the many enterprises of Mr. Alfred Jones, through whose indefatigable exertions the Canaries have entered a prosperous period after a chequered career under the proscriptive policy of Spain. Living is cheap in the islands, and at this palatial hotel it is possible to live in first-class style for 8s. per day inclusive.

The streets of the town are narrow but fairly clean, and the main thoroughfare is lined with pretentious looking shops.

What strikes one forcibly is the air of listless indolence that pervades everywhere. The proprietors of the shops sit lazily enjoying a cigarette at the door, drivers lounge on their carts with reins hanging loosely and horses going as they please; sentinels stand negligently at their posts leaning on their rifles and moodily smoking, while the people saunter in the streets in a languid but contented fashion of their own. The Canaryite is a lover of idleness, and shut off as he is from the outside world, he cares nothing for the rush and turmoil of the nations around him, but lives in perfect contentment, knowing he has enough for to-day and not caring what to-morrow may bring forth.

The chief food of the lower classes is gofio, a mixture of Indian corn and water. It is neither a difficult nor expensive meal to prepare, and the peasantry apparently thrive well on it with the addition of a little goat's flesh as an occasional treat.

The market presents a busy scene with rows of stalls heaped with fruit, and it is thronged by country people, who bring their produce to town on ponies or donkies which stagger under the combined weight of well-filled panniers and the lazy owner mounted on top.

The mantilla is the favourite head-dress of the women of all classes. The high-bred dames drape their heads in fine black lace, but their humbler sisters are content with black and white cashmere, the latter being the favourite, and serving to heighten the olive complexions of the dark-eyed senoritas.

Life is never dull in the islands, and if other things flag there are plenty of gay fiestas or semi-religious holidays, when the towns are brilliantly illuminated and the peasants flock in from the country, decked in glorious finery that has been purchased by many previous days of hunger. Then there are the plazas, where bands play every day, and golf, lawn tennis or cricket can be indulged in on well-kept grounds.

The houses are irregular but well built, enclosing many glorious little piazzas and gardens, shut out completely from the outside world. Here the children can play and the elders rest in shady bowers amid dazzling visions of flowering magnificence, with gushing fountains and gay music of the bright yellow little songsters which we hear only in captivity, but which flit from tree to tree in Canary as free as air. Passing down the streets dark eyes gleam and flash dangerously through the green postigos or shuttered jalousies, but a peep behind often shows the splendid eyes belie the owner. Young ladies from fifteen to twenty-one are exceedingly beautiful, but Spanish loveliness is transitory, and when they reach maturity the beauty so rapidly fades that in a few years they are positively—well plain.

Unquestionably, the one charm of the Canaries, or as they may well be called, the " Fortunate Islands," is the splendid and equable climate. They form the ideal spot for invalids as they have every advantage the health-seeker needs. The climate is warm, but dry and bracing, and the heat is not too great as it is tempered by the stimulating breezes from the sea. The islands are too far south to feel any effect from the north winds which have expended all their force before they reach such latitudes. The east winds have a thorough sweep of the desert, being thus warmed and dried before they touch the islands, and the gentle westerly and southerly winds agreeably temper the heat and sometimes produce a gentle shower of rain that keeps the ground fruitful and moist. The average temperature in the coldest period, *i.e.*, from November to March, is 63°, which is much higher than the average of the South of France during the same months. There is no excess of heat, no cold, little rain and no heavy night dews. Bathing is carried on all the year round, and while we in England are raving over burst pipes, plumbers' bills and perpetual fogs, the Canaries are enjoying glorious sunshine, invalids are able to sleep with windows thrown up, and the country round is gorgeously arrayed with flowers and fruit.

Thus as a winter resort for invalids they far surpass the Riviera, and though the journey has to be considered, a week on board one of the first-class Mail Steamers, under the management of Messrs Elder, Dempster and Co., is almost an added delight to the trip. This firm issues a ticket for Saloon passengers to the Canaries or Madeira for the low sum of £15 return fare, available to or from any of the islands for twelve months.

A few years ago the natural attractions of Grand Canary and the other islands were almost unknown, but their fame has now spread far and wide. Much has been done to improve sanitary conditions, and accommodation for travellers is provided in plenty. It will be well if the Spanish Government, realizing what a prize they have in these possessions, do all they can to assist the English enterprize now developing them, and seeking to attract the thousands who annually flock to a warm climate for the winter.

Many are the enjoyable excursions that can be made into the interior from Las Palmas. The scenery is varied, the vegetation so rich and tropical that a trip into the country is a series of delights. The roads are mountainous, but the sides of the hills and fertile valleys are industriously cultivated, lemons, oranges, figs, tomatoes, bananas, melons, cereals and sugar cane being grown in abundance. Cochineal once formed a staple industry in the islands, and though the trade has much dwindled, a large number of the insects are still collected from the prickly pear which is cultivated for the purpose.

SANTA CRUZ DE LA PALMA.

CAVE DWELLINGS OF ATALAYA.

Up among the peaks behind Las Palmas are many ideal spots for a picnic within walking distance, but the favourite drive is to Monte, which makes a delicious excursion a few miles inland. Driving up the steep winding roads, through patches of bananas, acres of delightful flowers, young vines, groves of eucalyptus and figs, with graceful trees on each side of the track, red flowered oleanders and the brilliant pepper tree, the eye revels in hundreds of acres of richly cultivated land, but broken with imposing barrancos, volcanic peaks of solid lava and stupendous cliffs around. A day spent among the mountains is one to be remembered. The curious hamlet of cave dwellings at Atalaya should also be visited, and the most interesting trip of all is to the Caldera, about eight miles inland. The first part of the journey may be undertaken by carriage, but the latter part must be performed on foot as the road is uneven and very steep. After a long and fatiguing ascent of the Bandana hill the crater is reached, and it gives one a good impression of the volcanic disturbances that have taken place on the islands. The Caldera is the most perfect crater in existence, and it is a mile across with a depth of over a thousand feet. As if in strong contrast to what is past, a small farm nestles securely in the centre of this yawning basin;—a charming Ceres resting in the arms of her thunderous brother Jupiter.

Visitors to Grand Canary would do well to extend their visit to the neighbouring islands, the chief of which may be easily reached by the coasting steamers which ply from port to port.

The Canary group is composed of thirteen islands, but six of these are very small. The origin of their name is attributed to the fact of Juba visiting them, and sending two large dogs to Rome from the islands, which he reported as clothed with eternal fire. Pliny mentions the existence of the Fortunate Islands, but in 1330 a French vessel was driven upon them by stress of weather and they were thus rediscovered, afterwards falling into the hands of Spain. Teneriffe is the largest of the group and is almost as popular as Grand Canary. It is chiefly remarkable for its lofty volcanic peak, which rises almost in the centre of the island, of which Santa Cruz is the capital, possessing a well sheltered harbour. It is a great commercial centre and the chief inhabitants of the town are engaged in trade with Great Britain; but it is, nevertheless, a delightful little place, built at the foot of high mountains, though not greatly patronised by visitors, who flock on to the more fashionable resort, Orotava, about thirty miles distant. The cathedral is specially interesting to Englishmen, for it contains two flags captured in 1797 from the English, and they may still be viewed, a solitary record of Nelson's one failure, which cost him his arm. The anniversary of this event is still marked by a grand fiesta to celebrate what they call, a glorious victory. The whole of the inhabitants turn out in the morning to attend solemn mass, which is followed by a bull-fight, and at night the city is illuminated with myriads of fairy lamps, the inhabitants gaily dancing and singing; and the sky ablaze with rockets and fire balloons.

The scenery round Santa Cruz is almost awe-inspiring, and within reasonable distance are glorious pine forests at Las Mercedes and Mina, with majestic mountains and imposing barrancos where the surrounding country rivals Switzerland.

Laguna and Orotava are the fashionable resorts; the latter especially should be visited, as it is situated in the midst of lovely scenery, wild and mountainous, but with richly cultivated hills and valleys between. The ascent of the lofty Peak or Teyde of Teneriffe can also be made. For days it is never visible, but occasionally a partial view can be obtained through a break in the clouds. The transparent atmosphere then enables one to distinguish even small houses and trees at a great distance, and a magnificent view can be obtained from the top of the crater, which attains an elevation of 11,950 feet above sea level. A vast expanse of ocean, studded with the whole archipelago, stretches away on every side, and it is perhaps the most extensive view in the world.

The western group of islands also includes Palma, Gomera and Hierro, but they are seldom visited by travellers, the two latter being practically unknown. The chief town of the first island, Santa Cruz de la Palma, is important from a commercial point of view and is lighted by electricity. There are some splendid medical springs in Palma which will prove a great attraction when the natural beauties of the island are better known to the health-seeker. The island is a mass of picturesque rocks and precipices, and the Caldera is the largest crater in the world, being nearly seven miles across and 7,000 feet deep.

## CHAPTER II.

THE GAMBIA—SIERRA LEONE—FREETOWN—THE WEST INDIA REGIMENT—
SHERBRO ISLAND—SECRET SOCIETIES—LIBERIA—THE KROO TRIBES—
CAPE PALMAS—THE GOLD COAST SURF—MAJOR PIGGOTT—VIEW OF
CAPE COAST CASTLE.

WE had dropped a number of passengers at the Canaries, and when we again steamed out of the harbour, all on board were more or less connected with the Expedition, except some officials and a trader or two returning to their unsalubrious posts on the coast.

On the way, the Pasteur Filters which we were taking out for use in Ashanti, were tested. The filter itself is a splendid one, the water, after going through an ordinary course of filtration, is drawn by suction through removable porcelain candles, thus being cleansed from all impurities. From some unexplained reason those on board refused to act. Many hours were fruitlessly spent by all the officers vainly trying to overcome the obstruction, and after much trouble and manœuvring, three emitted a meagre stream, others gave out a perceptible dribble, while two or three flatly refused to act. Utensils of this description being so essential for the health of Europeans, who have to depend on water of questionable purity, should have been carefully selected and severally tested before being shipped by Government. The filter was seen at work by Surgeon-Colonel Taylor, before the order was given, and he found it satisfactory in every respect, so in the present instance it seemed to rest rather with some technical error in the manufacture than any fault in the system of filtration. A cable was sent off as soon as we touched port, an expert being dispatched from England by next boat, and on his arrival some were put into tolerable working order, but a little care in the first place would have saved trouble and anxiety to all concerned.

We left Las Palmas on Saturday night, and on Wednesday morning we sighted Cape Verd. The land leading up to the Cape is low and flat, extending as far as the eye can reach in dull monotony, broken only by solitary palms dotted here and there. Passing a small group of islands, we had a distant view of the strongly fortified island of Goree, belonging to the French, and one and a half miles from the coast of Africa.

As we steamed through the glorious sunlit waters, with the awnings to keep off the glare of the sun, and a pleasant sea breeze tempering the heat, it was difficult indeed to realize we were near the deadly West Coast of Africa. Skirting the low shores of Gambia, we passed Bathurst, the chief town in the colony, built at the mouth of the river. The Gambia was annexed to Sierra Leone until 1888, when it was made an independent district, but the colony has had a chequered existence, and now ground nuts form the staple export, being shipped in large quantities.

On the troop-deck the men were busily engaged cleaning and sharpening their arms, while the officers spent much time in improving their shooting, revolver practice being the order of the day. When will revolver shooting be really looked upon by the authorities as a necessary qualification for an officer? It is essential for every officer to be a dead shot, and yet few facilities are offered for them to obtain the requisite proficiency, and few indeed of our English officers can even emulate the cowboy's feat of hitting a button at ten paces.

We had some very fair marksmen on board, and the bottles suffered accordingly, but it remained for Bennett Burleigh to take the palm by the only shot he ever tried on the voyage, in which he shot away a small portion of cork left hanging after the bottle had been shattered.

On the morning of December the 13th we sighted Sierra Leone, and turning into the wide mouth of the Roquelle, had our first view of "the white man's grave," a sobriquet which all the coast unfortunately seems to deserve. Passing the light-house, and steaming along the narrow strip of coast to Freetown, the country appears to be a perfect paradise, with its luxuriant tropical vegetation. Spreading palms and patches of bananas, intersected by enormous trees of great variety, extend right down to the water's edge.

Nestling at the foot of the famous range of the Lion Mountains is Freetown, but the whole appearance of the place is deceptive. The apparently substantial-looking white houses and wide streets, thrown in strong relief by the thick profusion of tropical bush, extending up the sides of the heights behind, and forming a many-tinted green back-ground, make one almost exclaim "Utopia," and, at least, you think such a lovely spot cannot be as black as it is painted.

Once on shore, the illusion is instantly dispelled. Many of these houses that appear so substantial and clean in the distance are found, on a closer view, to be but roughly built and coated with white-wash, rendered a dirty yellow with the damp. True, the streets are wide; there is now a good supply of water and the sanitary arrangements are the best on the coast, but there still remains that keen sense of disappointment which increases as you go further into the town.

When we also remember that this colony was ceded to the British in 1787, we fully realise how slowly the stages of civilisation have advanced. The slow rate of progress made in all our West African possessions is mainly attributable to the trying climate which soon shows its baneful effects on a European, robbing him of all his vigour, and sapping the vitality from his constitution. His energies are impaired, his life is a mere existence, and before he has had really time to thoroughly grasp the situation, and see his ideas of improvement carried out, he is invalided, or on long leave, and another man takes his place. This applies to Government officials and traders alike, for though the latter stay for longer periods, the mortality is much greater among them, and thus, by the ever changing of the white population, their sphere of influence is greatly narrowed.

The cause of the general unhealthiness of Freetown is apparent from its position. Freetown Bay forms a perfect natural harbour, which is the only one worthy of the name on the coast, and the town has naturally grown up around the port. Close behind the city the high crescent-shaped range of mountains completely shuts in Freetown, and prevents a breath of fresh air from that direction, while a series of ridges and spurs on the east keeps off effectually any breeze that may blow from the sea. Thus a north wind is the only one that can cause a leaf to stir near the town, and that blows across the river when it has lost all its force, and does not retain a trace of freshness after traversing the desert and the muggy tracts of country extending to the northern bank of the Roquelle. Freetown is thus left in a reeking atmosphere caused by the great heat, lack of fresh air, and the dampness of the low-lying valley in which it stands, and which also forms a cesspool for the drainage of the hills around. The strongest sanitary measures have been adopted, and have done a little towards making it habitable, but nothing can surmount the natural obstacles which render it so unhealthy.

Sierra Leone was ceded to Great Britain by native chiefs to form a colony for the many destitute negroes in England and America. Since then it has been used extensively as a settlement for those liberated Africans, set free in the West Indies and America, or found on board captured slavers. More than one half of the population consists of freed slaves, and is made up of a great variety of tribes, who have now so intermingled that they form almost a distinct race. There are sixty different dialects spoken in the colony, though for general intercourse, they have resource to pigeon-English, which all understand.

By an old system the younger fry were apprenticed to older residents, receiving an outfit of farm utensils when they had served their time. They were then located in the different villages, receiving for subsistence a daily sum of two pence for six months. Unfortunately, the people were too indolent to make use of these opportunities, idling their time instead of cultivating the land, and, being thus as badly off when their allowance ended as before, the scheme had to be abandoned. The ground is very fertile and a little judicious cultivation abundantly repays the labour bestowed on it. Some of the people adopt European dress, but a shirt and tall hat are considered by many to be an ample outfit.

A large proportion of the natives find employment in the transfer of the produce from the interior to the coast for shipment, sending up European goods in exchange. The exports consist chiefly of palm oil and kernels, but ground nuts, rubber, gum and benni seeds are also shipped in considerable quantities. Palm oil is extracted by simply treading out the pulp of the nut, but a better oil is produced by boiling the nut itself.

Education is now in a very advanced state in the Colony, and good schools are established in every village of importance. These liberated Africans have a strong desire to become members of a civilized religion, but though the haughty aristocrats of Sierra Leone attend the cathedral and will not mix with mandigoes, there are still a large number of converts to Mohammedanism, which allows a plurality of wives, and panders a little more to their taste for the marvellous by the mystic power of its charms and amulets. Without disparaging the excellent work done by the missionaries of all denominations, many of the so-called converts to Christianity are converts only in name. They assume a great outward show of devotion, but will have nothing to do with a religion which is not attractive and noisy. On Sunday they sing all day at the top of their voices, or pray with fervent emotion in a familiar manner, but it is only a thin veneer of Christianity laid over hereditary paganism, and behind which they are lazy, and think nothing of lying or stealing at every opportunity. There are many exceptions to this rule, but it seems the greatest difficulty for missionaries to instil into the native mind that religion should be more than a mere cloak to be adopted on occasions, and lightly laid aside again. Education is now, however, making very rapid strides, and if progression is slow, it is sure, and things are greatly improving.

When I landed at Freetown, I found every available approach to the quay crowded by thousands of brightly arrayed negroes, eagerly awaiting to see the Governor land from the "Loanda" and the effluvia of "nigger," aptly described as the "bouquet d'Afrique" was much in evidence as they perspired freely under the glare of the midday sun. A Guard of honour was drawn up to receive Colonel Cardew, and when he stepped on shore, the natives went mad with excitement. They rushed, *en masse*, to get a closer view of the gallant Colonel and his lady, who were entering their hammocks, and judging from the display of popular feeling, His Excellency must be highly esteemed by all classes. The enthusiasm of these niggers did not appear in any way damped by the hard knocks they received from the batons of the police, who were vainly trying to keep the surging and yelling crowd from closing round the small procession.

On the heights behind the town are the barracks of the West India Regiment, and these, with other houses and quarters dotted on the cliffs, make a scene anything but African, and one could well imagine it was Switzerland, with the chalets perched picturesquely on the ridges.

The Cathedral is a small building in the centre of the town, and there are also several chapels and schools of various denominations. The Bishop of Sierra Leone, the Rev. Ernest Graham, resides in Freetown, though his tenure of office is almost expired.

The Governor is assisted by Executive and Legislative Councils, and among many well-known names in official circles may be mentioned, the Hon. E. Brice Kindley, the Chief Justice; Captain A. F. Tarbet, Inspector-General of Police; Mr. E. Faulkner, Assistant Colonial Secretary; Mr. P. Crampton Smyly, and many others.

The colony is one hundred and eighty-five miles long, and has an area of four thousand square miles   The imports in 1894 amounted to £470,025, and the exports to £426,499. The population of Sierra Leone is stated at 136,000, of which 30,000 live in Freetown.

Some of the houses are substantially built of a red iron stone that abounds, but these are chiefly the stores connected with English firms, and under the management of a white agent and staff of natives. Many pretentious looking places, however, are under the sole ownership of negroes whose parents were probably rescued from the horrors of slavery and set free by the English.

A commodious Market Place stands in the centre of the town, where fruit can be purchased in almost any quantities at a cheap rate, and plenty of rubbish cast from the English market is also sold at exorbitant prices to the credulous niggers, who all delight in flimsy trinkets of every description.

The fish market is held in the open, on the sides of a steep and narrow gorge leading up from the river. The canoes unload at the foot of the cliff; the women sitting in various positions and selling their shimmering wares on the rugged steps leading to the road above. The presence of the market reveals itself to the olfactory nerves at a long distance.

On Saturday morning, the market being in full swing, I innocently allowed myself to be rowed to the foot of the cliff and landed, intending to pass up through the market into the town. It was a blazing morning; much of the fish was stale, and, to put it mildly, very high; but in addition to enduring that stench, I had to clamber up the rugged ascent, pushing through hundreds of vile smelling, perspiring niggers, who crowded round till the effluvia became unbearable. I reached the top with tongue cleaving to my mouth, throat parched, and lungs gasping for a breath of air. The patches of grease on my clean suit of khaki showed where I had come in contact with some oily fishwife, and the combined smells clung to me for hours.

Missionaries, when conducting a service, are obliged to let the blacks take their seats with all the doors and windows open before they can go into the hall. They also do not encourage the natives to stand up to sing, as in that case a European would have to leave the building, the smell being unbearable.

The news of the Expedition had already arrived, and many of the people were as well informed as we on all subjects—" à l'Ashantie."

While on a short shooting excursion into the interior, after a hot tramp in the bush with little sport, I came across a small clearing and farm near a lagoon. The only occupant was a tall negress, whom I surprised in a rather alarming state of dishabille, because of the heat of the day she afterwards explained, but she retired for a few moments and re-appeared attired in a long plain garment of gaudy print, and redolent of patchouli. I was agreeably surprised to find she spoke English fluently, with little of the usual negro twang. She had come over from the West Indies with her husband some years before, and had settled in Sierra Leone, but being left a widow, she carried on the farm with the aid of three bushmen. She was very voluble, indulging in a long tirade against the French and the trouble they have caused in West Africa. The collision the previous year between the English and

## A CIVILIZED NEGRO.

French forces in the interior was a very sore point, and many were the maledictions hurled at the head of the French commander. It will be remembered, the West India regiment, then on a punitive expedition inland, under their late commanding officer, Colonel Ellis, were mistaken for Sofas by the French, who opened fire on them. Both sides blazed away for some minutes before the mistake was discovered, and by that time our Lieut. Lindsay and a French officer were shot, and several of the troops killed and wounded on both sides.

The farm was a picture of neatness and fertility, showing what could be done if the lazy natives would only do a little work in clearing the bush and planting, for the ground is so rich that anything once started requires little care. The farm in question was chiefly planted with the cassada or cavassa, a poisonous tropical shrub, a species of manioc. From the fleshy tubers of the plant tapioca is prepared, and a superior starch can be made in the same manner. It is grown largely in the West Indies, but is also cultivated in some parts of Sierra Leone, where it obtains a ready market and is much used as an article of food by the better class natives. The outskirts of the farm were fringed by huge palm-trees while there was an abundance of oranges, pineapples, and also paw-paws, a small cucurbitaceous fruit, peculiar in taste but very refreshing.

On the main road near the landing stage stands the Wilberforce Memorial Hall, built in commemoration of the abolition of slavery, and named after the man whose untiring efforts were chiefly instrumental in bringing about the desired result. The lower hall, used as a reading room, is stocked with numerous English papers, sent in the first place to some of the European residents in the town. As this hall was thrown open directly to the street and was unoccupied, I went in to glance through the papers, when a crabbed-looking negro appeared, and in peremptory but unmistakable tones, ordered me out, adding that if I wanted to use " dat dere 'all " I had better lay down a subscription. I smiled and went on reading, only to be regaled with much startling information. " You tink me niggah ? I no niggah ! My fader, he be West India man bred an' barn. I'se a Christian, an' a citizen, knowed by ebbery golly bounder in Freetown," and so on, *ad infinitum*, till, finding I was unmoved by the recital of such estimable qualities, he left me with the parting admonition that I was a d——n brute. He was only a reliable type of the civilized and educated negroes of Sierra Leone, whom England has rescued from slavery and found a home for.

On the eastern side of Freetown the Kroomen have formed a settlement. This Kroo-town is under the rule of a headman, the inhabitants being constantly employed to work on the various vessels as they discharge cargo down the coast. A certain number have been induced to settle here as they are then ready for those boats that do not intend calling on the Kroo coast lower down. Close to the village is a large inlet, Kroo Bay, which forms a harbour for many of the small fishing boats and canoes. Fish are very plentiful in the mouth of the Roquelle, but it is also infested with sharks, and if a frail craft upsets, a common occurrence, the occupants are rarely, if ever, seen again.

The "Loanda" stayed two days in Sierra Leone, and on Saturday afternoon the Ashanti contingent of the West India regiment was embarked for Cape Coast Castle. This embarkation was a picturesque sight viewed from the ship. The slopes and steps leading down to the water's edge, and the quay were crowded with thousands of natives, who, dressed in every variety of colour under the sun, turned out to see the troops off. The band of the regiment, their dusky faces thrown up in striking contrast by their white zouaves and puggarees, played suitable airs as each barge load of men was towed off to the ship by the little tug of the Coaling Company. The music was the source of much gratification to the assembled masses who danced, clapped their hands and halloed to the different airs, but "Auld Lang Syne" seemed to cause special delight, probably because many of their well-known hymns have been adapted to it.

We weighed anchor just after dinner, and steamed out of the river through inky darkness, increased by the miasma rising off the land, and obscuring all the lights in the town. The scene on board was a striking one, with four hundred dusky warriors swarming over the decks, singing, chattering in pigeon English, and laughing as only a plantation nigger knows how. There is something particularly simple and child-like about the sons of our West Indian possessions, but when offended in the slightest degree they show their deeper character of cunning, cowardly brutality. Thus, while they retain their negro simplicity, they are strongly tainted with the curse of slavery that brutalised and crushed out every spark of manliness in their forefathers. There is splendid material in the two regiments raised and recruited mainly in the West Indies, but the white officers in command require a large amount of tact in dealing with their men, who are over-sensitive, and will resent any supposed affront, regardless of consequences, and will stoop to most despicable means to obtain their revenge. Major Bailey, who was in command, appeared to understand them perfectly, while the men in turn seemed to regard him as a father and would follow him anywhere. The strict laws of military discipline could never be rigidly enforced, and it was a common thing on board, when orders were being read on parade by the officer, to hear a perfect chorus of "We no heah you heah, Sah!" "Kindly speak more loud, Sah!" from those who were in rear, though they were all drawn up at "attention," when a white soldier hardly dreams of winking, much less speaking.

It was impossible to find quarters for these four hundred men on an already crowded boat, so they had to make themselves as comfortable as possible with a single blanket on the decks, and down the forehold, which had been cleared for them. They lay in every conceivable position, singing far into the night a corruption of "Daisy Bell," and some of their own plantation ditties, their voices rising in perfect unison, despite the themes. A powerful spray of electric light, rigged to the mast, shone down on their upturned ebony faces, surmounted by their red caps, making a most weird scene as contrasted with the surrounding stillness of night on the ocean. Many interesting sketches of those last days on board were made by Mr. Seppings Wright, most of which were reproduced in ensuing numbers of the *Illustrated London News*.

Steaming down the coast we passed Sherbro, which forms the southern part of the Sierra Leone colony. This district is noted for the various secret societies formed among the inhabitants, and about which a great deal of mystery exists. The most interesting of these is an order of native freemasons called " Poro " which is a Sherbro institution peculiar to the Imperri country. The particulars given here were culled from a narrative of Her Majesty's Commissioner at Sherbro, Mr. T. J. Alldridge, who was present in his official capacity at the recent crowning of the Sokong or head chief in the Imperri Land, when a curious and rare native custom was observed which had not been previously witnessed by a European. This consisted in the appearance of the Tasso men who are the head of the Poro order. Such is the power invested in these Tassos, that they take precedence of the Sokong himself in some matters, and it enables them to raise objections to the laws made by the chief if they think fit. They assume a most barbarous costume, including a head-piece of enormous weight. This head-gear is over three feet in height, consisting of a foundation of plaited cane, covered with skulls and leg bones of defunct

Tassos, and surmounted by a gigantic bouquet of feathers, three feet in diameter. On their body they suspend skins of various animals, and jingling charms which make a considerable noise as they walk. Beside these Tasso men, there is a subordinate rank called the Lagas, who attend the Tassos. They are bedaubed with large white spots on the body and have no head-dress. If a Tasso man dies in a town, he must not be buried there, but in the bush. No woman must look on a dead Tasso, and on the decease of one of the order, a law or "poro" is immediately declared, compelling all women to withdraw till the burying is over, the law being so imperative that the females have to drop their work and retire instantly to the bush. If curiosity prompts a woman to secrete herself, and she becomes acquainted with the mysteries of Poro, her superstition brings on an imaginary sickness, during which she confesses, and is at once taken to the Poro bush, where, like the famous English lady of yore who was caught eves-dropping at a Freemasons' gathering, she is initiated into the inner rites of the order, henceforth being regarded as a Poro proper.

There are, however, far more horrible societies than this existing in the low-lying country called British Sherbro, which comprises a large district, including Sherbro Island. A race exists there composed of professional poisoners pure and simple, and though their actions are somewhat retarded by their now being under British rule, many victims still fall yearly. These poisoners form a profession of their own, doing their deadly work with the greatest secrecy, and they are well versed in compounding and preparing most mysterious and deadly poisons from vegetables unknown to the European world, and therefore difficult to trace. In out-of-the-way districts, if any vindictive native has a grudge against another person, he has only to make a present to one of these diabolical fiends, and the selected victim is carefully removed, either suddenly or by a lingering illness that is difficult to locate. The hereditary methods of preparing the poisons are secretly handed down from generation to generation.

A most curious custom that is now dying out is the "Egugu," but this is a fraud practised by a few imposters who implicitly follow out the methods of the Mumbo Jumbo rites employed by Mandigoes and pagan tribes further south. The Egugu man is supposed to have unlimited powers by which the name and appearance of every woman who has been guilty of infidelity is revealed to him. This strange minister is sometimes consulted by a jealous owner of a house full of wives, and in that case his work of finding the offender is comparatively easy, but he also pays periodical visits to the different villages for the purpose of exposing the frail ones, announcing his arrival by loud and dismal screams on the outskirts of the surrounding woods. The women do not relish his visits, and consternation falls on a large portion of the feminine community, as they have nearly all been equally guilty, and there is little chance of his picking an innocent subject. When Egugu enters the town, presents are liberally showered on him, and he can easily mark down a victim by seeing the woman who seems most anxious to propitiate him by her gifts. No one dare absent herself from the parade that follows, and each lord and master takes particular notice that his wives, alias slaves, are present. When all are assembled at the "bentang" or meeting place, the ceremony is commenced by songs and dances, which continue till midnight, when Egugu suddenly pounces on his selected victim. The poor wretch is immediately seized, stripped naked, and tied to a tree, where this superficial quack inflicts a severe switching with his rod of authority, amid the derisive shouts of the assembly, the women being loudest in their exclamations against the unhappy sister.

The members of a secret society of which very little is known, but which still exists, use some imaginary charm or ju-ju, in the preparation of which, the heart of a virgin, plucked from the body of a living victim, is indispensable. Happily, now, this horrible rite is seldom, if ever, celebrated, though it is affirmed that girls are still sacrificed occasionally in the depths of the forest, the breast being cut off a living virgin, and the heart plucked out while still pulsating and throbbing in its last throes.

A few months before I reached Freetown much stir was caused there by the capture in the Imperri country of nine men belonging to the Human Leopard society. Covered with leopard skins, members of this faction are in the habit of secreting themselves in the bush, near various villages, and anyone who ventures out is set upon and killed, a cannibal feast afterwards being held. So serious had the depredations of this gang become, that the Sierra Leone authorities sent men to scour the country for these murderers. Only nine natives were arrested, and, on investigation, no proofs could be found against six of them, and they had to be liberated. The other three were brought to Freetown, tried before a jury, found guilty, and hanged on August the 5th, 1895. One of these malignant wretches named Jowe was formerly a coloured Sunday School teacher in Sierra Leone, but he subsequently adopted the more lucrative profession of trading in the Imperri country. Jowe, in his defence, said he had been compelled to join the society by threats. As, however, he had been a member for a long period, and was at perfect liberty to leave the country if he had chosen, his plea was not admitted. The defence of the others was, that the murders were committed to obtain special parts of the body, such as the heart, hand and leg, to make a certain fetish medicine. It was decided that their execution should take place at the scene of their crimes, and a force of police was dispatched with the prisoners and the scaffold to the Imperri country. The scaffold was erected and the execution took place in the public street, the bodies being allowed to hang forty-eight hours as a warning to the natives. The murders committed by these "leopards" are numerous; one girl who had recently been tied to a tree and was about to be killed and eaten, screamed till she attracted the attention of her friends in a village close by, and on their approach the miscreants fled. Eight more members of the "leopards" were afterwards arrested, and on arraignment, evidence was proved against two of them on the charge of murdering a Krooman named Jack Purser at Mabondo, about fifty miles from Freetown, in the Sherbro district.

Another atrocious outrage was recently brought to light at Bouthe, where a native of the Imperri country had been brought down the river to the St. Joseph's Catholic Mission there, for treatment of wounds, caused by these cannibals. He was working on his land when he was attacked from behind, and stabbed in the neck with a three-pronged dagger peculiar to this gang, gashes then being scored down his back in a manner which, to an unskilled eye, might suggest they had been caused by a leopard's claws. His cries attracted the attention of some other natives working in the vicinity, and on their arrival, his assailants made off. He was only just alive when taken in at the mission house, and succumbed to his terrible injuries shortly after.

On Sunday we could descry the dark outline of the Liberian coast extending monotonously in one long level line of vegetation and with no hills to vary the aspect. Liberia is an independent negro Republic of great pretensions and small exchequer. The Republic was established in 1823, the country being purchased in portions from time to time by the American Colonization Society, and it has an area of 20,000 square miles. A large proportion of its inhabitants are composed of freed blacks from the United States, and captives released from slave ships. Its population is said to number over 200,000. Monrovia, which is situated on Cape Mesurado, is the capital of the State and the seat of Government, where President Cheeseman reigns supreme.

## ARISTOCRATIC LIBERIA. 23

Large trade might be soon established with the rich products of the interior, and the country itself produces coffee, indigo, ginger, arrowroot and hides in abundance. The people, however, have little enterprise, and are content with producing the bare necessities of life. They evince the greatest interest in politics, and will stand for hours discussing the most trivial point with the extravagant flourish of language in which the civilized negro delights. They are very proud of their independence of which they make a great outward show, even to the extent of possessing a gun-boat, "The Rocktown," which they use to frighten the Kroo tribes on the outlying districts, who resent the rule of the little Republic. There is one obstacle in the way of making an effective display of the "Rocktown"—she requires coal for her engines, and unfortunately coal costs money of which Liberia has little, but on one or two occasions, enough fuel has been provided for her to steam down the coast and drop a few shells among the miserable mud-houses of the turbulent Kroos, who seek safety in the bush long before the gunners have their pieces loaded. As a rule the supply of black diamonds has been exhausted in the outward trip, so there she quietly rests till funds are forthcoming to again fill her bunkers and enable her to return to her proper anchorage.

The Colonisation Society paid an extraordinary price to the Dahie tribe when they purchased this land, though it was not such an extensive district as at present. The price paid in commodities was :—

    1 hd. of tobacco.
    1 puncheon of rum.
    50 pieces of cloth.
    25 kegs of gunpowder.
    1 case of muskets.

To this they added other presents of slight value in after years to purchase peace from the previous owners.

As the Liberian colony increased, duties were levied on imports and exports, but these the British traders refused to pay, as, by treaty, the American Government cannot colonise in Africa.

These negroes were now fairly settled, however, and many had been educated in America, so on July 29th, 1847, by a unanimous resolution, they threw off all yoke and declared the freedom of the country. They then assumed the American flag, but with only one star in the blue.

Their leading newspaper—for they have newspapers—would require a great deal of beating. Some of the other sheets published by educated negroes on the West Coast are good samples of egotistic verbosity, but the *Liberia Herald* is far ahead of them all. The sublime "Pott" and his "Eatanswill" production would have sunk into oblivion, if compared to these efforts of Africa's own journalist. The editorial "WE" has played an important part in the World's History, according to the *Herald's* modest articles; the irresponsible writer of which would make an ideal Senator for Buncombe.—*American papers please copy.*

The Liberians are a proud but simple-hearted people, and from the President downwards all enjoy some high-sounding title, many of them painfully incongruous. "Lord Chief Justice" and "Right Honourable" are adopted by the most unpretentious, while others aspire to even greater heights. A prominent Liberian lady is Mrs. Ricks, who, it will be remembered, recently visited England to see the Queen. She takes a keen interest in mission work and workers, and is a well-known figure in the religious world of West Africa.

The steamers generally call at Sass Town for Kroomen to work the ship to the southern ports, and to take on others as deck passengers to different places on the coast, where they are employed in many capacities by traders; but we were too full to take up more passengers this side of Cape Coast.

These Kroos are fine athletic fellows, with muscles that would put any of our so-called strong men in the shade. They will work day and night in discharging cargo when necessary, but without showing the least signs of fatigue. Yet, with the strength of lions, they have the pluck of chickens. Physically they are everything that could be desired as material wherewith to form a native force for service in our African possessions, but they are useless for fighting, and the very mention of war sends a thrill of terror through their puny hearts. They have, however, many tribal disputes, but these are always settled without bloodshed, though occasionally their temper gets up, and they indulge in a rough and tumble, tribe against tribe, when sticks and fists are brought freely into play.

Numbers of these men are constantly coming in contact with Europeans on the coast or visiting Liverpool when working on the steamers, but they still remain in a very backward state of civilisation, though they have few of the barbarous practices which still abound among other tribes who have long since professedly become christianised.

The Kroos have absolutely no kind of religion whatever. Marriage is unknown among them, and there are no rites or ceremonies of birth or death. The children are all marked by a strip of indigo, half an inch wide, tattoed from the forehead over the nose, so their nationality can be instantly traced, in common with many other African tribes who adopt distinctive marks. Curiously enough, salt is looked on in a holy light by these people, and on one occasion an interior tribe, who had journeyed to the coast to attend a palaver, imbibed such quantities of sea-water that they were rendered helpless for several days.

Among the Kroos we had on board, were individuals answering to the sobriquets of " Jim Block," " Cabin-boy," " Pea-soup," " Tar-bucket," " Paint-pot," and " Tom Stern." All of them adopt similar appellations, the character of which clearly points to their origin, and as soon as they scramble on board, they make a point of introducing themselves to the passengers, though some names are of very doubtful taste.

Leaving the Liberian coast, we passed Cape Palmas and came abreast of French territory. Cape Palmas is the healthiest station on the West Coast of Africa, its highest point being one hundred feet above sea level. On the little peninsula, nestling picturesquely among a clump of palms, are the European houses and lighthouse. The coast here is very dangerous in rough weather, owing to the numerous reefs, and, lying high and dry on the sand, the steamship " Monrovia " may still be seen, where she was run up after striking on a sunken reef, just off the point, many years ago.

After Cape Palmas, the French Ivory Coast is reached, extending to the Assinee river which marks the boundary between that and the English Gold Coast. On the Ivory Coast is the French settlement of Tabu, which consists of a native village of conical thatched huts and two European houses. The French have imposed a very foolish tax of £1 on every Krooman taken from their coast to work southwards. As these Kroomen spend all their earnings on every description of finery from the factories before returning home, only reserving just enough to pay their return passage, the French probably object to their subjects spending their money and bringing back goods from another market, but as the tax acts as a deterrent to the steamers calling on the coast, the diminution of exports and imports must make a greater corresponding loss to the revenue. Further down the coast is the desolate French settlement of Berebi, where the European community is made up of five French officials and one trader.

As we steamed along in sight of the coast, the heavy surf was plainly visible as it broke on the beach in long stretches of foam, like banks of snow, extending as far as the eye could reach, the whiteness being intensified by the dark background of vegetation behind. The surf right along this coast is ever a source of wonder and danger, as the rollers surge in and break with sullen and monotonous roar.

The whole length of coast-line extending from the mouth of the Roquelle in Sierra Leone to Lagos, a distance of 1,300 miles, is without a single inlet or harbourage where a ship can rest in safety or discharge her cargo. Vessels calling at the Coast are forced to anchor some distance from the shore, and all communication with the towns or trading centres is carried on by means of surf boats. These boats are specially constructed with a curved keel, which lifts the craft as it meets each advancing crest instead of cutting through the waves as an ordinary straight stemmed boat would do. If a boat is launched for any reason from a man-of-war or one of the mail steamers, they never venture near the range of the surf as it would be courting certain death. Fortunately, the tornadoes which rage in these latitudes are of short duration, and hurricanes seldom blow, or the list of casualties must have been much greater on this inhospitable shore. In sandy places where the beach is smooth and level, the rollers regularly break in straight unvarying line, but on rocky shores the heavy swell of water is broken and thrown up in immense columns of foam and spray as each wave surges up in mad confusion. The mouths of the various rivers that empty themselves on the Coast of Guinea offer just as serious impediments to landing as the uninviting shores. A bar is formed across each mouth, over which the water ever boils and fumes, and only an experienced native in his specially shaped canoe dare cross.

On Wednesday afternoon, December 18th, we had the welcome news that Elmina was in sight. After passing the white walls of the castle and town perched on high ground, the ramparts of Cape Coast Castle were plainly visible, and at six o'clock we dropped anchor about three-quarters of a mile from the shore. It was too late to land that evening, but we were immediately surrounded by boats and canoes whose occupants were soon floundering in the water, scrambling for ship's biscuits thrown from the troop-deck.

Lieutenant Blosse, of the West India Regiment, had contracted a sharp touch of fever on board, so he was lowered over the side and landed that evening, being invalided to England by the next homeward bound boat. He was the second officer invalided at the very outset of the Expedition, which gave ample proof of the trying climatic conditions to be yet undergone. The other officer sent back was Captain King, Army Service Corps, who was proceeding with Captain Matthews on board the "Angola," with the first consignment of supplies. Captain King went on shore at Sierra Leone and received a severe sunstroke, necessitating his being left behind at Freetown and sent to England by next mail.

The town of Cape Coast, as we viewed it that night, lit up by the last rays of the setting sun, made a scene of striking grandeur. Built on a solid rock is the castle, consisting of battlements and turrets, and with the main building and tower in the centre, while a blue sea rolls in great waves, which rise in crested walls of water as they break on the rock at the base. Low hills surround the town, while the white walls of the fort gleam from the heights beyond. The little whitewashed church and mission houses on the sea front, and the substantial houses of the traders, form a strong contrast to the native quarter, where the mass of square flat-roofed houses of red clay stand perched in every conceivable position below. Small clumps of palm trees on the east border a mass of half-ruined houses of the same description which stand tottering on the top of a green bank whose sandy base is ever washed by the waves as they break with a continuous roar. Behind the town, and extending right to the water's edge on either side of it, rise green masses of luxuriant vegetation, forming the ridge of dense African forest that stretches away to the interior. As the sun set in all its tropical splendour, throwing a crimson tint over the whole, the most prosaic could not fail to be struck with the rare and romantic beauty of the scene that would enrapture an artist and make a spring poet rave.

Anchored off the castle were the gunboats "Racoon" and "Magpie," rolling incessantly in the heavy swell, which must make things very unpleasant on board in those narrow quarters. The life of Naval officers and men, shut up in the confines of their floating home off the African coast, must be terribly monotonous, as they lie day after day continuously rolling with no outlook, save perhaps a few mud huts and impenetrable bush, and their resources for any kind of amusement are necessarily limited.

We were a merry party at dinner that night, the last we should spend on board. There were the usual speeches and leave-takings of officials going to posts lower down the coast; a couple of naval officers came over from the "Magpie" to dine, and we thus ended what had been a most pleasant voyage, thanks chiefly to Captain Jones and the other officers of the ship who had taken every care of our creature comforts throughout the voyage.

During the evening a boat came from the shore, and as it reached the ship there was a cry of recognition. "Here's Piggott!" An officer came on board in quiet serge patrols, but those cleanly-cut features, clear fearless eyes lit by a gleam of humour, the firm mouth and determined chin, revealed a striking personality—it was Major Piggott,—hero of a dozen fights, and with more active service records than any two officers on the expedition, though there were old campaigners there, and no feather-bed soldiers. Singularly his regiment is the 21st Hussars, who have the unenviable notoriety of never having been in action, but their motto "Thou shalt not kill" has been easily earned in the peaceful years since the regiment's formation, and their time is yet to come.

We were up betimes next morning, and after a hurried breakfast, clambered over the side into the waiting surf boats with our traps. We were paddled vigorously ashore by twelve muscular Fantees, who sat six a side on the gunwale, paddle in hand, giving a combined stroke as each wave lifted us on the crest, and watching their opportunity, the boat was rushed ashore on the curling top of a large breaker, the next wave dashing over the boat and drenching us. A dozen naked blacks were at hand, and seated on the shoulders of two gigantic specimens, I found myself at last deposited high and dry on the shore of Cape Coast Castle. The scene on the sand was a particularly animated one, as boat after boat arrived in quick succession, loaded with stores from the "Loanda," and as soon as one boat's load was landed, a gang of carriers, many of them young girls and boys, had each put a box on their head and carried it into the Castle courtyard, while superintending the work were Supply Officers, standing in the blazing sun with parched faces and dried lips. Once on shore the heat begins to tell, the sun beating down with merciless ferocity, and woe betide that foolhardy person who exposes himself without suitable head-gear, as sun-stroke is then inevitable to a European.

## CHAPTER III.

ASHANTI--KUMASSI DYNASTY--PREVIOUS QUARRELS--SIR GARNET WOLSELEY'S EXPEDITION—OSAI MENSAH—ADANSI—THE LAST TROUBLE WITH THE ASHANTIS—SIR FRANCIS SCOTT'S FORCE.

It will be well now to say a little on the cause of this Expedition to Kumassi, and for this purpose a short *résumé* of Ashanti history and our previous quarrels with them will not be out of place.

CAPE COAST CASTLE.

Africans have no written records, so to trace the past history of a savage nation and get reliable accounts of the various states of society, manners and customs of the people is impossible. Hereditary families hold the throne for centuries, and although in Ashanti primogeniture is by no means strictly adhered to, and usurpers have at different times seized and held the stool, the dependent chiefs have never given their real support to an outsider, beyond that exacted by fear, and sooner or later he has been put away by some secret method as poison, or by open deposition, and a descendant of the old stock reinstated. There are a few traditions handed down from generation to generation, but they are of the vaguest description and mere fables that cannot be classed with the records of the Arab tribes in the North, whose ancestry, and every detail of past history, is handed down regularly by word of mouth from father to son. The actual power of these kings is much exaggerated, though perhaps, with the exception of the absolute monarchy of a Dahomeyan Sovereign, the Kings of Ashanti have enjoyed greater despotic power than any other known African Potentate. By law the King could do no wrong, and had to marry into every family of note in his kingdom to keep the time-honoured standard of Ashanti ethics, and that fact gave rise to the rumour of King Prempeh having exactly 3,333 wives by law. This marrying into as many families as possible is not peculiar to Ashanti, and is a common thing among most African races. Khama, Chief of the Bamangwato, who visited England last autumn on a mission to the Colonial Office, caused the utmost consternation in Bechuanaland by breaking this long and invariable precedent, only marrying one wife and steadfastly refusing to further profit by his matrimonial privileges. So scandalised were the Bechuanas that they gave vent to their outraged feelings of decency, by making war on Khama, and for a time he was driven out of his country with the few faithful ones that chose to remain with him.

Little is known about the Ashantis till the beginning of the seventeenth century, when a great king and warrior, Sy Tutu, after conquering many of the sub-tribes and villages in the district, formed an extensive kingdom over which he ruled. Sy Tutu was afterwards slain when invading the territory of the King of Akim, situated on the south side of the Prah river. The memory of this great battle of Coromantee is still cherished by the Ashantis, who offer slaves yearly as sacrifices to the departed chief. After Sy Tutu's death his son Apukoo ascended the stool and conquered the Akims, adding their country to that of Ashanti. His son succeeded him and he tried to annex the neighbouring country of Dahomey, but obtained no success in fighting against so powerful a race. Kumassi flourished through the reign of several kings, and in 1823 we started a most disastrous campaign under Sir Charles M'Carthy, the then English Governor of the Gold Coast. The decisive battle was fought at Assamacow and raged fiercely for several hours, but through faulty arrangements, the reserve ammunition had not been brought to the front and this mistake proved fatal to the British forces. Our allies were cut up, and Sir Charles M'Carthy and most of his staff were captured, beheaded, and eaten by the Ashantis; the white men's skulls being cleaned, set in gold and used as royal drinking cups in Kumassi. Assamacow was immediately followed by an Ashanti invasion of Cape Coast Castle. The small garrison in the castle was powerless to aid the miserable Fantees, and terrific slaughter ensued during which over 25,000 natives were slain in our so-called Protectorate, and Ashanti power now extended right down to the narrow strip of coast line defended by our forts on the immediate seaboard. In 1826 a British force was collected at Accra to operate against the Ashantis, and a sanguinary conflict ensued which completely turned the tables. The Ashanti army was routed and fled, while many war-chiefs, rather than meet the disgrace and terrible death by returning defeated to their king, committed suicide on the field. In 1840 another king, called Kwaweda, caused trouble and again invaded the Protectorate, waging war on our allies, the Fantees, but beyond supplying them with arms and ammunition to fight with, the English did not have to interfere. In 1841 much interest was aroused in England by the departure of a Wesleyan missionary, the Rev. T. B. Freeman, for Kumassi, as a pioneer of missionary enterprise in Ashanti, Her Majesty and the late Prince Consort taking much interest in this dangerous mission. Mr. Freeman took with him a carriage and a plough as a present to the reigning monarch. The difficulties in taking vehicles through the dense forest and swamp would now seem insurmountable, but no doubt there was then a wide path of some description cut through the bush for the easy advance of the invading army to the coast. In any case the task must have been a stupendous one to undertake, but he reached his destination with his presents, and completely won over the king, who even gave a plot of ground for the erection of a mission house. In 1849 the English missionaries were forced to withdraw owing to the frequent outbreak of hostilities, leaving some converted natives in charge, but the mission had to be finally abandoned in 1854. On June 12th, 1869, some German missionaries of the Basle mission, while pursuing their religious duties, were captured by an Ashanti general, Adu Bofu, who took them as prisoners to Kumassi. The captives were Messrs. Kuehne and Ramsayer, the latter, unfortunately, taken with his wife, who was visiting him at the time. A French trader, M. Bonat, was also a captive, and these white people would have been sacrificed had they not assured the king that a large ransom would be given for them if their lives were spared. Governor Hennessey made a demand for their release, and though they were not British subjects, offered to ransom the captives. The Ashanti general demanded 1,800 ounces of gold; that is nearly £7,000. In 1872 the king sent a message to say that £1,000 would effect the release of the white men, the amount to be paid half in gold dust, and half in goods. In June a son of Adu Bofu was made prisoner, but was released by Governor Hennessey hoping in that way to obtain a reciprocal release by the Ashanti general, but without success. In October, 1872, the Ashanti King Koffee Kalkali despatched a message to Governor Hennessey saying he was shortly sending down envoys to arrange with the English, but the message was only made to temporize, and the following February the whole district was alarmed by hearing the Ashantis were preparing to invade British Protectorate. Colonel Hardy was at that time Administrator at Cape Coast Castle. The cause of the invasion was chiefly through the Dutch cession of Elmina Castle to the English. Koffee declared that he ought to have the place as a port to trade with and he meant to take it. Another cause that probably brought matters to a head so quickly was that an Ashanti chief called Atjeimpon, and uncle to Koffee, was held a prisoner in Cape Coast Castle. He was released in December, but by the time he reached Ashanti all arrangements were made for the invasion and three large divisions of King Koffee's army invaded the Protectorate together, each simultaneously attacking at different points.

The Ashanti warriors numbered about 40,000, and when Sir Garnet Wolseley arrived at Cape Coast Castle, he heard that this immense force were in the neighbourhood of Abracrampa and were evidently preparing to advance on Elmina, to seize the castle. Sir Garnet immediately advanced and suddenly came on the enemy, hiding in the dense bush, impenetrable to the European, but through which the Ashantis crept on all fours. So effectually did the dense jungle conceal them that no one in the English force suspected the presence of the dusky foe till volleys of slugs showered from the leafy tangle on each side of the path. There was no confusion, however, though many officers and men were seriously wounded, and the Ashanti fire was effectually silenced after two hours' hard fighting, and they retired. The Ashantis were at this juncture almost starving, and after the thrashing they got in this brilliant little affair, known as the Expedition from Elmina, they withdrew, many falling by the way and dying of starvation. Our coloured levies had come in slowly, but as fast as the companies were formed, they were dispatched under their own chiefs to Fort Napoleon, and soon a sprinkling of Mumfords, Kossoes, Winnebahs, and Houssas were extended along the road between Mansu, Dunkwa and Abracrampa, and also from Elmina to Fort Napoleon, while Captain Gordon took command of a gang of labourers to cut a road through the bush toward the Prah. Meantime the Ashanti General, Ammonquanta, swore a terrible vow of vengeance against Sir Garnet, though our forces still worked on the roads unmolested. On October 27th, news came that the warriors were again on the move, having evacuated their camp, but the main body were retiring, as the General had been recalled by the King, while a smaller force of about 10,000 men were moving westward. An expedition was speedily arranged, and a party of natives started with casks of water and the tents in hand-carts. Major Baker Russell went in front with 250 native levies, chiefly Winnebahs and Sierra Leone men, and about 200 bluejackets and marines with Captain Allnut completed the little force under Sir Garnet Wolseley. A halt was made near Assaibo for a rest, and before daylight the troops filled their water bottles and started on ahead through the bush. The heat was intense, and many of the bluejackets dropped by the wayside thoroughly overcome, but after a toilsome march, their destination was reached only to find the Ashantis had fled. Sir Garnet rested at Abracrampa, and leaving Major Russell's native corps, fifty marines and eighty Houssas to protect the King of Abra, he returned to Cape Coast. While he had been on this expedition, a most brilliant affair had taken place at Dunkwa by Colonel Festing, the commandant there. Hearing the Ashantis were in the neighbourhood, Festing made a reconnaissance toward their lines. After an hour's march, he captured an Ashanti cutting wood in the bush, and they forced him to act as guide to the enemy's camp. They came upon the Ashantis quietly sitting at breakfast, and rushing in on them, forced them to retreat *en masse*, capturing a large quantity of stores and ammunition which were destroyed. The Ashantis afterwards rallied, and suddenly a fierce fire was

## THE FIGHT AT DUNKWA.

opened from a hidden foe concealed in the bush round the abandoned camp. The West India regiment behaved with great gallantry, but the native levies began to lose ground, though Captain Rait got a gun and rocket tube into play. Had the enemy charged, it is probable that the levies would have broken at once and a terrible loss been inflicted on the English. Lieutenant Eardley Wilmot, of the Royal Artillery, was badly wounded in the arm, but afraid of disconcerting his force of Annamaboes, he stood his ground, and was then shot through the heart. Many other officers had been severely wounded, and when poor Wilmot fell, the cowardly natives under his command drew back, forcing the English officers to retire. Next day the enemy attacked Abracrampa, but the small force under Major Baker Russell held the place successfully, and before Sir Garnet arrived with reinforcements the little garrison had driven the enemy away. The Ashanti camp was afterwards attacked by Sir Garnet, the enemy suffering a signal defeat, when General Ammonquanta narrowly escaped capture. The whole Ashanti force then began to retire by the road leading from Elmina to the Prah. A large force of levies were formed, and having been reinforced by three regiments from England—the Royal Welsh Fusiliers, Rifle Brigade, and Black Watch—Sir Garnet started his famous march to Kumassi. Among many officers that took part in this expedition beside Sir Garnet were Lieut.-Colonel Evelyn Wood, Surgeon-Major Mackinnon, P.M.O., Major Baker Russell, Captain Buller, Lieutenant Maurice, and others whose names are now almost household words.

The forces marched through the bush unopposed and crossed the Prah, but the King of Ashanti, hearing of the approach of the English, set free first the missionary Kuhne, and afterwards the trader Bonat, Mr. and Mrs. Ramseyer, and their two children who were born in captivity in Kumassi, and they met the troops on the way up. Sir Garnet had sent an ultimatum to Kumassi, demanding hostages to be sent to him with an indemnity, but though envoys came from the King asking for peace, no other steps were taken, and nothing remained but to march on to Kumassi and enforce the terms there. The army crossed the Adansi Hills, meeting with no opposition till they reached Borborassi, which was strongly occupied by the enemy. Here Colonel McLeod, commanding the advance forces, met a spirited resistance, in which Captain Nicol was killed while leading the Annamaboes, who, this time, behaved splendidly throughout the engagement, and deeply avenged his death. The enemy were forced to withdraw with heavy loss, but on January 31st they again assembled in great force near Ejinassie and occupied strong positions at Amoaful. The fighting was commenced by several brisk skirmishes between the advanced posts at eight a.m., and a heavy fire was kept up continuously on both sides for more than four hours, during which the Black Watch suffered severely. Amoaful was captured, but long after the town was taken the Ashantis kept up a heavy fire from the bush till they were dislodged by the Naval Brigade. The enemy even now were not done, and hardly had the fire been silenced in front when reinforcements arrived and commenced an attack in the rear. The baggage column was fired at, and though it was accompanied by a large escort, the cowardly carriers dropped their loads and scampered in all directions. A part of the Naval Brigade was sent back, and brisk fighting ensued far into the night, when the Ashantis were repulsed and forced to retire to Bekwai. On February 1st, at mid-day, the English made an advance on this town, but the enemy rushed from the place into the bush on the first approach of the troops, where they recovered from their surprise and resisted vigorously. The advance column consisted of the Naval Brigade, Russell's Native Regiment, Lord Gifford's Scouts, and a small detachment of Engineers. A gun and rocket tube of Rait's Artillery were also pushed forward, and as volley after volley was poured into the Ashantis they again retreated; the town being captured and burned to the ground.

As the troops advanced through the different villages they found human sacrifices of both sexes in each place, the mutilated bodies lying with head severed in the centre of the path, but it is difficult to say what significance the Ashantis put on these ghastly exhibitions. Each village of any size was found to be occupied by the enemy, but in every case, after a hot fight with the advance-guard, the Ashantis were forced to retire. On February 4th the last gallant advance was made by our troops, fighting every step of the way through the deadly swamp surrounding Kumassi, and at six o'clock Sir Garnet and his staff were in the dreaded capital. King Koffee and a large portion of his army had escaped, taking their treasure and arms with them, and though constant messages were sent by the General, Koffee remained obdurate and would not agree to the terms of peace. The rains had started, rivers were rising, and nothing remained for Sir Garnet but to prepare at once for the return march to the coast, if he wanted to save his army. On February 6th Kumassi was burned to the ground; the troops at once setting out on their homeward march and encamping the same night at Egimum, fourteen miles from the capital. They returned by quick stages to the coast, the roads becoming more impassable every day by reason of the rains, but happily a serious disaster was narrowly averted. A few extracts from Sir Garnet's letters to the Colonial Secretary will explain his reasons for destroying the capital and his subsequent action. Speaking of the occupation of Kumassi, he says :—

" I immediately issued stringent orders for the protection of the inhabitants and the safety of the town, but in the darkness it was impossible to prevent some of the numerous camp followers from pillaging, and the result was the outbreak of many fires. Captain Baker, Inspector of Police, and several officers were engaged nearly all night in the suppression of pillaging and putting out fires. One policeman taken in the act was hung. I endeavoured immediately on my arrival to communicate with the King through Mr. Dawson, and through every channel that appeared to offer an opportunity. A chief having come into Kumassi, who was said to be sent by the King, I saw him myself and impressed on him my wish to spare the town, and my desire to impose on the King no severer conditions than those he had already accepted. Moreover, I told this man, now I had shown the power of England, if the King would make peace at once, I was ready to accept a small part of the indemnity, and not to exact half I had previously required to be paid down. All was, however, of no avail. The men whom I endeavoured to employ as messengers, and who came avowedly as envoys of the King, were found treacherously removing powder and gold dust from the houses. The whole scheme of Ashanti politics is so based upon treachery that the King does not either understand any other form of negotiation or believe it possible that others can have honest intentions. Under these circumstances it became clear that a treaty would be as valueless as difficult to obtain. Nothing remained but to leave such a mark of our power to punish, as should deter from future aggression a nation whom treaties do not bind. I had done all I could to avoid the necessity, but it was forced upon me. I gave orders for the destruction of the palace and the burning of the city. I had at one time contemplated the destruction of the Bantama where the sacred ashes of former kings are entombed, but this would have involved a delay of some hours. Very heavy rains had fallen, and I feared that the streams might have risen in my rear sufficiently to seriously delay my march. I considered it better, therefore, not to risk further the health of the troops, the wet inclement weather having already threatened seriously to affect it. The demolition of the palace was complete. From all that I can gather I believe that the result will be such a diminution to the prestige and military power of the Ashanti monarch as may result in the break-up of the kingdom altogether. This I had been anxious to avoid, because it seems impossible to foresee what power can take this nation's place among the feeble races of this coast. I certainly believe that your Lordship may be well convinced that no more utterly atrocious Government than that which has thus, perhaps, fallen, ever existed on the face of the earth. Their capital was a charnel house; their religion, a combination of cruelty and treachery; their policy, the natural outcome of their religion. I cannot think that, whatever may be the final fate of the people of this country, the absolute annihilation of such a rule, should it occur, would be a subject for unmixed regret. In any case, my Lord, I believe that the main object of my expedition has been perfectly secured. The territories of the Gold Coast will not again be troubled by the warlike ambition of this restless power. I may add that the flag of England from this moment will be received throughout Western Africa with respectful awe—a treatment which has been of late years by no means its invariable fate among the savage tribes of this region. The troops are now on the march homeward, and will embark for England immediately on reaching Cape Coast."

After the war, the Adansi King wished to be taken under the protection of Great Britain by joining our allies the Wassaws, and after a little hesitation, Sir Garnet allowed his request in a modified form. At Detchiasu, on February the 9th, fresh envoys reached Sir Garnet, assuring him that Koffee was most anxious to accede to the General's terms and make peace. They declared that the King could only send 1,000 ozs. of gold, instead of the 50,000 ozs. demanded, but that he would pay the rest in quarterly instalments. Refusing to accept those terms would not have improved matters, so Sir Garnet drew up a treaty which was signed by the envoys and himself. The treaty is too long to give in full, but the chief clauses were as follows:—

"The King of Ashanti to pay 50,000 ounces of gold dust as indemnity for the expenses of the late war, and undertakes to pay 1,000 ounces forthwith and the remainder by instalments.

The King on the part of himself and heirs to renounce for ever all pretensions of supremacy over Elmina or any tribes formerly connected with the Dutch.

The Kings of Ashanti will for ever renounce all right or title to any tribute or homage from the Kings of Denkera, Assin, Akim and Adansi, and other allies of Her Majesty, formerly subject to the Kingdom of Ashanti.

There shall be freedom of trade between Ashanti and Her Majesty's forts on the coast; all persons being at liberty to carry merchandise from the coast to Kumassi, or from that place to the coast.

The King guarantees that the roads from Kumassi to the Prah be kept open and free from bush to a width of fifteen feet.

As Her Majesty's subjects and the Ashanti people are henceforth to be friends for ever, the King, in order to prove his sincerity and his friendship to Queen Victoria, promises to put an end to human sacrifices, as the practice is repugnant to the feelings of all Christian nations."

By the end of February, the troops had all arrived at Cape Coast and were being embarked for England.

Thus ended the famous war of 1873-4, but the Ashantis, though taught a severe and bitter lessson, were not yet crushed. A town built of clay and wood, with the materials close at hand, is soon rebuilt. The Kumassi of 1895 was soon standing on the old foundations of the Kumassi (or Coomassie) of 1874. Shortly after the sack of the capital, a bloodless revolution took place. Koffee Kalkalli was removed, and his brother Osai Mensah reigned in his stead.

## A FRESH CAUSE FOR TROUBLE. 37

An officer was sent from the Gold Coast to collect the first instalment of the war indemnity when it fell due, and it was paid without demur. The Ashantis, however, have short memories, and when the second instalment was demanded, the King said it was not ready, and the officer had to leave without it. He paraded his Houssa escort, and marched out amid derisive hoots and cries of the Ashantis ; but, afterwards, wiser counsels prevailed, and the King becoming frightened at the probable consequences of his act, sent runners with the gold. After that date it was not considered safe to send for any further instalments without a large force, and as that would be too expensive a mode of collection, a message was sent to Kumassi to say the remainder must be paid at Cape Coast Castle.

The Ashanti power having been tamed, one of their most powerful feudatory chiefs seceded shortly after and formed the independent Kingdom of Juabin. The Ashantis, enraged at the establishment on their border of a rival power recently subject to them, immediately threatened war on the Juabins, though it was only a few months after their own defeat by the English. An officer was sent from the Gold Coast to Kumassi to preserve order, and he met with a good reception, exacting a promise from Mensah and the Juabin king, Hsafu, to keep the peace.

For the next few months the Ashantis kept steadily at work repairing their shattered fortunes, reforming their army, and collecting ammunition, which had been nearly all expended. In 1875 fresh friction took place between the two rivals, and in October the Ashantis invaded Hsafu's territory and attacked Juabin. The conflict raged for a few days when the Juabins were worsted and put to flight. Seeing that the invasion was a breach of good faith, and also gave back to Ashanti much of her old power, the Colonial Authorities ought to have sent a force at once to occupy Juabin and take the country out of Ashanti yoke. Not only was this neglected, but no steps were taken in assisting the Juabins to retake their own possessions. Arms and ammunition were obtained by the Ashantis from the French traders at Assinee, while the importation was forbidden on the Gold Coast, which was the only market for the Juabins to get the much needed munitions of war. The Ashanti kingdom thus again flourished in less than two years after Kumassi was burnt, and Mensah at once repudiated the war indemnity, reinstating the old power that Sir Garnet Wolseley thought he had broken for ever. When it was too late to repair the injustice to the Juabins the Gold Coast authorities removed the embargo on the importation of arms, finding it simply reduced the revenue and gave the trade into French hands. The Ashantis were thus encouraged to purchase breech-loaders at Cape Coast itself, so they thoroughly re-armed their fighting men with modern weapons right under the eyes of the British Government, and if internal dissensions had not convulsed Ashanti, owing to the deposed King Koffee intriguing against Mensah, war would have been made on some of the border tribes. Mensah had an efficient body-guard and was able to hold his own against the revolutionists, and as a further proof of his power, he indulged in human sacrifices to a much greater extent than his predecessor. The Ashanti war party was very anxious to remove the stain caused by the '74 defeat, and, at any rate, force the king of Adansi again under their rule. Adansi had thrown off the Ashanti yoke after the war, and become an independent state and ally to England. When things had quieted down a palaver was held in Kumassie where the Bekwai chief publicly swore to the King that he would force Adansi to again become subject to Ashanti. This would be an open breach of the article of the treaty dealing with the Adansis and other allies who were not to be interfered with by the Ashantis, but unfortunately England herself seemed only too ready to repudiate the claim the Adansi people certainly had on us. If we were not actually bound to protect these people, we had a signed treaty forbidding the Ashantis to attack them, and any breach of that was surely an open defiance to England, and one she ought to have taken the strongest measures to nip in the bud. The Colonial Office, however, seemed determined to a strict policy of non-intervention, and Adansi was certainly at that time proverbially between two stools. At this juncture, however, having allowed the Ashantis to re-arm themselves, the Gold Coast authorities became seriously alarmed by fresh friction with Mensah early in 1881. An Ashanti prince named Awoosoo having incurred the displeasure of the King, sought safety in flight, and, on arrival at Cape Coast, claimed protection which was accorded him. On January 19th envoys arrived from Kumassi bearing the golden axe, supposed to signify it was a matter of peace or war, and demanded an interview with the Governor. After the usual compliments had passed, the chief envoy Amanquah demanded in the name of King Mensah that Awoosoo should be given up. The Governor replied that Awoosoo, being in British Protectorate and not having committed any crime, was free to go or stay where he pleased, and would never be given up to them, whereupon the envoys said that if Awoosoo were not forthcoming, the King would invade Assin. This message probably did not really come from Mensah, but was a surmise on the envoy's part, and beyond that threat, and also the fact of the embassy bearing the golden axe, no actual cause for alarm was given. A panic, however, took place on the Gold Coast, and an Ashanti invasion was considered imminent. All the available forces were massed on the coast to defend the forts there, leaving the whole country open to the ravages of the dreaded foe had he been seriously considering such a step. Alarming reports arrived constantly at the coast as to the rapid Ashanti advance, but all these rumours constantly turned out to be false, though definite news was received that the King had an efficient army fully organized, among which were 1,000 men armed with Sniders.

Reinforcements were ordered from Sierra Leone, and 200 of the West India Regiment were dispatched to Cape Coast. Fresh envoys arrived at the castle, saying the King did not want to fight, and they appeared greatly surprised at the Governor's warlike preparations. Prince Ansah was at this time employed on the coast, and he also was astounded to find the steps that were being taken to defend the place, and though it had been previously proved that no reliance could be placed on the word of an Ashanti monarch, there seems this time to have been little need for such excitement and dismay when the King was quietly resting in his capital. A large majority of Ashanti chiefs were ready, burning for revenge when the envoys returned to Kumassi without the prisoner, and some advised war at once, but Mensah strongly advocated a delay till he had received an answer from the second ambassadors. These arrived in due course with a decisive refusal from the Governor to deliver up Awoosoo, and that, coupled with the report that the English Government were arming their old and despised enemy, the Fantee, and was going to invade Ashanti, threw Kumassi into an uproar. The war drums were beaten and slaves sacrificed amid signs of excitement, but next day a messenger arrived from Prince Ansah saying that reinforcements had arrived from Sierra Leone, and that thousands of white soldiers were on their way from England. This report, though false, considerably damped the recently kindled war-feelings, and King Mensah decided to take no further action, but to keep his troops ready for emergency in Kumassi if war were forced on him. The second West India Regiment had also by this time arrived at Cape Coast from the West Indies, and when this fact was duly notified and exaggerated in Kumassi, Mensah thought war was inevitable, and he called out his full army to oppose the English if they crossed the Ashanti border.

An expedition was now determined on by the authorities at Cape Coast, and a force about 1,000 strong marched up country to Prahsu with the Governor. On April 16th, Ashanti messengers arrived at the Prah, a palaver was held, and the troops returned to the coast having had a useless and needless journey. Here the envoys paid over to Government an indemnity of 1,000 bendas of gold-dust and the matter was ended, clearly showing that Mensah desired peace. Further trouble from this matter was prevented on July 16th, when Awoosoo committed suicide by leaping from the wall of Elmina Castle, and thus dramatically ending any anxiety the Ashantis felt about him and his supposed intrigues.

Following the example of the Juabins in 1878, the movement of disintegration continued, and many of the provincial kings and chiefs of the principal southern states migrated, taking their people into the British Protectorate, and Kumassi found itself surrounded with deserted or disaffected provinces. In 1888 an attempt was made to restore the Ashanti kingdom by the selection of King Prempeh, or Kwaku Dua, as the rightful heir to the stool. Some of the states rallied for a time, but the ambition of the young king and his mother to re-establish Kumassi supremacy over the whole of the revolted kingdoms led to a series of inter-tribal wars which lasted for several years, and threw Ashanti into the utmost confusion. In 1891 it was proposed to take the whole territory under the British flag, but no friendly arrangement could be arrived at with Kumassi. Negotiations were again entered into in February, 1894, but Prempeh became enraged and alarmed at the surrounding states becoming friendly with the British. Many complaints were received from various sources, and in 1893-4 Houssas had to be dispatched to protect our borders on the north of Ashanti and to prevent the raids from Kumassi.

Sir Brandford Griffith dispatched two ultimatums to Prempeh, but he continued his policy of prevarication and double dealing, and the mission returned to the coast with nothing done; the Houssas being fired at and one killed on the return journey. Prempeh was told to send his reply to the Governor of the Gold Coast, but he sent envoys direct to England, though, no doubt, these princes and chiefs were only too eager for a little jaunt at the expense of their country, and used every means in their power to induce the King to dispatch them direct to the Queen. Governor Griffiths was succeeded by Governor Maxwell, who was on his way out from England when the envoys started. They were warned at the coast that they would not be received in London, and told if they waited a few days they could see the

SIR FRANCIS SCOTT, K.C.M.G.
*From a photograph by Elliott & Fry.*

Governor who was deputed to receive them, but that meant no England, and no fun. They must go at all risks, and go they did in face of warnings. A last ultimatum was afterwards taken to Prempeh by Captain Donald Stewart, the Special Commissioner, who left on September 26th, 1895, escorted by a force of Houssas under Captains Cramer and Irvine. Kumassi was reached on October 7th, and Captain Stewart read the letter which was translated by the interpreter, Mr. Vroom. The letter described the various offences of the King, his violation of the Fomona treaty, his vicious practices, and the constant molesting of tribes friendly to the English. It demanded that the King should receive a British resident, who would see the reforms carried out, but not interfere with the details of Prempeh's government. He was told that the ambassadors he had sent to England would not be received there, and that his answer must be sent to the Governor at Accra. Prempeh, who was surrounded by his chiefs and 5,000 of his people, took the letter and said he thanked his " good friend the Governor " for sending it to him. He would see his chiefs to talk over the matter, and then reply to it. Presents were exchanged, and the little force returned to the coast. The Ashantis took no further notice, and as the day of grace expired without a sign from the King, nothing remained but to enforce our demands. A military expedition was decided on, consisting of a special corps of picked troops from different regiments at home, also the Second West Yorkshire Regiment, 700 Houssa troops, 400 of the West India Regiment, and a levy of friendly natives to act as scouts. The officers of the Expeditionary Force were:—

*In Command.*
Sir Francis Cunninghame Scott, K.C.M.G., C.B.

*Staff.*
Lieutenant-Colonel F. J. Kempster, D.S.O., Munster Fusiliers, Second in Command.
Lieutenant-Colonel Ward, Army Service Corps, Assistant Adjutant-General.
Major Belfield, Munster Fusiliers, Chief Staff Officer.
Major Ferguson, Royal Horse Guards, Camp Commandant.
Colonel His Royal Highness Prince Henry Maurice of Battenberg, K.G., Military Secretary.
Major C. B. Piggott, D.S.O., 21st Hussars, Aide-de-Camp.
His Highness Prince Christian Victor of Schleswig-Holstein, G.C.B., King's Royal Rifles, Aide-de-Camp.
Captain H. D. Larrymore, Gold Coast Constabulary, Aide-de-Camp.
Mr. Haddon Smith, Private Secretary.
Mr. Reginald P. Knollys, Interpreter to the Force.

## Other Officers on Special Service.

Surgeon-Colonel Taylor, M.D., Principal Medical Officer.
Lieutenant-Colonel Leggett, Senior Ordnance Store Officer.
Major Wolfe Murray, R.A., Commanding Lines of Communication.
Major Baden Powell, 13th Hussars, Commanding Native Levy.
Major Sinclair, Royal Engineers.
Major Gordon, 15th Hussars.
Captain Graham, 5th Lancers.
Captain E. W. Blunt, Royal Horse Artillery.
Captain Montanaro (Local Major), Royal Artillery.   Base Commandant.
Captain Williams, South Staffordshire Regiment.
Captain Benson, Royal Horse Artillery.
Captain Phillips, Royal Engineers.
Lieutenant Pritchard, Royal Engineers.

## Special Service Corps.

Lieutenant-Colonel Stopford, Commanding.
Major Hamilton, East Yorkshire Regiment.
Lieutenant Hon. G. A. Hood, Grenadier Guards.
Captain Drummond, Scots Guards.
Captain W. H. Sitwell, Northumberland Fusiliers.
Lieutenant E. Fitzgerald Wood, Devonshire Regiment.
Major Barter, Yorkshire Light Infantry.
Captain Reade, Shropshire Light Infantry.
Captain Kays, 3rd King's Royal Rifles.
Major J. W. A. Marshall, Royal Irish Fusiliers.
Major Northcott, Leinster Regiment.
Captain Fuller-Acland Hood, Rifle Brigade.

## The 2nd West Yorkshire Regiment.

Lieut.-Col. A. J. Price, Commanding ; Major A. W. St. George ; Captains H. Walker, G. W. Swaine, W. de S. Cayley ; Captain and Adjutant F. W. Towsey ; Captains F. B. Pearce, J. O'B. Minogue, T. P. Barrington, T. H. Berney ; Lieutenants G. F. Gardiner, E. P. Purchas, C. Mansel-Jones, W. M. Hall, L. H. Spry, J. B. Paget, P. E. H. Lowe ; 2nd Lieutenants B. A. Thompson, C. J. Deverell, H. L. Mourilyan.

## Royal Engineers—Field Telegraph Detachment.

Captain R. S. Curtis ; Lieutenant MacInnes ; Lieutenant Faber.

## Army Service Corps.

Colonel Ward ; Major F. Clayton ; Captains C. H. Donovan, E. Bernard, E. E. D. Thornton, E. C. Thring, D. K. E. Hall ; Lieutenants Wilson, Armstrong, Atkins, Atcherley ; Quartermasters Edwards and Challoner.

## Army Medical Staff.

Surgeon-Colonel W. Taylor, M.D., Principal Medical Officer ; Surgeon-Lieut.-Colonels Townsend, Blennerhassett ; Surgeon-Majors Hughes, Wolseley, Dodd, Porter, Wilson, Beatty, Bartlett, Hickman ; Surgeon-Captains Wilson, Beevor, Maher, Josling, Burke, Eckersley, O'Callaghan, Cummins, Corcoran, Hilliard ; Surgeon-Lieutenant Spencer ; Hon. Lieutenants Arbeiter, Lines.

THE GOLD COAST. 43

*Ordnance Store Department.*
Lieutenant-Colonel Leggett; Captains Sherwood and Mathew; Hon. Lieutenant Cox.

*Army Pay Department.*
Lieutenant-Colonel Compigné; Major Dolby; Captain Westmorland.

*2nd West India Regiment.*
*Regiment—Sierra Leone. Right Wing—Gold Coast and Ashanti.*
Colonel Caulfeild; Major Bailey, Commanding Right Wing; Majors Egerton and Lowry; Captains Jackson, Stansfeld, Henstock, Wilson, Baines, Climo, Liston, Davies; Lieutenants Barchard, Falcon, Alone, Hardyman, Woodman, Litchford, Drury, Fulton, Thorne, Blosse, Bliss, Davies, Poole, Davis, Martin, Peacock, Beamish, Magan, Chill, Murison, Prideaux, Hewett, Swabey, and Robertson.

*Officers holding appointments in the Gold Coast Constabulary (Houssas).*
Captains Aplin, Cramer, Buchanan-Boyd, Irvine, Matthews, Annesley, Houston, Grant, Hawtrey, Pamplin-Green; Lieutenants O'Donnell, Middemist, and Parmeter.

A Company Lagos Houssas under Captain Reeve-Tucker

---

## CHAPTER IV.

THE GOLD COAST—CAPE COAST CASTLE—FILTH AND NEGLECT IN THE TOWN—THE SPECIAL SERVICE OFFICERS—CAPTAIN LARRYMORE—THE WHITE RACE—KING TACKIE—FOREIGN COMPETITION—MISSIONARIES—A FANTI WEDDING—A FETISH FUNERAL—A NATIVE BALL—CHRISTMAS IN FANTI LAND—MATERNITY.

HAVING in the previous chapters roughly followed up the affairs in Ashanti to the causes of the 1895-6 Expedition, a few words on our Gold Coast Protectorate will not be out of place. The Gold Coast proper comprises the coast of the Gulf of Guinea from 3″ West to 1° 10′ East of Greenwich, with a Protectorate calculated to include an area of 30,060 square miles, and a population of 1,500,000; a large proportion of which are pagans. The first trading centre was established in the 16th century by the Portuguese, who built a castle at Elmina, but it was soon taken from them by the Dutch. In 1618 English merchants built a fort at Cormantyne, and subsequently many forts and factories were built along the coast by English, Dutch, French, and Germans. In 1662 the first English company was properly chartered, and ten years later, they were succeeded by the Royal African Company who enlarged and strengthened Cape Coast Castle, making it the finest on the coast, and also established stations at Dixcove, Secondee, Commendah, Annamaboe, Winnebah and Accra. In 1750 the African Company of Merchants was constituted by Act of Parliament to trade right down the West Coast, and in 1821 the Gold Coast settlements were transferred to the Crown and placed under the jurisdiction of Sierra Leone, but in 1874 the Coast became an independent district under the title of the Gold Coast Colony. In 1872 the Dutch had transferred all their forts to Great Britain, and it was this exchange that led to the Ashanti invasion of Elmina, and the subsequent war.

The merchants of the seventeenth century named each section of the coast of Guinea after its special product. Thus we had the Grain Coast, now the Republic of Liberia; the Ivory Coast, merged in the French possessions of Grand Bassam and Assine; the Slave Coast on the east, which has also lost its distinctive name, as slaves are no longer exported, but the Gold Coast still retains its name and trade, and a considerable quantity of the precious metal is shipped yearly.

On the edge of this harbourless coast stand various settlements and forts. The first place of any importance on the west is Beyin, and the next settlement, nearly thirty miles away, Axim, stands at the mouth of the Ancobra river, down which a large quantity of mahogany and other valuable timber is floated. Owing to the difficulties of loading, the timber trade is not developed to the extent that the resources would justify were a better harbour possible. Near Axim are the gold mines of Wassaw, which are now being further developed at a considerable sacrifice of the lives of the Europeans engaged in prospecting. Thirty miles from Axim is Dixcove; then Chama at the mouth of the Prah, and forty miles east of Axim, Elmina, the oldest station and once the most important on the coast. Eight miles from Elmina is Cape Coast Castle, once the seat of Government, but superseded in 1875 by Accra, though it is still a most important trading place. About eighty miles further east, passing Annamaboe, Cormantine, Salt Pond and Winnebah, we reach Accra, the chief town and settlement on the coast, with a population of about 18,000. The township includes the villages of Christiansborg and Victoriaborg, and is

## TRADE IN THE COLONY. 45

the seat of Government. Sixty-seven miles from Accra is Addah, at the mouth of the Volta, and thirty-five miles from there our eastern-most settlement, Quittah, is reached, built close to a lagoon, which makes it a most deadly station for Europeans, though it has an important trade.

The Gold Coast Protectorate has many rivers, but they are of little use for communicating with the interior owing to the bars formed at the mouth, and the numbers of rapids to be encountered. The most important is the Volta, which in some seasons is navigable for small steam launches, while the smaller river, Ancobra, is the best from a commercial point of view, being much used to float down timber from the interior. The historical Prah, the most famous river, and which forms the border of the Protectorate, is the most useless, being a succession of rapids and projecting rocks.

There are two wet seasons, from March to July, and October and November. The Harmattan wind blows from December to March, and the dry season prevails.

Owing to the terrible climatic conditions, and the number of lives sacrificed every year in keeping up the Government and trade on the coast, some naturally are inclined to ask if it is worth the trouble expended on it. From a purely commercial point of view there is undoubtedly a splendid future in store for the Gold Coast, but much remains to be done before its great natural resources can be fully developed. Trade is now largely carried on, and the country, besides producing considerable quantities of gold, also exports ivory, gum copal, monkey skins, cotton, camwood, guinea-grains and palm seeds. A great increase on the rubber industry is reported, and though in 1882 only 7,168 lbs. were exported, in 1894 the figures had risen to 3,027,527 lbs., valued at £232,550. In 1894, 4,213,935 gallons of palm oil, to the value of £237,623, were produced and shipped from the coast. The timber trade also promises well, but the difficulties of transport still greatly hinder its development. The imports consist chiefly of hardware, spirits and Manchester goods. The total imports in 1894 amounted to £812,830, and total exports £850,343.

The Governor is assisted by a Legislative Council, consisting of six official and two non-official members.

Cape Coast Castle was in an uproar with the preparations for the advance on Kumassi. I had heard before I arrived that the place was the most filthy and neglected town known under a civilized government, and therefore did not expect to find things particularly flourishing. Such an assertion as the above is perhaps too sweeping to describe the present state of the town, but even now it would rank among the worst types of places with all the improvements which have taken place since 1874. The town has been in English hands now for two hundred and thirty years, and yet, beyond a few minor improvements, it remains as it was, with the addition of a few larger and more substantial houses, built by traders who have settled there. The town lies in the hollows at the base of three hills, the centre immediately behind the Castle being occupied by the Government House, chief trading houses, post office, church, mission-house and schools, and on each side over various little undulations and hollows are massed the squalid mud hovels of the Fantee population proper.

To the east of the town rises Connor's Hill, which was used as a hospital and sanatorium for the troops, and from the top, by the white wooden houses and marquees forming the hospital wards, a fine view is obtainable. In front is the mighty expanse of the ever-rolling Atlantic, to the right stands the Victoria tower, and nearer at hand on the top of the centre hill, Fort William, a round whitewashed little place, resembling a Martello tower, and now used chiefly as a lighthouse. Behind the fort is Prospect House, while all around, closing right into the very outskirts of the town, is the bush, so thick and tangled as to be almost impenetrable.

The little water obtainable is stored in wells outside the town, and there is no system of drainage in Cape Coast Castle. There are 12,000 inhabitants, none over clean, and many living in a horrible state of filth; so imagine what condition a place in ordinary latitudes would be in under such circumstances. Added to that there is the intense heat, and not a breath of air stirring in the lower parts of the native quarter, where the stench is unbearable. There is one large surface drain cut right through the centre of the town; but, whatever use it may be in the wet season, in the dry it is simply a convenient repository for all the filth and offal that the natives wish to get rid of. The authorities do what they can to prevent the depositing of offensive matter in the streets, and a strict ordinance is in force by which all delinquents caught in the act may be heavily fined. This may have a little effect in bettering matters, but the natives easily evade the law by keeping the refuse in their hovels all day and throwing it outside at night when darkness has set in. With sanitation in such a state in an otherwise deadly climate, small wonder that Europeans sicken and die if they stay in the place any length of time. Undoubtedly a very great deal could be done to improve matters, but the authorities are not alone to blame, as the lack of water is a great defect, and the filthy habits of the natives, if restricted, cannot be altered by law, however rigidly enforced.

On landing at Cape Coast, on December 19th, I found the whole place in a glorious state of bustle and confusion. Long lines of carriers were taking stores from the shore to the castle. Fresh gangs were being loaded and sent off up country to Mansu, where the intermediate depôt on the road to the Prah was formed. Everything was in a very forward state, though the first contingent had arrived less than a fortnight before, and Sir Francis Scott and his staff had only landed a few days previously. Colonel Scott had certainly an efficient staff of officers under his command for Special Service. He himself served in the last Ashanti war, and was also in the Crimea and through the Indian Mutiny. In 1892 he was in command of the expedition against the Jebus on the West Coast, and is at present Inspector-General of the Gold Coast Constabulary or Houssas. Colonel Kempster, D.S.O., Second in Command, has served in the Egyptian Army, and was also in the Bechuanaland Expedition. Major Belfield, Chief Staff Officer, had seen no previous war service, but he is a Staff College man, and has a very high reputation. Surgeon-Colonel Taylor, Principal Medical Officer to the force, when he was selected for Ashanti, had only recently returned from special service with the Japanese Army, during their late war with China. He was present at the capture of Port Arthur and Wei-hai-wei, and he was for some years on the staff of Lord Roberts, in India. Lieutenant Colonel Ward, A.S.C., Assistant Adjutant-General, served in the Soudan. Major Piggott was in Zululand and served in the Transvaal, but it was in Egypt and the Soudan that he made his name and gained a list of honours in the many engagements he passed through, and in 1886 he was second in command in the expedition against the Yonnes. Major Piggott and Prince Christian Victor were aides-de-camp to Sir Francis Scott. The latter volunteered his services, and his appointment was sanctioned by the Queen. He has seen service in India, where much of his military career was spent. Captain Larrymore, Adjutant of the Gold Coast Constabulary, has a medal for the Jebu expedition, and was eminently fitted for aide-de-camp, as his duties on the coast have brought him into close contact with Sir Francis, and he is thoroughly acquainted with the tribes in West Africa, both on the coast and in the interior.

*Apropos* of Captain Larrymore's connection with Sir Francis Scott, a story of that young officer's pluck may not be out of place. In February, 1892, while on a tour of inspection, Sir Francis Scott and Captain Larrymore, with a small party of Houssas, called at Asuom, where there was much excitement among the natives over the death of their King. After a long march in the heat of the day, the officers settled down in a native shanty to rest, having put their men into quarters.

Sir Francis was suddenly disturbed by a great clamour, and going to the door of the hut he saw his troops surrounded by an armed, howling mob, mad with drink. The Houssas had formed into line and were loading their rifles, while the natives, who numbered a thousand or more, had loaded also, and in another minute shots would have been exchanged, when the little force must have been annihilated. Captain Larrymore, however, dressed only in a suit of pyjamas, rushed in between the two bodies of men with his umbrella open. He gave orders to his men to unload and go into the hut, while he quietly stood, umbrella in hand, confronting the horde of savages. Such prompt presence of mind had its effect. Quiet was restored, and the natives, after yelling considerably, retired. Had the Captain seized his arms and rushed out showing signs of alarm, the niggers would have instantly opened fire, and no one would have been left to tell the tale; but such quiet pluck is not without an effect even on the dark minds of African savages.

Another digression may be of interest in connection with Captain Larrymore, who had recently returned from the Koranza country in the interior. While there he gleaned further information about the existence of a white tribe in the interior of Africa. He found it was an accepted tradition among the Houssa tribes, that on a strip of the desert to the N.E., there lived a tribe of white men. As this desert was dangerous, attempts had been made by the Koranza people to avoid it, by passing through these white men's country, but they were found to be so fierce that the dangers of the desert were preferred to the hostility of this tribe. He afterwards met a Mohammedan priest and Hadji; a man of great integrity, who had been to Mecca and had seen one of this white tribe on his return journey. Captain Larrymore suggested that the man was simply a light-coloured Arab, but the Hadji said "Oh, no! I saw him close at hand. He had light hair and blue eyes, exactly as you have, and was armed with a bow and arrows." This region is practically unknown to European travellers, but for some years, reports have constantly been brought down by the

## SPECIAL SERVICE OFFICERS. 49

natives as to the existence of this white race, and there seems now to be substantial grounds for believing there is a foundation for their story.

Beside the officers I have mentioned, there were many others working up towards the Prah, or superintending the dispatch of stores up country. Major Montenaro, R.A., Commandant of the base at Cape Coast; Major Wolfe Murray, an experienced Staff Officer, in charge of the Lines of Communication; Major Baden-Powell, of the 18th Hussars, in charge of the native levies, and who had served in Afghanistan and South Africa. He was Intelligence Officer in the Zulu operations of 1887, and also commanded the flying column which captured Dinizulu. Major Gordon, 15th Hussars; Major Clayton, Army Service Corps; Captain Benson, R.H.A., a Staff College man; Captain Blunt, another well-known Horse Artillery Officer; Captain Williams, South Staffordshire Regiment, who served in the Zulu war; Captain Mathews and Captain Bernard, Army Service Corps; and Captain Graham, 5th Lancers.

Major Sinclair, R.E., was hard at work preparing a pontoon bridge over the Prah, barrels for which had been taken up country with considerable difficulty; Captain Curtis, R.E., was pushing on with the telegraph cable, which was at this time laid almost to Prahsu.

Lieutenant Edwards and Sergeant-Major Johnson, A.S.C., were the first to advance up country. This first advance was published in many of the newspapers, headed "Gallant Exploit of a British Officer," and referring to Quartermaster Edwards plunging alone into the interior and penetrating as far as Mansu, &c., &c., when, as a matter of fact, he was accompanied by Sergeant-Major Johnson. The Houssas also were ahead at Prahsu, and the journey to Mansu is frequently done by traders and officials, who think nothing of it, the road being good and quite as safe as many a country road in England, with less chance of being molested than in Cape Coast itself.

Things were kept very lively in the Castle by the constant arrival of various kings who came in from the surrounding districts with their followers to act as carriers. Each arrival was announced by a fearful uproar; shouting, singing, horn-blowing, and beating of tom-toms; the rank of each chief and the number of his followers being easily decided by the amount of din made. As an officer pertinently remarked, "You could first hear them, then smell them, and afterwards see them," as they marched down the main street to the Castle. The present

E

power of many of these kings and chiefs is purely nominal, so a special ordinance was brought into force, conferring upon them the power to enrol their able-bodied subjects for service with the expedition, and under this enactment, all kings and chiefs were liable to heavy fine for neglect in collecting their men, and their subjects also liable to punishment for refusing to obey orders.

This ordinance quite did away with the stern necessities of martial law, and was a sort of compromise between that, and making service optional, in which case the required number of carriers would never have been collected. The arrangement proved satisfactory in every respect, causing great excitement among the natives as soon as it was published, and they willingly rallied round their chiefs. The Governor certainly acted wisely in reaching the people through their own head-men, who were thus backed by the authority of the Government. Their loyalty to the British is only prompted by fear, but they still keep up a semblance of their former devotion to their kings, whose legal power, in most cases, is absolutely *nil*. The case of the Accra King Tackie may be cited as an example of this. In 1881, he was a prisoner at Elmina Castle, and his people steadfastly refused to join the expedition then being formed, unless Tackie were released. When he was ultimately set free, he had no legal control left over his tribe, and latterly he seemed to have so allowed his moral influence to wane, that his power had practically ceased to exist. But when the enactment came into force, and temporary power was vested in him, the Accras rushed *en masse* to their chief, and he suddenly found himself in a position of perfect authority over his people, whose latent instincts of loyalty were stirred to the utmost.

They arrived at Cape Coast Castle on the 21st in full force, amid scenes of great excitement. It was so long since the Accra people had been regaled by a Royal Procession, that they determined to make the most of it, working themselves into a state of enthusiasm bordering on frenzy. The poor old king, finding the excitement infectious, was so beside himself with his newly-found power, that he indulged in a penny bottle of palm-wine from a roadside merchant, and after drinking a carefully measured half, he distributed the remainder among the head-men while his people danced round, wildly shouting most extravagant and adulatory encomiums to the dusky monarch, amid a deafening accompaniment of drums, tom-toms and horns.

In the streets of Cape Coast, the one topic was the war; and the niggers were all squatting on their hams, gravely discussing the ins-and-outs, and probable consequences thereof. Many of

## CAPE COAST WATER SUPPLY.                       51

them remember the last war, and a few, who had served in some capacity in '74 and obtained a medal, were proudly exhibiting the precious bit of silver, pinned on an old European coat or shirt donned for the occasion. Meanwhile, up country, things were being pushed forward. Major Baden-Powell was at Prahsu with his levies, and rest camps were being formed at intervals along the road to the Prah. Stores were being rapidly sent on ahead, and it was evident that, when the white troops arrived, everything would be in readiness for a rapid advance to the frontier, beyond which, progress must be slow and difficult.

An ever-absorbing difficulty on the West Coast is to keep the water in tolerable order. Just outside Cape Coast are large wells, or closed underground reservoirs of puddled clay, with a small opening to the surface, and there is a more substantially made tank in the town. These wells are filled in the rainy season, the water being stored for subsequent use, but after standing for some time in such a climate, it is totally unfit for European consumption, and is doubtless a great cause of sickness among white men on the coast, though the natives apparently suffer no ill effects from it. Many of the officials and traders have private tanks to store their water, in which it is kept free from contamination, but nothing can prevent it becoming stagnant and tainted by the surrounding unwholesome influences.

There are a great many pretentious looking stores in the town, but most of the commodities consist of old stuff, shipped from England or Germany, calculated to catch the negro eye, and little can be purchased that is of service to a European. English money is now more freely circulated, though many places of business still retain their scales for weighing the gold-dust which, until recently, formed the staple currency. Coppers are looked at with disdain, the smallest article being threepence, and thus the modest silver bit is in great demand.

The Market stands on the front, but it is only a corrugated iron shelter with open sides and no fittings. The bush people flock down with their supplies, and barter is much carried on with their stock and coast commodities. There is an air of bustle and activity there all day long as the dusky vendors, dressed in gaudy wraps of Manchester print, ply their trade, while perspiring women stagger round with a heavy load balanced on their heads and a nodding brown babe or two tied behind. Thus loaded, they thread their way through the crowd, vigorously pushing the sale of their stock of bananas and plantains.

The horse is a greater curiosity in Cape Coast than an elephant at home, for in the narrow environs of the town there is little use for them, though the total absence of suitable forage alone forms an insuperable barrier to their introduction. There are a few light hand-carts or buggies occasionally to be seen flying through the streets, drawn by half-a-dozen stalwart Fantis; the occupants being some white official or trader going to make a call, or a haughty gentleman of colour, who looks disdainfully on the pedestrian *canaille* around him. The approved method of travelling is by hammock, for this means of locomotion is available, and fairly comfortable, under the most difficult conditions of road, through forest or swamp, where all other mode of transport is impossible. The hammock is slung on a stout bamboo with cross pieces fixed at each end, and an awning over the whole. The four bearers stand, one at each corner, and placing the ends of the cross pieces on their heads, walk with a swinging stride, the weight being evenly distributed and the hammock hanging suspended between them. The jolting is trying at first, and until confidence is gained, the nervous inmate feels at every step one end will slip from the bearers head, in which case a nasty fall is inevitable, but so practised do these hammock boys become that they rarely make a false step, and if one trips, his hand is up instantly to keep the load firm till he recovers his equilibrium.

One half of the West India contingent was encamped on Connor's Hill, the remainder being sent forward to Mansu. Many of the former daily reported sick, and no doubt they suffered as much from fever as any of the white troops, though the attacks were shorter and had less effect. Many of the cases were trivial, and I am afraid the close proximity of the hospital gave vent to a great deal of malingering among these lazy negroes, in the hope of getting admitted as a patient, with a few additional luxuries and no duty to perform.

On December 21st, the smart detachment of Artillery non-commissioned officers, under Captain Benson, left to take charge of the Houssa battery at Mansu. The butchers and bakers of the Army Service Corps also started, under Sergeant-Major Sparks, to get field ovens built, and a batch of fresh bread ready for the troops when they marched up country.

The accommodation in the Castle was severely taxed, many officers having to find quarters in the Wesleyan Mission House. The school-rooms afforded shelter for the men of the Engineers, who made themselves as comfortable as possible on the stone floor, and if the bed were hard, at least it was dry and cool.

The one sight in the Castle was the massing and numbering

## COLONIAL FREE TRADE.

of carriers as they were formed into gangs. Large cases of police armlets, with numbers attached, were sent out, and the possession of one of these gaudy bandages was the cause of much inward joy and gratification to the dusky burden-bearers. Each native lost no time in strapping on his number, there being little fear of his discarding the valued insignia of office as enrolled carrier to the Queen, and the work was much facilitated thereby, for each man's number was always visible, denoting his position and gang without difficulty or palaver. The Army Service Corps certainly earned fresh laurels for the efficient arrangements of transport, and before the troops had landed, there were 11,000 loads of supplies safely deposited at Prahsu; a feat of no small magnitude, over an indifferent track of seventy-three miles.

The more that is seen of Cape Coast and its surroundings, the greater wonder is created as to what the Government has done for the town and its inhabitants. True, there is a fairly efficient force of native police, who walk about, baton in hand, ready to crack the skull of any offending nigger. There are a few oil lamps sprinkled down one or two of the principal streets, but any other road or track is left in total darkness, and from one end of the town to the other there are numerous holes and pitfalls into which any traveller, who has the temerity to walk abroad after dark, is sure to come to grief. Then the stench and pollution in many of these slums are a disgrace to any town whose inhabitants profess to be under the British Flag.

On a previous page I have referred to the total imports and exports of the Gold Coast Colony for 1894. From these figures I find that from the total imports valued at £812,830, the value of English imports only reaches £582,273, thus leaving a surplus of £230,557, or over one-quarter of the whole amount, for goods from foreign markets. The total exports, value £850,343, show the sum of £278,956, or nearly one-third of the total, was sent to foreign markets, and the remainder to England. Recently the German Colonial Authorities on the West Coast decided to grant no further concessions to English traders, and the French place many obstacles in the way of alien merchants, but on our Gold Coast the foreign trader has every facility offered him, after paying the regular ten per cent. *ad valorem* duty imposed on all imports. Free Trade in England and Free Trade in a colonial possession is a different thing, and, with a few restrictions, all the interests might easily be kept in British hands, to the benefit of our traders, and without injuring the Revenue. The smaller stores are filled with flimsy rubbish of a decided German cut, and these foreign traders have a great advantage over those who supply *bona fide* English goods, though the staple trade in Manchester stuff and prints is kept well in British markets. Jam, so-called, tinned provisions of very questionable quality, and mineral waters which taste like dish-water, all have foreign labels attached, and when purchasing such articles as these it is very difficult to obtain British brands.

On my first Sunday evening in Cape Coast, I was present at the service in the Wesleyan Mission Church, and was much impressed by the scene in that little place of worship. The preacher that evening was the Rev. Mr. Somerville, a very earnest young missionary, who afterwards acted as the Chaplain to the troops on the way to Kumassi. The building was crammed, including the galleries, but the congregation was not composed of the overdressed and arrogant Fantis, always ready to show off their superiority and advanced state of civilization. Here, indeed, was a congregation to feel interested in. Many of the people were of the poorest class, in scanty native dress, and there was a strong sprinkling of well, but quietly dressed negroes, sitting with their wives and children by their side, all paying fixed attention; while the singing, though hearty, was marked with little of the usual negro shouting and gusto. The first part of the service was in English, and the latter half in the vernacular, being conducted by the native minister. The Wesleyan Mission on the Gold Coast is certainly a pattern worthy of imitation, which, unfortunately, is more than one can say of many other foreign missions run on much more pretentious lines, and boomed far and wide. Personally, I have little sympathy with foreign missions as a whole, and the large amounts annually subscribed and expended in keeping them up, might be far more judiciously spent in elevating some of our semi-heathen at home. A large percentage of the missionaries are prompted to volunteer their services by the romantic prospects thus opened to them, and the same men would look askance if asked to labour in the slums of our large cities, among their unfortunate countrymen. Others, especially native preachers, spoil all the good influence they might have, by embarking in trade with the natives, but the Wesleyan Mission is a notable exception, which, perhaps, goes to prove the rule. I am not a Wesleyan, and hold no briefs for them, but simply state facts as I found them. In the first place there is not a single redeeming feature to attract Englishmen to labour on the insalubrious surroundings of a town on the West Coast of Africa, and to the few white men who are daily risking their health and life, it is essentially a labour of love. Trading on the part of any Methodist minister, white or black, is strictly forbidden. Among their followers also a strict discipline is exercised, forming a great contrast to many other missions, where the sole object is to swell the list of new converts. If any member is inconsistent in his private life, the discipline is put into force, and the result is, that a negro who simply adopts a civilized religion in the same matter-of-fact way that he gets into European dress, and only to obtain social advantage, soon finds there is something more required than mere outward show and Sunday profession, and he does not remain a member long. Thus there is no large increase in the annual numbers published, for though many fresh members are yearly enrolled, large numbers of inconsistent ones are removed from membership. This fact spoils elaborate reports as to progress, but gives a far more convincing proof of reality in the work than any of the startling papers often published on foreign missions, which show the annual return of members double or treble the numbers of the preceding year. Their churches, too, all endeavour to be self-supporting with the native ministers, so they do not have to depend so much on outside help from England.

Wesleyans began their work in 1837, and now own the most palatial residence in Cape Coast for a Mission house and training college for native ministers. A book room is also established in the right wing of the building for the sale of books and stationery at a moderate price, and over £1,000 worth of books and papers are disposed of annually, which alone speaks volumes for the advance of education among members of the community on the Gold Coast. The Rev. Dennis Kemp is the Chairman and General Superintendent for the Colony, and he and his colleague, Mr. Somerville, have their hands full in directing the work of such an extensive sphere. In the Cape Coast Sunday Schools, over 1,000 children are on the rolls; the day schools have an attendance of nearly 400, and there is now a flourishing industrial school in which lads can, at any rate, pick up the rudiments of a trade.

While the Wesleyans are doing so much in the Western part of the Colony, the labours of the Basle Mission in the Eastern districts are worthy of note, especially their work in the Acropong district. The first Basle missionaries came to the coast in 1828. Their headquarters are at Accra, and besides their purely religious work, they have done much to promote technical education, industry and agriculture. Doubtlessly these German Swiss have gone in largely for trade, but it has been trade for a good purpose, and their efforts are perhaps more successful in advancing commerce and civilization than in moral and religious training, though the latter is part of their curriculum. They have a large establishment at Christiansborg, where the pupils are trained as blacksmiths, carpenters, coopers, tailors, etc., and thus in after-life the students have the means of earning an honest livelihood. Most of the skilled labourers employed under Government have been taught their trade in this Accra Mission.

Despite all the labours of the missionaries, or God-palaver men as they are called, and the constant intercourse of Europeans, the majority of the people in Cape Coast are still in a dark uncivilized condition, and as barbarous and superstitious as if they had never seen a white man's face.

The Fantis are the inhabitants of the town of Cape Coast and its immediate neighbourhood. They are a fine-looking tribe, but about as cowardly a race of blackguards as could well be found, and with all their bombast, the mention of an Ashanti makes them tremble. As allies, they are perfectly useless for fighting, and are greatly despised in consequence by the tyrants on the northern boundary. Their outward fetish worship is not very powerful now, but still flourishes, one curious fetish being the mass of rock called "Tahara," on which the Castle stands. At regular periods this is washed and swept by the women, and offerings are piled up on it.

Many were the queer customs and bizarre ceremonies that I daily witnessed in the streets, in which the ugliness and boniness of the semi-nude hags that jumped and yelled, did not tend to remove the sense of disgust felt amid such scenes of downright savagery. Numbers of the women had fetish to perform as their husbands had gone to the war, and one most singular custom was to make clay with their saliva, and anoint their shoulders and face with long stripes of white mud each day.

Before the authorities interfered, a wedding marked one of the most disgusting orgies that it is possible to imagine. In one part of the ceremony, the young virgin was stripped quite naked, and carried round the streets loaded with jewels, till the multitude had gloated its eyes on the maiden, who was then conducted to the house of her husband, accompanied by the howling scum of the place. The one wedding that took place in the town while I was there, was a very different affair, for the hymeneal pair belonged to the select upper ten of Cape Coast Society, and were therefore married in orthodox European fashion, or in a near approach to it. The service was conducted in the little English Church by a native clergyman, the bride being attired in a flowing white veil and crimson satin gown, the bridegroom in faultless European dress. The church was crowded by the wealth and beauty of Cape Coast upper classes, the youths chiefly in European clothes, and many comely maidens decked in full dress, or rather undress, of the latest native fashion, which allows no costume above the waist, unless a few rows of beads around the neck could be thus described. When the ceremony was over, the happy pair bowed themselves down the aisle to the door, and entering a hand gig, were soon whirled, amid clouds of dust, by a dozen willing pairs of arms, to the bride's residence. Owing to the difficulties of travelling, honeymoons are necessarily dispensed with.

The next afternoon was marked by an even more lively ceremony, to wit—a funeral. For two days previously a monotonous chant and tom-tom beating had been kept up in the native quarter, and the reason was explained when a horde of men and women appeared, dancing and shouting to the accompaniment of the everlasting drums and horns, and bearing in their midst the body of a minor fetish priest, rolled in a shroud. With much din and hubbub was the gruesome burden taken to the beach, where a disgraceful scene was enacted. The body appeared to be used for a tug of war between two parties, each scrambling for the possession of the corpse, and racing it through the surf, and many were the capers cut with the remains before they were laid to rest in the native burying place. This ceremony constituted some of the obsequies of the water fetish, the ocean being worshipped right down the coast. In some out-of-the-way places human sacrifices to the water still take place. A young girl is tied to a stake at low water, for the rising tide to sweep her away, unless a shark ventures in to seize the prey before the sea comes up. The King of Dahomey used to be even more liberal in this respect, handing over some prime minister or high official to the tender mercies of the Dahomeyan Amazons, for ocean sacrifice. The King's wives, as these dusky daughters of Mars were called, promptly marched the victim to the coast in his full regalia, and when he had been rowed some distance from shore in a canoe, he was thrown overboard to drown, or to make a meal for the waiting sharks.

The sunrise of December 24th was heralded by a fearful din in the town, and on enquiring the reason of the hubbub from a dignified gentleman of colour, who condescended to act as a clerk to the Government, I was told that it was "Christmas Eve," in a tone that plainly showed how I was to be pitied for my ignorance, though it was only just 7 a.m. The natives keep up the day before Christmas, or "Christmas Eve," as they call it, in grand style, but it is only a forerunner of the day that is to come. In the terrible heat of West Africa there is nothing suggestive of the festive season, and the bare idea of Christmas seems a glaring incongruity in the un-English surroundings. The natives have copied Europeans in making a general holiday of this season, but their notions of "Peace on Earth and Good Will to Man" take the form of a disgraceful debauch, and settlement of private feuds. Should any resident in Cape Coast, be he black or white, have given offence to any person, he is always on the alert at Christmas-time. The individual wronged quietly nurses his injuries till this holiday when, inflamed with spirits, he remembers his insult, and accompanied by a crowd of friends, lies in wait for his victim, who gets a severe mauling with sticks and fists should he fall into the clutches of the mob. Probably the intended recipient is warned, and as a precaution takes a bodyguard of partisans with him, and many a sanguinary faction fight takes place on the coast during the season we look on as Divine.

Bands of young men and maidens in the scantiest costumes, paraded the town all day, but sunset was the signal for the orgies to commence in good earnest. The streets were packed; the din unbearable; drums and tom-toms of every description were beaten, the night air being rendered hideous by the screeching of native horns, penny trumpets and tin whistles, without regard to time or tune, and all the niggers were more or less maddened with excitement and drink as they danced, screamed and howled in mad frenzy. Skinny old hags were grinning hideously, revealing their toothless gums; nude children hopping inextricably between the legs of their elders, and the men dashing about madly with coloured fires and torches in their hands. Squibs and crackers were also flying in all directions, for the surplus fireworks of our English November festival are shipped to the coast for December, and the Saturnalian celebration was indeed pandemonium let loose.

A Government clerk, a gentleman of colour, had sent me a written invitation to a ball to be held in the town that evening. I have, unfortunately, lost the important missive, but the contents ran as follows:—" A grand ball under the height of the patronage pertaining to the aristocracy and official circles of the district, was postponed on the same date to the date of a later period, and will take place this evening, at the hour of eight, in the residence of H. —— Esq. The patron of the auspicious event will feel indebted to great honour of your presence in great condescension, and if the bearer of enclosed ticket brings it himself to the door, you will be admitted. A charge of two shillings for each person is made at the door to pay voluntarily for the band." Enclosed was a ticket with my name written across, and as a friend of mine, an English trader, had promised to drop in, I decided to go. The wording of the letter was decidedly ambiguous, but I grasped the gist of it, and in due course set out. Being a white man, the doorkeeper did not attempt to collect the subscription, and I was ushered into the ball room, a spacious whitewashed chamber above a large trading store. A giddy waltz was in progress, but just as I entered, the band ceased, and the afore-mentioned clerk introduced me with much ceremony to mine host, a fat, greasy nigger, in a tolerable dress suit and pumps, shipped expressly for the occasion from England. As I gazed down the ball-room the gaudy vision and coloured magnificence of that brilliant assemblage dazzled me, for the colours of the rainbow were not in it. The dusky beaux were arrayed in coats and waistcoats of satin of every shade and pattern, with a wide expanse of shirt-front; their nether extremities cased in black and coloured stockings and the orthodox pumps. The ladies were redolent with patchouli, and magnificently attired in silk and satin wrappers of most brilliant hues, and more modest proportions than usual. Hair oiled and dressed in spikes or knobs, and bedecked with gaudy artificial flowers or glaring pins, stuck fantastically into every corner, and their ebony complexions—well, not painted and powdered, as soot would be the only preparation suitable, but heightened and polished by fish oil, which gives a beautiful finish, but vile effluvia. The ladies were all young and comely, most of them between fourteen and seventeen, after which age they are usually mothers of families and decidedly *passé*. The guests were leading residents of the town, coloured officials, native traders and clerks, all absurdly dignified and scrupulously polite. The grandiloquence of the males was the cause of much envy on the part of the ladies, and they vainly tried to emulate the fluency of their lords and masters, but invariably had to relapse into pigeon-English. " Miss Martha C——, may I have the ineffable felicity of the next dance?"

" Oh, Mr. —— I'se mortal sorry, but hab jes' given it to that ther Mr. A—— N——," naming a prominent post office official.

The music was supplied by the drums and fifes of the Cape Coast Volunteers, and though it was possible to dance to the measured beat of the drums, the so-called harmony was simply a discordant fanfaronade. I was introduced to the principals, by mine host, with much flourish and flowery speech, while the compliments showered on my poor head by him, would have made the most brazen *reprobate* blush; but at last it was over, and the dancing restarted. Like an English ball-room, there were a number of " wallflowers," but not so much from the lack of eligible partners, as the fact of many prominent men bringing their wives and sisters, the former not being supposed to dance with any, save her lawful spouse, though he was free to lavish his attentions on any lady he pleased. I was earnestly pressed to pick a partner from one of these forlorn maidens, but my feelings of gallantry were not sufficiently strong to go through the ordeal, though the waiting belles felt I was showing a total lack of good taste in failing to appreciate their respective merits. The dance had hardly started when there was a sudden disturbance. A certain gentleman was assiduously paying his attentions to a showy little damsel in the far side of the room, when "*horrendum dictu!*" he suddenly noticed his wife, a modest-eyed maiden of fifteen, was dancing with another man, who, as subsequently proved, was her cousin. He quitted his partner instantly, and dashing across the room, roughly dragged his poor little slave aside, and with murder blazing in his eyes, faced the now enraged chevalier. Bursting with righteous indignation they could find no words to express themselves, but if looks would kill, ·both would have instantly departed this life. They found tongues at last simultaneously, and then ensued such a flow of rhetoric, in Fanti and English, that had I a speed certificate for Pitman's, I could never have kept pace with their tongues, neither would the report be fit for publication. Terrible were the maledictory threats and solemn imprecations hurled from side to side with much bombast of " blood alone wiping out the stain on their honour," till they were both exhausted, and turned away, about to resume the festivities.

It is now my pleasant duty to record the gallant action of the one hundred and fifty guests who had crowded round the two principals while the uproar was on. The fierce arguments had hardly ended, when the crowd of friends heroically flung themselves in the breach, frantically holding apart the late combatants in the wordy war, begging them to desist, and not injure each other. The two heroes, finding it was now impossible to come to blows, immediately made a brave show of resistance, and piteously begged to be allowed to take summary vengeance, and fly at each other's throats. They vainly struggled to get from the grasp of the peacemakers, but when some of them seemed inclined to let the

## AN AFRICAN CHRISTMAS. 61

irate husband have his way, and loosed their hold, he was suddenly seized with an unalterable determination to pass it over that time, and reserve reprisals for a future date.

It was a relief to get into the air again after the hot stuffy room, but in the streets the row had increased tenfold; the orgie was at its height, and the din unbearable. As we stood and looked into the lower part of the town, the glare of the torches and coloured fires, the sombre stillness of the surrounding bush, the hordes of nude savages flying madly around, and the different flares lighting up their naked bodies as they twirled and turned, made a most weird scene, and one could well imagine it was the very haunt of demons. We had hardly gone a hundred yards when whiz! came an empty bottle past my ear, smashing on the road in front, another broke at my friend's feet, followed by a shower of stones, and it was lucky we had not discarded our helmets, for mine was knocked over my eyes by a large lump of flint, which would have smashed an unprotected head. We scrambled up the bank to dislodge our unknown assailants, who were lurking in the ruins of an old mud house, and when we rushed in, there was a dash and scuffle, as a dozen dusky figures clambered over the walls and were lost in the labyrinth of clay ruins. This little ambush was no doubt intended for some white man, and as we were of the same colour, they thought we should make as good recipients for such favours as the intended quarry, providing it gave vent to their pent-up feelings.

As we got into the main thoroughfares the crowd became denser than ever, but we managed to push through into the Ashanti road where a fresh crowd was gathered, and some well-dressed nigger clerks greeted us with a string of insults. We took no notice till the rabble sent a volley of stones after us, when we turned on them, and I grasped my stick, expecting to be involved in the thick of a fight, but to my surprise the crowd melted, scattering in all directions; two hundred instantly put to flight by two white men. Our troubles were not yet ended, as in the square by the Wesleyan Mission Church, we encountered a fresh mob. In the centre were two more highly civilized negroes in European dress, making melody on an old banjo and concertina, the crowd dancing round the centre pair, who were almost revered for their adoption of civilized attire. Wishing to make a further show of their vast superiority, they made various offensive remarks about white men, and finished it by shouting "you two white niggers, &c., &c." Had we passed on, the rabble, thus encouraged, would have sent a volley of stones after us, so we turned sharply, and made for the educated specimens, who precipitately fled, followed by the crowd running like a flock of frightened sheep, many falling over one another in the panic.

Christmas day brought no relief from the row; the respectable few attended service, but the majority kept up the drunken debauch till night, when they ceased their noise from sheer weariness.

So much for these wretched Fantis, who are practically useless, being the most cowardly, indolent, toil-hating tribe to be found on the coast.

Among negroes, conscience really does not seem to exist, unless the wholesome fear of the law, and its far-reaching arm when they have transgressed, can be so termed. They have no true sense of right or wrong in themselves, but know that if they are found out in certain things they will be punished, and keep a little straight in consequence, though they do not abstain from law-breaking for any moral sense of wrong. The Fantis have a terrible dread of the law and police, while the logical deductions which often enable the white commissioner to bring a crime home to a man, is looked on by many as the wonderful power of fetish; for their own dull brains can never put two and two together.

When returning from Elmina early on Christmas evening, I saw a group of people gathered round a prostrate figure, while another man was tearing at his wool, and beating his forehead on the ground in a way that would be perfectly suicidal if other than a negro's thick skull were concerned. As I drew near, the man, hearing the approach of booted feet, sprang up with a cry and disappeared in the bush. I found a youth badly stunned, with blood oozing from his nose and mouth, and was told by an intelligent-looking negro that the man who had dashed for the bush had beaten this youth on the head with a club. Thinking he had killed him, he was told by the crowd, who had coolly watched the proceedings, that the police would take him, and he would be hanged. Not till then did he feel any compunction for his brutal conduct, but he at once set to work to kill himself rather than be captured, though he would have taken a long time to fracture that thick skull of his. He was, however, cutting his face badly on the gravel, till hearing a European tread, he made off.

"Where has he gone? Why did you not stop him?" I asked.

"Oh, sah, him go to bush plenty far, but white man strong medecin find him ebbery where he go. Dat dere fool nebber escape, no fear ob dat."

I did not seek to underrate their belief in the secret power of the white man and his Sherlock Holmes' methods of procedure when unravelling simple crimes.

GOLD COAST WOMEN.

## GOLD COAST CHILDREN.

The feelings of maternity are strong among African women, and form a wonderful contrast to their utter indifference on all questions of morality. For two or even three years the mother's whole care is devoted to her little one, though probably she has one or even two more children before the first is weaned. Thus she slaves and never separates herself from them, and even when going through the most laborious occupations, one or two children will be suspended on her back, with their little heads alone showing over the tight folds of her wrap. Thus encumbered, she will trudge into the bush, and collect her supply of yams and plantains for the day's use. Many procure a second load, and trudge to market, with sixty or seventy pounds balanced on their head and child behind, to exchange the fruit for other wares. Yet these children soon return this marked devotion with perfect indifference, and when once they can do for themselves, the mother is treated as an absolute stranger.

The brightness of these little savage children presents a striking contrast to the dull expressions of their elders. The active little boys and girls, with their naked bodies, fat corporations, and bright fearless faces, roll about in a perfect state of happy innocence. On seeing a white man they instantly stand to attention, gravely saluting, as they have seen the Houssas do to white officers. As you pass, there is a shrill little chorus, "A good h'evening, sah," "Good h'evening, sah"; you look round with a smile, and a dozen little paws are outstretched, "Dash me frepence, sah," "Dash me frepence." Who could resist such an appeal? You dash, *i.e.*, give them a couple of threepenny bits to scramble for, that being the smallest coin current on the Gold Coast, and go on your way; but another hundred yards, a fresh group of urchins require "dashing," and it soon becomes wearisome. This charming naïveté of character is lost as soon as childhood's days are past. There is little of the bloom of youth in Africa, especially with the women. Children develop at a very early age, and at thirteen or fourteen, the girl is married, and soon sinks under the degrading slavery of her position. The male degenerates by the life of apathy, and the excesses he indulges in, long before man's estate is reached.

There is a newspaper on the Coast, published at Accra, a weekly production — *The Gold Coast Independent* — of which the inhabitants of the coast towns are very proud. The price is threepence, for which you get two small sheets of large print. The modest aspirations of this delightful

F

paper are "To create and foster public opinion in Africa, and make it racy of the soil." To accomplish this small task, which you are reminded of by the motto appearing in large type, in three different places, you pay threepence, and we obtained, on December 31st, 1895, one column and a half devoted to an Ordinance, a copy of which could be seen posted up in a dozen places in the town, and the remainder of that page filled with a school report and remarks on Ashanti, taken from the *Standard*, of Nov. 15th, 1895. Two pages of advertisements, and the last columns containing some startling information under the heading of "Latest War Intelligence," in which we are told "All people are taking much interest in the forthcoming war." "Many men from Axim are running into Cape Coast to see the troops land," etc., etc.

The British trading companies on the Gold Coast have a white agent, and one, or perhaps two, white clerks to superintend the working of the staff of native assistants. The clerks are generally young men who hear of an opening on the West Coast of Africa, and immediately are filled with a romantic longing for a change. Visions of lion and elephant hunting, travels among cannibals, and a life of adventure, loom in the distance, and they engage for periods varying from two to three years, at a salary that is not munificent at home, and is certainly inadequate compensation for a life on the Gold Coast. They arrive fresh from home, and what a terrible disappointment is in store. Before a week has elapsed, they are longing to return, and after a few months on the coast, their energies have become impaired, and they go on in a mere sort of day-by-day existence, and hope dies within them. To spend three years in the pestiferous environs of a town like Cape Coast, with a miserable craven-hearted tribe like the Fantis, is little better than a living burial were the climate healthy; but the risk of health and life is also so great, that I should strongly advise those intending to accept a situation on the West Coast of Africa, to think well before they decide, and to take a small post in England, rather than an apparently good one in the tropics. If they manage to live three years, they return home broken in health, and probably ruined for life. With Government officials it is entirely different, as the conditions are better, the pay is good, and future prospects assured; with chances of seeing the surrounding country, and six months' leave in England, after every twelve months on the coast.

## CHAPTER V.

ASHANTI ENVOYS—THE PALAVER—WEST AFRICAN SQUADRON—THE WHITE TROOPS—TO THE FRONT!—BICYCLING IN AFRICA—AKRAFUL—NIGHT IN THE BUSH — COWARDLY NIGGERS — AFRICAN VILLAGES— MANSU — ATTEMPTED MURDER.

FINAL arrangements were now made for a rapid advance on Kumassi. On December 16th the Ashanti Envoys arrived at Cape Coast on the "Roquelle," and had an interview with the Governor before returning to the capital. Governor Maxwell, Sir Francis Scott and Staff, and the Naval Officers from the Gunboats took their seats in the Castle, many of the Kings and Chiefs of the Protectorate also being present; for a palaver is a function that the African Kinglet delights in. The Ashantis were ushered in, but they were not the two Ansah princes who had made such a stir in Portland Crescent, but their subordinates, Kwaku Fukoo, Prempeh's gigantic linguist, Kwamin Boatin, Kwakoo Inkruma, and Kobina Bondah, who all appeared to be of little importance in London, but lounged in rear of the royal princes. The Ansahs evidently did not mean to run unnecessary risks, and sent forward the lesser lights to bear the brunt of their monarch's displeasure in Kumassi, while they waited for a later boat.

Kwaku, who acted as spokesman, leaning on his gilded staff, with his retinue, and gorgeously arrayed in striped toga and Moorish trousers, tried to appear at his ease with a forced smile and fixed carriage.

Mr. Croome acted as interpreter, and through him His Excellency promptly came to the point, nonplusing the Ashantis who, in common with other African tribes, delight in hyperbole and flowery rhetoric.

"I understand the Envoys who have been to England wish to speak to me!"

Kwaku then looked ill at ease, but after a prolonged pause, rejoined to Mr. Croome, "Some time ago you brought a letter to the King saying the Governor wished to send a white man to govern his country, and the letter also said six nations had accepted British protection. The King told you he would consult his chiefs and reply to the Governor, and he held a palaver, but he could do no business with Governor Griffiths; he was not a safe man, for he had been offering British protection (when asked for) to tribes that owed allegiance to Prempeh. The King therefore sent messengers to England to see the Queen, but when we got there Griffiths had interfered between Prempeh and the Queen, and she would not see us, so we had to come back, as we were told to see the new Governor. Thus we are here and the other Envoys return soon."

"Am I to understand he brings a message to me?" asked the Governor.

"We took a letter to the Queen," was the reply.

"Has he anything to say to me, then? If so, let him say it."

Kwaku pondered, and began a rambling statement about Governor Griffiths, who was not a good man to settle with, but His Excellency interrupted:—"I have been in the Colony since April last, and the Envoys left for England only three days before I arrived. They have wasted eight months, and if they had a message from the King why did they not await my arrival?"

Kwaku attributed that to Governor Griffiths, but Mr. Maxwell stopped him. "In defiance of prohibitions, and in spite of advice you Envoys proceeded to England. You were distinctly told before you started that you would not be received, and you were not received. In your absence it was necessary to send a further demand to Prempeh in Kumassi, to which he has not replied. Have you any instructions from the King as to that?"

The Envoys shook their heads and grunted, Kwaku saying, "The King will accept a resident, and we will take him with us to Kumassi."

The Governor then told them to return at once to the capital, and tell the King, if his promise were sincere he must prove it by:—

1. Meeting the Governor on the border of the Protectorate.
2. Signing a fresh treaty with England.
3. Paying the expenses to which the Government had been put by his defiant conduct.

The Envoys smiled contemptuously. They evidently thought such terms perfectly ridiculous, the idea of Prempeh coming to meet the Governor being specially preposterous.

## A USELESS PALAVER.

Still there seemed a possible chance of the expedition being stopped on the border of Ashanti, though it was generally thought that Prempeh would never leave his capital to meet the Governor. To satisfactorily overcome the difficulty, it was no use treating the Ashantis as spoilt children. The Ashanti policy had ever been a mixture of open treachery, insincerity and procrastination, and in the interests of trade and civilization alone, Kumassi would have to be crushed. A section of the Press in London howled and fumed, but surely the Government, through fear of condemnation, were not hesitating before striking a decisive blow. Expedition after expedition had been sent during the last century, and yet all had failed to enforce obedience and respect from the truculent Ashantis, who had been a menace to the Gold Coast Colony only too long. British prestige alone demanded that Kumassi be taken once and for all, and kept in our hands. The abject submission of a dozen sham envoys or of Prempeh himself, would not have been worth the paper it was written on, as our past dealings with Ashanti have too clearly shown. There was only one course open, and that was for a force to march right into Kumassi, capture it, and leave a garrison there, unless we wanted to be made a laughing stock of the Ashantis, and all the surrounding tribes, who would thus be shown how even a savage king might twist the lion's tail with impunity. Governor Maxwell no doubt meant to have no shillyshallying, but it was little use attempting any compromise, or giving the King loopholes of escape, to cause subsequent trouble.

On December 24th, the West African Squadron arrived and dropped anchor off the castle. The vessels anchored in the roads were the Flagship " St. George," H.M.S. " Philomel," " Blonde " and gunboats " Racoon " and " Magpie." In the afternoon Admiral Rawson, commanding the squadron, came ashore. He was met by Sir Francis Scott and Prince Christian, a guard of honour being formed by a company of the West India Regiment. The warships were to remain in order to operate in case of need on the coast, but officers and men, " Jack Tars " and " Joeys," were very disappointed at having to remain everlastingly rocking in their narrow quarters on board, without a chance of gaining fresh laurels in Ashanti. Both bluejackets and marines on these ships are continually being called upon to summarily deal with some turbulent coast tribe. The men are landed; there is a sharp fight; an officer and a man or two are killed, and an entry made in dispatches. Owing to the absence of the ubiquitous

Reuter in these out of the way villages, and the fact that the mail takes perhaps months to get home, the brisk little affairs cause small interest, being soon forgotten amid the excitement of more recent events.

The duties of the men-of-war on both the East and West of Africa are arduous and trying, and the vast importance of the work devolving on them, in maintaining order, and protecting life and property on the coast, should not be underrated. The authorities are rather guilty in that respect, and they have been particularly stingy in granting medals for some of these little affairs, which, in proportion to the size of the respective forces engaged, would rank above some much lauded engagements.

During the afternoon 100 Houssas from Lagos arrived under Captain Reeve Tucker, and proceeded directly to the front.

The wildest rumours came down continuously to the coast; there had been sharp fighting: Kumassi was undermined with powder: Prempeh was dead: the Ashanti army was being formed to invade the Protectorate: also many other reports so conflicting that no reliance could be placed on any one of them. Two of our Adansi scouts were found with their throats cut, but that had little significance beyond shewing that the Ashantis were on the alert; and could not be looked on as the actual commencement of hostilities as some thought.

The surf was very heavy during Christmas week, and communication with the mail boats dangerous. Anxious to get a letter on board the s.s. "Volta," which had just signalled for departure, I hurried to the shore to find the surf boats had ceased running for the evening. To wait for a crew would be out of the question as the steamer would be gone, so I foolishly decided to cross in a canoe. The two boatmen flatly refused to go at first, but the promise of a good "dash," or bribe, at last prevailed, and the sorry craft was duly launched. Time after time we attempted to get through the surf, but were driven back, till we broke through the crest of an advancing roller, which all but swamped us, and by vigorous paddling, got clear of the breakers, into open sea. Our troubles were, however, only just starting, for every moment tremendous seas threatened to overwhelm us, and while the niggers slaved at the paddles, I baled continuously with helmet and calabash, to keep the canoe afloat. We reached the ship, and by means of a rope thrown over the side I managed to scramble on to the ladder and deliver my letter. The difficulty was now to get back into the frail craft that was one moment alongside, the next, swept far away, but after a dozen tries I dropped, luckily, fairly in the centre, as the boat was swept right below me, and we then headed for the shore. Drawing near the jagged bar of rocks off the Castle, we steered for the narrow opening through them, but the rush of water swerved us violently on one side; a huge wave came behind, completely enveloping us; there was a dull scraping, a jolt; we were swamped, twisted over and over in mad confusion till I was suddenly thrown on shore, half choked with sand and water. The darkies were also safe, and we scrambled out of reach of the next wave, which brought up the canoe. Soaked and bruised we waded on shore with it, happily little the worse for the small adventure. The wave had carried us right over the bar, and brought us up almost high and dry, but had our frail canoe struck on one of those jagged spurs, we must have been dashed to pieces, as no one could live in a boiling sea, against those rocks.

On Christmas day the transports, "Coromandel" and "Manilla," arrived with the white troops. The surf was still very heavy, and little communication could be held with the ships, but a surf boat went over, bringing back the mails which had been put on board instead of being sent by the ordinary and slower mail boat, not due till four days later, when many of us would be on the way up country. There was naturally much rejoicing over the unexpected piece of good luck, an instant rush being made to the Commandant's little post office in the Castle. Letters were none the less acceptable by arriving opportunely on Christmas day, when one's thoughts would revert far over the sea to the various home circles gathered in England.

Two fishermen had rowed down the coast in a canoe, but on attempting to get through the bar, they came to grief on the same spot that we were capsized on the previous evening. Their boat was smashed, the men vainly battling with the waves that mercilessly battered them against the rocks. Happily, the surf boat was returning from the "Manilla," and under the direction of Sergeant-Major Bamford, A.S.C., who was on board, they were rescued with great difficulty, suffering from severe contusions.

On board the Hospital-ship "Coromandel" were the Special Service Corps, with detachments of the Medical Staff and Engineers, and the "Manilia" brought from Gibraltar the 2nd West Yorkshire Regiment under Colonel Price. Only Prince

Henry of Battenberg landed, the troops all remaining on board till required.

On Boxing-day, everyone was hard at work making final arrangements for the landing of the troops and the advance up country. Special stores were landed from the transports, also the two donkeys Prince Henry had brought with him for use on the march, though there was much surmising as to the effect of the dreaded teste-fly on them. The landing of these animals was difficult, but after their feet were tied, they were safely lowered into the surf boat. The twelve stalwart Fanti boatmen were in a ludicrous state of funk at the presence of these uncanny beasts, and every time they started to plunge or kick as they lay in the bottom of the boat, over would go every nigger head foremost into the sea. It took some time before they could be induced to resume their seats, and as these dives took place several times, the voyage ashore was unduly protracted. Once beached, the donkeys were turned out on the sands, this proceeding being watched by a large crowd of Fantis, but when one of the asses lifted up his voice in a glorious succession of ear-splitting brays, the crowd bolted *en masse*, not stopping till they were out of sight or perhaps sound. I much doubt if that animal's historic and voluble brother, Balaam's mentor, could have created a greater sensation.

On December 27th, the Headquarter Staff started for the front, Prince Henry and Major Piggott being first off, and leaving Cape Coast Castle at 4 a.m. Sir Francis Scott left at 7 o'clock, accompanied by Prince Christian and the remainder of the Staff, except Colonel Ward, who was left to superintend the landing of the troops.

For the first four miles the road was smooth and wide, the bush being a variegated mass of vegetation composed of small palms, [green scrub, lilies, acacia and flowering creeper, tangled together in a glorious profusion of colour, and rising shoulder high on either side of the road. As we mounted the densely-wooded hills that skirt the coast, the early morning sun was just gaining power and dispelling the mists; but white and glistening far below lay the town, already like a smouldering furnace, and we heaved a sigh of relief at the thought of the smells now left behind in that pestiferous place.

After gaining the summit, the sun began to make its presence forcibly known, beating mercilessly down on our backs, and as there was not a vestige of shade, it was a relief to turn into a hammock. The regular jolting as the bearers step stolidly together makes reading or writing impossible, and is trying at first, but one soon grows accustomed to the motion, and a nap may be indulged in, if the bearers will only hold their tongues for a spell.

The first rest camp was formed at Jaycuma, or Inquabim as it is often called. Prince Henry was waiting here for the other members of the Staff, who halted for breakfast and a short rest during the heat of the day. The camp was built in a clearing, and consisted of rows of roughly built huts for the use of the troops on the march. These shelters were about 40 feet long; a framework of bamboo covered with palm leaves interlaced, and kept in place by long strips of fibrous creeper. The interiors were fitted with long, gridiron shaped platforms, running from end to end, and made of six-foot strips of bamboo, tied to trestles at top and bottom. These formed a rough and knotty bed for the troops to spread their blankets, and if the couches did not err on the side of comfort, they at least saved the men from sleeping on the ground, and the palm leaf thatch effectually kept off the worst of the deadly night dew.

Our rest was only a brief one at Jaycuma, for we were doing two ordinary stages each day to Prahsu, leaving the troops to march up in the short daily distances. "Chop," which, by the way, signifies any meal or food, being finished, we re-started on the road to Akraful.

The road visibly narrowed, and as the level macadam developed into a rough track, with traces of recent widening for the advance of the expedition, the first impression that in this highway was at least one useful piece of work of the Colonial Government was rudely dispelled. Mr. Bennett Burleigh intended to ride to the Prah on a bicycle; perhaps he had made his decision after reading of this road in the official accounts, which, if they cannot lie, equivocate to a near degree; but I pity a cyclist scorching over such a track. As we subsequently heard, he pluckily managed to pedal to Mansu, in spite of ruts big enough to bathe in, and an occasional trunk resting serenely across the path, but at that village the "bike" had to be abandoned. This was a pity. Judging from the effect on the coast niggers, who fled at its approach, had the valiant Burleigh taken his machine to Kumassi, and entered the capital sounding his siren, his presence would have been more effectual in subduing the Ashantis than twenty Special Service Corps; for Prempeh and his merry men would have instantly succumbed at the apparition of such a powerful fetish giving its aid to the advancing white man.

As we proceeded on the road, the bush increased in density, and in some places the trees, meeting overhead, formed a perfect archway and shelter from the sun, while huge cotton trees, with massive buttresses, reared majestically above the surrounding bush. The low dense undergrowth parted at intervals, opening into shady dells, containing stagnant pools, overhung with a choice profusion of flowering plants of all hues. In these lovely glades splendid and rare orchids abound, and a botanist can revel for hours in any one spot in an African forest. Floating on the surface of the water are various aquatic plants, and the beautiful African lily abounds; flocks of many coloured birds flit on the surrounding branches, brilliant lizards run up the trunks as one approaches, and myriads of glittering little creatures flit on the surface of the stagnant pools. What a glorious picture! How you would like to linger and revel in its beauties for —— Faugh! A loathsome smell assails your nostrils as you approach, and you instantly turn back to the road, inwardly vowing never to venture into these elysian glades again. This deadly smell comes from the rotting vegetation of ages, that forms a rich strata in which all plants flourish luxuriantly, but it also charges the air with the germs of malaria that, sooner or later, act on the system of the white man who enters that fatal country, and it pulls him to the very verge of the grave, if he escapes with his life.

Nearing Akraful the road widens, and as we reached the village, the smell of an extensive piggery played havoc on the olfactory nerves, making even the Sierra Leone hammock bearers break into a trot, with a vigorous hum to expel the noxious effluvia. All these villages are in a filthy state, the bush on the outskirts being terribly defiled; and the gangs of carriers passing to and fro had not improved matters in that respect. The natives seem impervious to smells, but the Sierra Leone men were an exception, though the odours in Freetown would want a deal of beating. Smart, active fellows, these Sierra Leone men are—made for hammock carrying, with their flat heads and bull necks—and they have a stock of ready wit and repartee that would vie with any cockney 'bus driver, both for pointedness and vulgarity. All other tribes are as dirt to them, especially the cowardly Fanti.

## FIRST NIGHT ON THE ROAD. 75

"Out de way, Fantee man!" "You Fantee fool! He no good 'tall, sah!" "Let us pass, you Fantee fool!" "Go to bush, you pig!" and woe betide the carrier who did not hastily step on one side to allow the hammock free progress, for the nearest bearer seized the offending nigger by the nape of the neck, and over he went, load and all, into the prickly scrub at the roadside. There were a few gangs of women carriers employed on the early stages of the march, and to these they were very polite and gentle. If we overtook a dusky beauty, the nearest bearer's arm was instantly placed round her waist to remove her gracefully on one side, after which he bestowed a smacking kiss on the ebony lips as he passed, and that without jarring his corner of the hammock, or losing his equilibrium.

After hurrying through the village, we reached the second rest camp on the road, and halted for the night. The shelters here were similar to those already described at Jaycuma, the camp being in charge of a white officer and guard of the West India Regiment. The surroundings of this camp at Akraful were very beautiful, and as cocoanut palms abounded in the vicinity, we were able to refresh ourselves by a good supply of the green fruit, which contains a cool and luscious drink, long before the hard nut is formed inside.

Our long strings of carriers were still straggling in, when the sun disappeared behind the high masses of foliage spreading around the clearing, but camp fires were soon blazing, cooking pots on, and every one started to settle down and spend the first night in the bush as comfortably as possible under the circumstances. The water was a dirty brown hue, and very thick even after twice boiling, and passing through the crude but fairly effectual dripping-pot system of filtration.

Here we had the first taste of the preserved Government vegetables, and they were very savoury, despite the ominous label, "Made in Germany." The latter fact gave rise to a deal of small talk among some would-be patriots at home, and even formed a theme for a question in the "House"; but as vegetables in this form are unobtainable in England, these busy-bodies could have easily turned their attention, with more profit, to the hundreds of articles that can be produced at home, but which are thrust out of the market by the inferior, if cheaper, products of the wily Teutons.

The leafy thatch of the shelters served the double purpose of keeping off much of the dew, and harbouring myriads of lizards and small insects that invaded everything and everybody alike. The first few nights in the bush, sleep, to the novice, is impossible, for beside the tortures of prickly heat, various little pests persist in crawling over him, and inflicting a series of judicious but maddening nips and stings. Enormous crawlers, horny beetles, lizards and spiders occasionally drop from the thatch upon one's upturned face, and a deafening chorus is kept up incessantly till morning by thousands of crickets.

A thick mist was hanging over everything when the march was resumed next day. The dew dropped from the trees like rain as we passed beneath them, and the musty smell of rank decaying vegetation was almost overpowering in the heavy humid atmosphere. Prince Henry was the first to start, and evidently believed in a morning constitutional, for he always tramped stolidly in front of his hammock for the first few miles, till the sun began to gain power. His bearers exchanged many glances of mutual satisfaction at their luck in being attached to so indulgent a master; for they thought it was done for their special benefit.

The first two miles on the road to Mansu were very trying, but as we reached higher ground, things became more favourable, and the sun at last dissipated the miasma, and shone forth in all its glory and power.

The soil right up from the coast is a bright red colour, and highly ferruginous, and the road is so strewn with quartz crystals that walking is difficult. This ferreous strata has a marked effect on compasses, the needles being tilted and rendered perfectly useless.

In some places the water had risen right over the road, or had washed it away, but these gullies were being rapidly bridged over to facilitate the advance of the main body. The pools were a great temptation to the natives, who were panting and perspiring under their loads, and the moment they thought themselves unobserved, down went the burden, off came the scanty wrap, and in two seconds they were splashing about in the delightfully cool but stagnant water. Many of them deliberately stooped to drink deep draughts, ignoring the green slime on the surface, and the filthy state of the water from the constant washings; but the nigger argues, "I am thirsty. Thirst requires water, and if I cannot get it pure I must take it as it comes," and they arrive at

## A TYPICAL VILLAGE SCENE. 77

all their deductions and rules of life by such simple but questionable logic. Numbers of natives die of dysentery, but it is chiefly caused through living on raw unripe fruit; and the consumption of this foul water, which would be death to a white man to drink unboiled, has no serious effect on them.

Passing along the road we met many women returning from the forest with their day's stocks of yams and plantains. The Fanti carriers made short work of these, stripping every woman and child of their day's provisions which had only been gathered at the expense of much personal toil and trouble. One comely maiden, about 15 years of age, attempted to run into the bush, but some cowardly Fanti struck her a blow which knocked her down, and her head striking a tree, she lay helpless and half stunned. I heard her scream, but was not near enough to see who struck the blow, and when I arrived the poor little creature lay dazed and bleeding, while a dozen lusty negroes were scrambling to get the biggest share of her stock, someone having even stripped her of her only print robe or wrap. So much for your civilized, educated and Christianized natives of Accra and Cape Coast, where these cowards came from. Yes, my Exeter Hall friend! these are members of the black brotherhood you are so fond of pitying; and they would call themselves enlightened members too.

Happily they were so absorbed in plunder that they did not hear my approach, and glad was I that a good stout cudgel was handy. The track was narrow, my hammock nearly blocked the way, while every stinging blow I struck filled me with unholy exultation, and before they had all got clear, my arm was powerless, and some of them were marked in a way they would not forget in a hurry. A little lime juice brought the poor girl round; her goods had all been dropped by the niggers in their flight, so she got back her stock intact, and the present of four bright new threepences to go on her necklace, made her forget her troubles. Little scenes like this speak volumes for the cowardly despicable nature of the negro, even if he has been brought up and educated in a town—the seat of the Government and the home of the English official, missionary, and trader.

We reached Dunkwa, the next rest camp, shortly before 10 o'clock. The huts and camp were similar to the previous ones, with sleeping accommodation for 500 troops provided. This halting place was only five miles from Akraful, and it was sixteen miles to the next camp at Mansu, thus giving the troops very unequal marches on succeeding days, but the water supply had much to do with the selection of sites at such awkward distances.

After a brief halt for breakfast, we resumed the march at midday. The heat was intense, the path anything but shady, and many a poor carrier lay thoroughly exhausted on the wayside with his load beside him.

We passed through several small hamlets, but all unimportant except Daman, which is a flourishing and dirty township. The only difference in these African villages is the size, for they all consist of a collection of mud huts, built on similar lines in a forest clearing; the people squatting on their hams, moodily dozing in the sun, and a few dozen naked children tumbling in the street with half a score of skinny fowls, and a few pigs. The women ran and hid themselves on the first approach of white men, but even these ebony daughters of Eve are inquisitive, and unable to restrain their curiosity, they could be seen furtively peeping through the holes and crannies in the mud-plastered walls. The young men had all been engaged at Mansu as carriers, but the old men squatted about and looked on with listless indifference, while hideous old hags grinned at us as they stood by the roadside, with short pipes between their toothless gums.

Most of the villages have some horrible monstrosity which is assiduously pushed forward in full view of any passing stranger. Here was a woman with her face half eaten away by a loathsome disease, a ghastly and terrible picture to behold. At Dumassi, the next village, a boy was strutting about, perfectly nude, but his hair and skin of a sickly white hue, though his parents were niggers black as night; and his appearance was not improved by festering sores covering his body.

In the centre of each of these forest townships are the palaver trees, with trimmed logs laid round under the shade of the spreading branches. The rustic seats are occupied by the " big men " of the village, and the most solemn palavers take place in these leafy parliament houses, during which the most trivial questions are discussed with weighty argument and flowery speech, under the presidency of the local chief.

The road dips suddenly as it crosses two valleys, with a low hill between. From the summit of this eminence a splendid view opened out, showing a vast stretch of vegetation extending on every side.

## A DAMP CLIMATE. 79

The track in several places was washed away by previous floods, but the gaps had been roughly filled, or bridged with logs, by the advance party. Passing through some swampy districts, the road suddenly plunged into pitch darkness, as it passed through magnificent clumps of bamboo. These clumps may be viewed from a distance, their presence being distinguished by a soft cloudy outline of bluish-green vegetation, differing greatly from the surrounding masses of foliage. The darkness was intensified by entering into it suddenly from brilliant sunlight, and as each cluster of canes rises at first perpendicularly, and then curves gracefully over to interlace with the tops of the adjoining clumps, a series of beautiful archways are formed. The atmosphere thus closed in is so humid, and saturated with malarious vapour, as to be almost unbearable, and a feeling of relief is experienced as you again emerge into the light of day.

The climate had already made its mark on our things, and every metal article was oxidized a few hours after cleaning, so that constant care alone prevented arms from being rendered useless. Pen nibs were rusted together, watches had refused to act, and my stock of paper, though carefully packed, was in a pulp from the damp, and this only our second day on the road.

At 5 p.m. we sighted Mansu, Prince Henry and Prince Christian being the first to arrive.

It was a late hour when the whole of the carriers had come in, having straggled much on the road. Here was one officer vainly waiting for a change of clothes, another searching for his "chop" box, but all turned up safely at last.

The camp at Mansu was larger than the previous halting places, as it formed the half-way depôt to the advanced base at Prahsu. Three large compounds of bamboo formed the storehouses, and stewing in the heat during the previous fortnight, a little band of officers and non-commissioned officers had been working from morning till night, receiving the everlasting streams of carriers with stores, and organizing fresh gangs to transport the loads to the Prah.

Being an important station, a hospital of several beds had been built, and a field bakery was almost completed. A company of the West Indians formed the garrison.

A few days previously, a West Indian private of the Mansu force was reported for insubordination by a sergeant, and sentenced to some trifling punishment. His trial was hardly over, when he seized his carbine, loaded it, and walking to the hut where his accuser sat writing, deliberatly shot him. The ball struck the sergeant in the shoulder, completely shattering it, and going through the flimsy wall of the hut, it passed through the arm of a carrier who stood just outside. The sergeant's life was at first despaired of, but he subsequently recovered from his terrible injuries. Such an event happening on the opening of a campaign, requires no comment, and, unfortunately, the West Indian soldier is not always a model of good discipline, for with the best treatment he is a grumbler, easily aroused. In this case the would-be murderer was tried by civil power, and sentenced to seven years' imprisonment, but had he been tried by court-martial, under the rules of active service, he was liable to be shot. This latter sentence might have seemed harsh, but it would have had a salutary effect on other of his disaffected comrades, and the term of imprisonment he received was certainly a light one.

Near Mansu there is a stream of quite respectable proportions, and the water free from the terrible Guinea worm. It was pitch dark when I heard of this pool, but immediately a longing for a refresher came over me, and as the feeling increased, I set out with a couple of niggers to act as guides. There was only a narrow track leading through the forest to this so-called lake, and that was fringed with tall grass that completely overshadowed the path, but after stumbling over various obstacles, a gurgling revealed the whereabouts of a stream. As I reached the bank, three dark figures rushed from the water; for this bathing place was set apart for Europeans, the natives having a strip lower down. There was a large patch of sand, clean, but infested with ants, and just as I had stripped, my guide suggested crocodiles. Reassured, however, by the presence of the three niggers two minutes before, I took a header into the inky darkness, only to run my head into, fortunately, soft mud at the bottom; the depth of the water had been exaggerated, for it was barely four feet deep. But what a treat that deliciously cool stream was, and how one revels in the luxury of sufficient water to wallow in, after some time on a very restricted allowance. The stream and its approaches were swarmed with thousands of fireflies, and the effect was both startling and beautiful. The trees met overhead on the higher reaches of the water where the stream was narrower, and swarms of these luminous little creatures flitted in the leafy avenue and

## A ROYAL RESIDENCE.

settled on the branches, making a rare and wonderful display of nature's own fireworks.

Sir Francis Scott had happily arrived in Mansu too late for the never failing palaver with the king of the place, though we were not so fortunate next day.

I paid a visit to the huts forming the royal residence, but there was little of interest save some elaborate war drums covered with leopard skin, and bedecked with a goodly supply of skulls, dried ears and eyes. All these petty African kings seem to revel in an osteological collection that would form a pretty decent graveyard or a first-rate bone museum.

Major Piggott who arrived with the staff at Akraful the previous day, returned to transact some business at Cape Coast the same evening. He arrived there at midnight, left again at 3 a.m., and reached Akraful soon after the Staff had started to Mansu. He pushed on, however, and arrived in camp during the afternoon, having established a record for hammock travelling. The double journey to Akraful, and then on to Mansu, made a total distance of 64 miles, almost without a break; a rate of transit that the hammock bearers would not appreciate too often.

## CHAPTER VI.

SUNDAY IN THE WILDS—PRINCE HENRY'S DONKEYS—LOST KIT—THE ARTILLERY—ASSIN YAN COMASSE—AFRICAN ROYALTY AND EUROPEAN IDEAS—A KING—FETISH CEREMONIES—PRAHSU—CROCODILES—NEW YEAR'S DAY—THE ANSAH PRINCES—THE ASHANTI IN WAR—STAFF OFFICERS DESCRIBED—ARRIVAL OF THE TROOPS—THE HOUSSAS—THE MOHAMMEDAN NEGRO.

ON Sunday, December 29th the sweet clear notes of *reveillé* were echoing among the trees when the column again got in motion; the long line of carriers wending their way like a long moving snake as they followed the sinuous windings of the path through the bush. As we left the camp the strains of a plantation hymn came stealing through the trees from the West Indian lines, reminding us it was Sunday. These men show a national trait in their fondness for hymns and part songs, and well they sing too, though some of their songs are coarse. They are outwardly very pious, and on the "Loanda," *en route* for Cape Coast, being unable to sleep much, they were singing the lowest songs till midnight on Saturday, when the theme instantly changed to the Church Service which they chanted till 3 a.m. without intermission. Quietness then reigned till daylight, when they started the service again from beginning to end, mingled with many well-known hymns, this being kept up all day. Sunday and its observances, with them, is a mere outward form to be adopted for a fixed period, *i.e.*, from twelve p.m. Saturday till twelve p.m. Sunday.

The road between Mansu and Kwaita was rough, but remarkably open on one side, and frequently intersected with large streams. The bridges over these were very crude, being simply three or four huge trunks thrown across, but the water was shallow in most instances, and easily forded by the natives. Crossing one of these bridges, Prince Henry's largest donkey came to grief, getting his foreleg fixed firmly between two trunks. The niggers would soon have made short work of it, for being afraid to approach too near, a dozen started to pelt the poor brute with stones in the hope of making it struggle to its feet. It vainly kicked and plunged, and must have broken its leg had not Major Ferguson arrived on the scene and stopped their pranks. Even then he could not induce the niggers to approach and lift the poor beast up, and he had to wait till others arrived, when half a dozen willing hands lifted Jack from his awkward position. These donkeys were the cause of much cogitation on the part of the bush people, and for once the much despised ass evoked a considerable amount of anxious interest and fear. An animal whose voice will beat even the roar of a lion is certainly a marvellous creature, and we were much amused when passing through a village in which the headman and numerous suite were seated in state to receive the white men. Suddenly the donkeys appeared on the scene, marching in solemn file. At once the regal party were visibly agitated, being half inclined to bolt, but they bravely sat, however, awaiting the approach of the animals, till a glorious bray broke the stillness of the forest, and chief, wives, courtiers and children, fled precipitately, overturning stools, and throwing aside every article in their flight. Nor did they stop till they were far from the source of danger.

Much is said on the coast of the teste-fly whose bite is so fatal to domestic animals, but the donkeys seemed to suffer little inconvenience from this cause; the total lack of forage seems to be a greater drawback to their introduction.

Passing up a rugged incline through Akrofuma, we reached Suta at 10 a.m., and halted for a couple of hours. The surrounding country is beautiful, and though the so-called bush is a misnomer, the trees having attained a sufficient height and density to fully exhibit the majestic beauties of a tropical forest,—the landscape is bright, with plenty of sun and sky, which quite removes the feeling of solemnity and gloom experienced in the dense forest further north.

The Colonial Authorities had an overhead wire in course of construction, which had been completed as far as Mansu, and from that place, the Engineers had started with their field cable already laid well on the other side of the Prah.

Passing through several villages, we reached Assin Yan Comasse just before sundown, after a trying march of twenty-two miles over an indifferent road. The long journey had severely taxed the endurance of the carriers, who straggled much on the way, and dragged themselves wearily into camp one by one, at all hours of the evening. At last all the loads had safely arrived but one, which was, as chance would have it, a bundle containing my only changes of clothes. Tired of waiting, I walked into the bush to see if there were any traces of the missing man, or the kit lying by the road-side, but after going a long distance fruitlessly, I began to retrace my steps. The sun set suddenly, and darkness came on, so my return journey was difficult and protracted, through swamp, and over fallen trunks, rocks, and other obstacles. In the solemn stillness of these vast forests at night, there is an awesome and appalling feeling of loneliness and depression that will not be shaken off. In the denser part of the bush it was impossible to see a foot ahead, but the dead stillness was occasionally broken by a dismal howl from a jackal, or the rustle of leaves, as some animal wended its way on a nocturnal prowl.

Hearing a breaking of twigs, and the creaking that denoted the approach of a human being, I stood in the shade on the edge of a large roadside pool, and in a moment a native figure, clad in white robes, cautiously emerged from the gloom of the trees, and proceeded to fill a chattie from the pond. The outline of his figure was shown in relief on the gleam of the water, and from his large head-dress and flowing robe he might have been a Mohammedan Priest, but for the long spear in his hand and sword in his girdle. I stepped out of the shadow suddenly, when the figure with a bound reached the bush and disappeared among the trees.

On return to camp there were no signs of the missing kit; my clothes were sopped through with perspiration and dew, and passing a night under such circumstances is not only uncomfortable, but well calculated to give one the necessary chill for a dose of malarial fever. In a country where the difficulties of transport are many, no one takes more than their absolute requirements, but happily I found one good Samaritan in the person of Mr. Ward, of the *Pall Mall Gazette*, who had a spare rig, of which he generously gave me the loan.

On Monday, December 30th, the Staff halted for the day at Assin Yan Comasse; Prince Christian and Major Piggott going on to Prahsu, about sixteen miles distant. Captain Benson had got his Artillery mobilized in camp, and during the day the contingent was inspected by Sir Francis Scott. They marched into the bush with guns slung, carriages in pieces, and carried on natives' heads, making a brave show with the long train of ammunition bearers. The order was given to come into action, and the whole movement was done in splendid style. In an instant each man deposited his load in its place, guns and wheels were unslung

## A SMART DISPLAY.

from the poles, ammunition placed handy, and on the carriers retiring to the rear, the native Houssa detachments, each in charge of a smart Royal Artillery sergeant, had the guns mounted, rocket tubes fixed, and all in readiness within one minute after the first order was given. This display of efficiency was a great credit to Captain Benson and his subalterns; one of whom was Captain de-Hamel, a well-known officer of the Londonderry Artillery, also Capt. Irvine, Donegal Artillery, and Capt. Hawtrey, 4th Royal Munster Fusiliers.

The gunners were evidently ready to give a good account of themselves should occasion require, though with the native carriers there is the fear of stampede or confusion when really under fire, and at such a time disorder may prove fatal to the best efforts of the officers and troops.

A big drumming and commotion in the distance plainly bespoke another palaver. Kings are as plentiful in Africa as Colonels on the other side of the "herring-pond," and every one was heartily sick of the constant palaver on palaver, all to no purpose, though it is most impolitic to refuse such honours, and the officials have to endure them with inward groanings but smiling exterior.

On the Gold Coast, a visit from one of these dusky monarchs is regarded as a necessary but unpleasant function, to be endured but not encouraged; but when some king or chief, who owns a bit of swamp and a few mud huts, with half-a-dozen wives thrown in, is able to get enough gold dust collected by his people to don European dress, and betake himself by deck passage to England, how differently he is received. His arrival and subsequent doings are duly chronicled by the Press; he dines with my Lord Mayor, and is petted and pampered to a degree that plainly shows how little African royalty is consonant with European ideas. The young kinglets that yearly come over to this country for education seem to move freely in superior circles of Society, and they are specially patronised by moneyed nobodies, whose snobbish instincts revel in the fact of having a real live Prince in their train, though he comes from a stock of brutal niggers that no person could see in their natural state, without horror and disgust. Yet with all the luxury and civilization that is crowded into them in England, the majority of these, when they have exhausted their finances, return to the old habits, with a bit of print and a swish hovel as evidences of the very thin veneer civilization has put over their patrimonial barbarism. It is a common thing in Africa to find young chiefs who have been educated in England, but have now thrown off the trammels of civilization, and are living in a blissful state of barbarity that would vie with any of their less enlightened subjects.

The King who turned up that afternoon for palaver was Attafuah, King of Akim, a more important personage than many of the same species who abound in the vicinity. His retinue was large and influential, and he was well aware of the fact. Had not his Prime Minister a large bunch of old rusty keys tied to his girdle? Was not the royal stool studded with brass-headed nails, and had he not a few rusty old flint lock guns in his possession?

They formed a dusky but picturesque crowd as they were grouped beneath the shade of three enormous umbrellas of silk and leopard skin. And after a short prelude on three drums, all skull-bedecked, the business started. The King had a long yarn to spin about Prempeh, and complained that many of his people had gone to the 'Shanti country to collect rubber, and had never returned, having been sacrificed in Kumassi. Sir Francis informed the king and his chiefs that he was going to Kumassi to enforce the demands of Queen Victoria, that Ashanti would be annexed, and the country opened up for trade. His remarks made an evident impression on the assembled chiefs, and then Prince Henry of Battenberg was introduced to the King as the husband of the Queen's daughter. All the chiefs, headmen and commoners immediately got on tip-toe to get a glimpse of His Royal Highness, and by their expression, they were evidently disappointed. That a Royal Prince! Why, he was wearing his own sword, instead of having a sword bearer, and worse still, holding a small white umbrella over his own head; then he had no slaves! no stool bearers! no war drums!: he did not come up to their African ideas of royalty, and they could not understand a Prince laying aside all considerations due to his rank, and sharing the same hardships and dangers as the rest of the force. A fawn was afterwards sent to Prince Henry from the King as a present, and the Akims took themselves away; King, noise, and stench.

On Tuesday, December 31st, we were all on the alert before sunrise. Major Ferguson was always one of the first up, and, with his able assistant Quartermaster Sergt. Toye, gave an eye to the arrangements for moving camp. Sir Francis Scott also was always ready to move with the lark, and little time was lost in the

## FETISHISM.

early morning. The scene at sunrise was an animated one, all the carriers bustling about, the native servants working or pretending to work, and the officers superintending the packing of their things till, everything ready, the march was resumed. Meanwhile, the light would be rapidly increasing; the thick miasma moving slowly up till the top of the trees were visible, over which the orb of day soon rose and beat down relentlessly.

The first village on the road to Prahsu is Anowia, which contains a curious fetish house. My presence so alarmed the priests and little group of men whom I disturbed when I entered the compound, that I did not push my investigations too far, but the fact of my being in the vicinity was regarded as gross sacrilege. Some of the carvings done in red and black clay were very well executed, the chief one representing the male and female figures, denoting the important genital symbol of fetishism, but a glimpse of the interior of the house revealed nothing more interesting than some medicine heaps and earthen pots containing food offerings for the gods.

The fetish religion flourishes in many different forms throughout the whole of Western Africa, and seems to consist mainly of the worship of the immaterial, existing, or supposed to exist, in material things. Thus, any odd article may contain some marvellous virtue. An old wooden doll, a horn, a tooth, a bit of snake skin—all may be endowed by a hidden power, transmitted through the medium of a fetish priest, to cure diseases, bring good luck, wealth or happiness, on the lucky owner; or on the other hand, to call down ruin and destruction on the head of an enemy. If a charm refuses to act, the native loses no faith in fetish, but knows the influence of his charm is counteracted by the more powerful charm held by some enemy, who is bent on acting against him. This gives the fetish priests abundant opportunity to impose on the credulity of the people. Present after present is exacted and cheerfully given to enable the priest to propitiate the gods in the suppliant's favour. More potent charms are purchased till the priest has extracted as much as he thinks prudent, and if natural means have not brought about a satisfactory ending, the trusting victim is told that there is a combination of fetish spirits joined against him, whose influence no power can break.

The consultation of the Fetish constitutes one of the most remarkable ceremonies possible, and animals are frequently sacrificed in the Protectorate in lieu of human beings. If a man feel ill, the fetish priest, or medicine man, is consulted. Should he think the illness slight, he demands a large present, and mutters some incantation which causes the evil spirit to take its departure within the next day or two. Should the case appear unsatisfactory, he is clever enough to procrastinate, reserving judgment till the symptoms are more developed or decreased. If he fears the illness will be fatal, he is at once endowed with so keen a sense of perception that he sees whole strings of spirits joining hand to rob the sick one of life. He is not quite disheartened, and accepts all the presents he can get to try and break the circle of uncanny influence. Should the patient recover, "Wonderful Fetish man!!" If he die, " Bad patient to make the spirits combine so strongly against him that even the priest's efforts are unavailing." To the dark native mind the fetish priest is as infallible as the old clock of Jedburgh, for though the sun or moon might be a few minutes wrong, that old timepiece never varied a minute.

A novice wishing to devote himself to the service of the gods must have sufficient goods, or influence, to open the eyes of the chief priest to the fact of his being endowed with the supernatural powers, and if a would-be priest is rich or influential it is wonderful how the gods swoop suddenly down and put the spirit of divination on him. There are many classes of deities, and the novitiate has to work himself into a frenzy in the presence of all the tribe, with emblems of the different gods grouped in the centre. The wily old priest, previously bribed, watches till he sees the dancing convert approach the pre-arranged symbol, when he immediately declares that the spirit has attracted the subject toward it, and henceforth he must devote all his services to that god.

A Fetish priest is not held accountable for any actions when the spirit of divination comes over him. He is at perfect liberty to violate most sacred laws, and indulges in fearful enormities. There is little need to add that everyone is careful to conciliate the holy man, or surely a speedy vengeance descends on their innocent heads when next he becomes inspired. It is also surprising how quickly a fit of piety will come upon him if he has cause for offence.

On the coast, religion is often simply a mixture of Christianity, the Koran and fetish mixed; the last named usually predominating.

Fetishism is deeply imbued, missionaries have introduced Christianity, and the intercourse with Mohammedans has left traces of the religion of the faithful; but many of the negroes follow a compromise between the three, which makes a curious combination.

Barraku was reached about midday, the latter part of the march being particularly hot and trying. After a halt for lunch and the issue of chop to the carriers and hammock boys, the march was resumed through Dumassi, a large hamlet which contained some of the best clay houses to be seen on the way up. Some of these residences even boasted of roughly-carved wooden doors, swinging on common iron garnets; an advance in civilization which few of the natives in the enlightened precincts of Cape Coast have arrived at; for many there are quite satisfied with holes in the wall for the double purpose of door and window.

Nearing Prahsu the track gradually widened, and the road into the wretched village was a well-made level highway, with extensive clearings on each side used as squatting camps for carriers. These places were in a very clean state considering the large numbers of natives constantly using them, or they might have been a serious nuisance and source of danger to health in camp.

Prahsu village is now a miserable collection of mud huts, though at one time it was a town of fair size. It derives its name from the river Prah; the suffix "su" meaning "resting on" or "built on." This termination is very common in West Africa, and thus Fumsu means, town on the Fum river, likewise Bannisu on the Banni; Mansu on the Man, and several others. Unfortunately such nomenclature often causes confusion, as there are possibly three or four towns on the same river, and all therefore named in the same way. The system of naming towns after their situation or some special feature, is also extended far beyond rivers; duplicate names being very common in consequence.

The camp was formed on the bank of the Prah, or more properly Busum Prah, which is roughly reckoned as the boundary line of the British Protectorate and Ashanti, though since 1874 the latter country has never regained her lost power over territory south of the Adansi hills.

The Adansis who used to inhabit the portion beyond the Prah, have removed to safer quarters on the south bank, and the district beyond is a waste or no-man's land, dotted with a few hamlets occupied by miserable settlers, while the sites of many old towns are now only marked by a heap of ruins.

On entering the camp, we passed the hospitals which were just being completed, though one ward was already nearly full, for the dreaded fever had attacked the advanced party of the Army Service Corps and Engineers. There were six of the latter corps in hospital, all of the telegraph department. Their work in laying the cables had been particularly arduous, slaving from morning till night, exposed to the hot sun one minute, and in the damp shade of the trees the next. The little body of the Army Service Corps, who had been toiling and steaming under the leadership of Captains Barnard and Matthews in receiving and checking loads of stores from sunrise to sunset, had also suffered, and several had been obliged to give in. These two Departmental Corps usually bear the brunt of the "kicks," but do not always get a full share of the "halfpence."

The Hospital buildings were large and airy, built of bamboo, and raised three feet off the ground. The interiors were fitted with rows of small bamboo rests, so the patient, brought in on a stretcher, had simply to be lifted to a stand, the body of the stretcher forming the bed. There were also small separate wards for officers, a native ward and dispensary under the charge of Staff Sergeant Ormiston, a genial and sturdy warrior who had seen much service.

Under the watchful eye of Surgeon-Col. Taylor, the P.M.O., who arrived with the Staff, things were soon put into perfect order, and it was evident that the Medical Authorities at home had a thorough grasp of the requirements for the Expedition. Nothing had been forgotten, even the smallest details having received due attention.

General Mackinnon, when Surgeon-Major, was entrusted with the medical supervision of the '73 Expedition, and, doubtless, the evidence of forethought and care taken in the present arrangements under his directorship, were mainly attributable to the knowledge of the climate he gained at that time.

This also applies to Lord Wolseley, assisted by the Adjutant-General, Sir Redvers Buller, V.C., and the Quartermaster-General, Sir Evelyn Wood, V.C. They used their previous knowledge, gained in the country, to the best advantage, and nothing was lacking.

The Army Service Corps had gathered piles of stores in the compound at Prahsu, and long lines of carriers were constantly

## THE BUSUM PRAH.

arriving from the coast. The road was particularly lively with the thousands passing to and fro continuously, and the whole route was often blocked by the moving mass. They worked in gangs, each under its own chief, and wearing distinguishing armlets. One gang with cases of *bouilli* beef, another with lime juice, pressed vegetables, or biscuit. A few lady gangs were also used to take supplies to the Prah, and these worked far harder than the men, and were more cheerful, notwithstanding they had often an additional load in the person of a little brown baby, nodding behind in the ample folds of the mother's wrap.

Near the bank of the river stands the European Frontier House, used by any Houssa officer or official that might have cause to occupy the station. In this two-storied building, once white, but now a dingy yellow, the Staff took up their quarters. Such a thatched residence would not be classed as a good barn in England, but it is considered quite palatial in West Afric's sunny clime, where even a royal palace is of mud. A long apartment on the ground floor was used for a mess-room and offices, while access was obtained to the upper floor by a rough outside ladder, up which Sir Francis Scott and Prince Henry had to climb when retiring.

Skirting the camp, its yellow waters flowing on in stealthy silence, is the Busum Prah, a beautiful stream of about one hundred and eighty yards in width. The current is swift, and, in the rainy season, it is a surging turbid flood, but in the dry months it is fordable in many places. In December its waters were quietly flowing between high banks clothed in luxuriant foliage; the motionless forms of the trees dully reflected on the unruffled but dark waters, as they flowed through a region of densest forest.

Singularly, the aspect of the fringe of forest verging on the north bank opposite Prahsu, is not particularly tropical, and from the south side the landscape has a most English appearance, resembling rather the outskirts of a well-wooded estate in Hants than an African forest. This is mainly due to the entire absence of palms and other tropical plants close to the bank, but the moment the river is crossed, and the forest entered, the English idea is dispelled by the thick and rich profusion of undergrowth and dense bush immediately encountered. Above and below the camp the river flows through a glorious tangled mass of luxuriant bush, with graceful feathery palms and long creepers hanging right to the water's edge. The river is worshipped by the natives in the vicinity as being the abode of the Busum or fetish, the rivers inland, beside the sea, being held as a sacred haunt of the gods of West Africa.

The stream of humanity had seriously disturbed the equanimity of the crocodiles in the Prah, and by way of protest, they removed themselves from the vicinity, leaving the river safe for bathing by the bridge. The scaly brutes had congregated a little lower down the river, but were too much on the alert to give a chance to the few keen sportsmen, who pushed through the jungle on murder bent. There were one or two fruitless excursions undertaken by different officers, and Surgeon-Captain Cunninghame, Correspondent for the *Lancet*, and an ardent sportsman, made several difficult trips through the bush in his endeavours to secure a bag, but he was unsuccessful each time.

When on a botanizing expedition within a few hundred yards of the camp, I had a golden and unexpected chance of a pot at the amphibious game. Emerging from a dense tangle to the river bank, I espied a wily old beast who, more daring than his fellows, had come up the river, possibly to reconnoitre. He was quite unconscious that a bloodthirsty two-legged monster was in the vicinity and who, though not looking for game, was none the less seized with a desire to kill when the unsought opportunity arrived. He lay like a log on the water, his gaping jaws facing the bank, and offering a beautiful target. Alas, I hesitated to alter my position for a steadier aim, and was lost. He spotted me almost as I fired. Bang ! His lordship sank like a stone, with a derisive wisk of his tail as he disappeared, and my bullet was received in the responsive bosom of the Prah. He put two little snail-like nostrils up to breathe shortly after, but far out of range of my revolver, and doubtless he gazed at my retiring form with a twinkle of mingled scorn and amusement in his armoured eyes when he had slunk to a safe retreat. And I? Well, I went home in a sadder if not a wiser mood, for had I not been offered a chance denied to far more deserving sportsmen, and yet made a grievous hash of it.

Prince Henry, Prince Christian, and Major Piggott had several shooting excursions in the vicinity of the camp, but the density of the bush interferes greatly with sport and large bags were not obtainable.

## A FOREST CEMETERY.

Close behind the huts built for the detachment of Houssas is a spot that has a melancholy interest to all Englishmen. A narrow pathway opens through the bush, its entrance being marked by a huge cotton tree, in the bark of which is cut a large cross and an inscription, now almost indistinguishable. As far as I could trace it, it read as follows :

```
T.      381.    T.A.
2.      R.B.    1874.
        2.      W.
```

Passing up the path there is a second tree whose bark bears the initials $\frac{T. H.}{W.}$ A little further on is a large mound planted with a grove of small trees, and beneath this, sleep the soldiers who fell from wounds and sickness during the last war. On one side of this mound is a single grave surrounded by a plaited cane fence which marks the place where Captain Huyshe was buried, and in the centre of the small cemetery, a splendid tree spreads its branches as a canopy of dense foliage over the melancholy forest graveyard, in which another inmate was to be laid to rest only too soon.

The days at Prahsu passed quickly. On December 31st we arrived, and a considerable number of congenial spirits gathered to welcome the New Year in true Caledonian fashion, though the wiser or less enthusiastic ones retired early to rest. When the strains of Auld Lang Syne aroused the niggers from their midnight slumbers under the trees, they wondered what fetish custom was being kept up, as the forms of the white men, with hands clasped, were revealed by the flickering of the camp fire.

Usually the Prah has to be crossed in a long dug-out canoe made from the hollowed trunk of a cotton tree. Major Sinclair and his Engineers, however, had built a substantial pontoon bridge which was safe enough in the dry season, but how it will stand the rain when the river is twenty feet higher, remains to be seen. The work of transporting the casks through the bush to form the pontoons was a very difficult one, and by making use of the large trees on the banks, a suspension bridge would have been more expeditious and much more durable.

Prahsu is certainly not an ideal spot for a camp as it is very damp from its proximity to the river, and therefore unhealthy. A thick mist hangs like a pall, completely hiding the trees round the clearing, and not till the sun is high, does this veil rise. At ten o'clock in the morning, the tree tops were often not visible, and though at last, as the sun gained power, the mists would gather in heavy wreaths, and roll away to seek a hiding in the swamps till night, there was a feeling of dampness and mustiness which the fierce heat of midday never quite dispelled. Before the dewdrops were evaporated from the blades of the jungle grass, the miasma would gradually rise, and by sunset, perpetual fog again enveloped everything.

The Artillery arrived in Prahsu on January 1st, but they received special orders and crossed the Prah a few hours after to advance to Kwisa, to support the levies.

During the morning, a nigger darted up to me, and seizing my hand, literally leaped round in transports of joy, and I recognized the carrier who was in charge of my missing kit. There sure enough was the bundle lying intact close by. He had missed me in the last camp, but had never rested till his load was safely delivered; for the honesty of the natives is proverbial when dealing with a white man's things. They have a wholesome fear of the law, and a few days before, two carriers, probably worn out or ill, deserted, leaving their loads by the roadside. When these were found by a patrol, each man's badge, armlet and day's subsistence money was laid on top of the load. Unfortunately this rule does not always apply, and the civilized negro is usually a terrible thief, for his enlightenment has made him cunning, and he does not fear betrayal from any occult power or fetish of the white man.

About midday the Ansahs arrived from the coast where they had landed on December 27th. They had an interview with Governor Maxwell there, and submitted their credentials and a document dated September 8th, 1894, purporting to bear the mark and seal of King Prempeh.

The Governor is not a man to be taken in by natives, even if they have been educated in English schools, and after an attempt at bluff, the Ansahs confessed that the document had never been seen by King Prempeh, but was drawn up on the coast, and the seal, manufactured in England, had been affixed in London by John Ansah.

So much for the talked-of envoys, who (*vide* a section of the

ARTILLERY CROSSING THE PRAH.

*From a sketch by Mr. H. C. Seppings Wright, Artist Correspondent to "The Illustrated London News."*

Press) were shamefully treated in London by Mr. Chamberlain, who wickedly refused to negotiate with them, and thus rendered an expedition necessary, when it could easily have been avoided. Such random twaddle requires no comment, for subsequent events speak for themselves. *Respice finem !*

The Ansahs were at once told by the Governor that the Colonial Government would not recognise their statements or declarations as binding on King Prempeh, so they had better set out at once for Kumassi, and advise the King to accept the terms which had been sent to him by the other envoys. They were, however, in no hurry to leave Cape Coast, being afraid of the consequences when they reached their King, and they made every excuse to delay their departure. They started for Prahsu eventually, having much trouble with their carriers on the road, who did not relish working for " Shantee-man," and deserted at every opportunity. They came into camp in hammocks, having, among other things, a tin of children's biscuits, some bottles of sweets, and two pounds of candles, as presents to mollify the wrath of the tyrant in the capital. They both seemed weighed down with anxiety, which was not feigned ; for their royal master would have thought nothing of beheading the two of them if he supposed they had neglected his commands in the slightest degree.

The Ansah Princes are grandsons of the late King Osai Tootoo, Quamin, Bonsoo. Naturally, when one has recovered from the shock of that stupendous announcement, little wonder is caused that these Princes refused to take in letters from Sir W. Brandford Griffith ; for the Princes were actually addressed therein as " Messengers to the King of Kumassi," instead of " Royal Ambassadors of Ashanti," which the *Princely* John Ossoo Ansah said was a " breach of civilized etequette" *(sic)*.

Singularly on the morning of their arrival, envoys came in from the subsidiary Ashanti King of Bekwai saying that this important ally of Kumassi would accept the English flag if we could send troops up to protect him from Prempeh's forces. A palaver had been held in Kumassi to which all the Ashanti chiefs had been summoned. The King of Bekwai, Yow Boatin, did not attend. Thereupon Prempeh sent men to bring him by force, but the subordinate monarch so forgot his good manners as to allow his people to beat Prempeh's myrmidons out of the town, and then, fearful of the consequences, he dispatched these ambassadors to the English for help.

The Bekwai messengers were terribly alarmed when they heard of the Ansahs' arrival, and the consequent risk of the discovery of their double dealings. However, by various subterfuges, the Ansahs were detained in front of Headquarters while the trembling ambassadors, hastily stripping off all badges of office, were hurried over the Prah, and they were well on their way home again before the Ansahs re-started.

These Ashantis from Bekwai were evidently types of a far superior race to the Fanti people on the coast. Our allies are contemptible cowards in war while the Ashantis have been hardened by years of constant fighting. Lord Wolseley, speaking in 1874 on the negro as a soldier, dwelt on the many instances of personal bravery among the Ashantis in the late war. On one occasion an Ashanti was found guarding the path, but he stood till the officers, leading the advancing troops, were within five yards of him, when he coolly fired point blank at them, and such acts of individual reckless bravery were common throughout that campaign. It was the habit of Ashanti generals to post certain men behind the fighting line, and their special duty was to kill every coward who fell back during the battle. The burden of their war song is:

> If I go forward I die.
> If I go backward I die.
> Better go forward and die.

If an Ashanti general were defeated it meant death to him; for he paid the forfeit with his head when he returned to Kumassi, and they usually committed suicide on the field rather than suffer the disgrace of public execution.

On January 2nd, the Bearer Company, Medical Staff Corps, arrived under Surgeon-Major Wolseley. These "Poultice Wallahs," as they are playfully dubbed by brother "Tommies" of other corps, marched into camp in fine style, despite their sixteen miles' tramp. Though they may be deemed, by some, to be better fitted to make out diet boards in a hospital ward, than to endure the rigours of a campaign, the Medical Staff Corps always show they have real grit in them, and on that toilsome journey to Kumassi, they marched and endured as well as any of the picked troops in the force.

The next few days they were actively engaged in getting their seven hundred odd native bearers drilled into order. The niggers thoroughly entered into the spirit of the thing, and when once

## SPECIAL SERVICE OFFICERS.

they grasped the different words of command, their movements were very creditable. Hammocks were brought up in good order, the counterfeit wounded picked up, medical store boxes unslung and opened, while spare members repelled the supposed attack. The acting patients were bundled into the litters with scant ceremony, the natives being excited in the heat of the moment, but sharpness of action is required above all things on some occasions, so it could hardly be counted a fault.

A mail reached us at Prahsu, bringing a fresh batch of newspapers. Some of them contained amusing reading on Ashanti subjects. The remarks made in certain quarters were absurd, and some of the personal attacks on Prince Henry, made in specially bad taste, were totally uncalled for. Certainly he ought not to have been indulged in a pleasure picnic at the country's expense; that is if an expedition through the bush, amid endless morass and stinking swamp, in a deadly climate, constitutes a picnic. Prince Henry fared exactly the same as any other officer; he was there as a soldier, not as a prince. He drew the regular Government rations as laid down for every member of the force, and as an old veteran remarked, "There was nothing but bully* beef and biscuit one day, and biscuit and bully beef for a change the next, in that ungodly country," unless you took tinned stuff yourself.

The Staff were hard at work at Prahsu planning out the details of the campaign, which, to sum it up roughly, seemed to require more commissary than strategy. The Ashantis had a far more powerful agent acting for them than their hordes of warriors with Dane guns and pot-leg shot, and any neglect in looking after the troops would soon give that enemy full play; for the malarious poison present in the very air we breathed, required constant care to defeat.

Sir Francis Scott made an ideal commander, showing untiring energy and determination, but marked with a kindliness of disposition that made him beloved as well as respected by every member of the force—officer, soldier, Houssa, or even the humble carriers who had been brought in contact with him. He was indeed wisely chosen to take command, for he knew the country, the people, and all the requirements for dealing with the climate and its drawbacks.

Colonel Kempster was admirably fitted for his duties as Second in Command, and Major Belfield, who worked so hard to

* *Bouilli.*

complete every arrangement, proved himself to be an officer with tact and discretion. He is one of those hard-working, energetic men whose example infuses fresh life into everything he takes in hand.

Colonel Ward also filled an onerous and most responsible post. Under his direction, and thanks to an efficient staff of supply officers at various stations at the coast and on the road, everything went without a hitch, and nothing was wanting.

Surgeon-Colonel Taylor was constantly employed, inspecting the hospitals on the way, testing the drinking water available, and directing by telegraph all the arrangements for the sick on the coast and at various camps up country.

Major Victor J. F. Ferguson, the popular Camp Commandant, was also an officer beloved by all ranks. The eldest son of the late Colonel John Ferguson, 2nd Life Guards, he entered the Army in 1884. In 1890, he went in charge of the special mission to King Lobengula, in Matabeleland, and he attained the rank of Major in the Royal Horse Guards, in February, 1895.

Prince Christian Victor is, perhaps, too well known to need describing, but he is a smart officer, highly popular, and noted for his considerate treatment of subordinates. He showed unflagging zeal and energy throughout the march, and frequently pushed forward to the advanced posts with the indefatigable Major Piggott, doing long journeys with little sign of fatigue, and being always to the front if there were dangers scented. The officers ahead with the scouts were also doing excellent work. Major Sinclair, Captain Curtis, and other Engineer officers were cutting a road through the dense forest north of the Prah, building bridges, placing corduroy over impassable swamps, and laying the cable up toward Kwisa. Major Baden-Powell and Captain Graham were pushing on with the scouts, and Major Gordon, late Commandant at Prahsu, to whom the cleanliness and good order of the camp were due, was marching up to form a camp and advance depôt at Kwisa on the other side of the Adansi Hills.

On January 3rd, the Special Service Corps marched into Prahsu in splendid condition, under Colonel Stopford. On December 27th an advance party disembarked under Major Northcott, and drew all equipment, proceeding to Jaycuma to make things ready. The main body landed next day, and marched at once up country. That first day's march to

A BURIAL IN THE BUSH. 101

Jaycuma proved terribly trying to the troops. Numbers fell exhausted by the wayside, and two men succumbed to the heat, Sergeant Arkinstall, Scots Guards, and Corporal Dickeson, Army Service Corps. Physically, these two poor fellows were perfect specimens of manhood, though the latter suffered with his heart, and never ought to have been passed as fit by the Medical Authorities. Yet it is strange that the climate should pick two of the finest men as first victims, before they were five miles in the interior. They were buried in the bush by their sorrowing comrades before the march was continued.

There is something particularly touching in a soldier's funeral at all times, but in the solemn stillness of the forest, amid the haunts of savages, the effect is indescribable. There are the dense masses of vegetation, the roughly excavated grave, that still form sewn in a blanket, the troops drawn up in line, small groups of blacks peering in wonderment through the trees. The burial service is read by the senior officer; the body is carefully lowered; then short words of command, and three ringing volleys in the air, wake up the echoes in the far recesses of the forest; the bugles softly sound the last post, and we leave the quiet form to sleep till the last *reveillé* shall sound.

The Special Service Corps marched up by easy stages to Prahsu, and though many fell by the way during the first few marches, they got more into form afterwards, and scarcely a man fell out. Prince Henry and Captain Larrymore proceeded some distance down the road to meet them, and on arrival, the battalion was drawn up and inspected by Sir Francis Scott, who complimented the men on their appearance.

The West Yorkshire Regiment disembarked from the "Manilla" on December 29th. This fine regiment suffered severely on the first march up country, when over eighty men fell by the way, thoroughly exhausted. The authorities seem to have shown little consideration in selecting this battalion for service in such a climate as the Gold Coast.

The West Yorks had spent many years on foreign service in India and Burmah, and they were then moved to Aden; perhaps the worst British station occupied by white troops. They were on their homeward voyage, when instructions were wired out for them to disembark at Gibraltar, to be picked up by the "Manilla" for the Gold Coast. The men were all suffering, more or less, from previously contracted fevers and ague, and their constitutions were so undermined by long sojourn in hot climates, as to be totally unfitted to battle with the trials of West Africa.

The one plea was, that the men would be able to stand the heat better than troops fresh from England, but in the bush the heat is a secondary consideration. Experience shows that the man most likely to brave the malarious climate is he who is sound, organically and physically, and certainly not those whose health is already impaired by wretched climes.

This fine body of troops were only too eager to win fresh laurels, and struggled right manfully to do their duty, but it was at much personal suffering and inconvenience. The first day they fell out like "rotten sheep," and many an instance came to hand of officers loading themselves with carbines and ammunition, to ease some of their men, who each had to march with seventy rounds of ball cartridge in their pouches, no light weight for those suffering from weeks of knocking about and rough diet on board ship, apart from the previous climatic drawbacks. They marched, however, into Prahsu in capital form after a sixteen-mile tramp, but the yellow, drawn faces, and glittering eyes of many officers and men showed they were still suffering, and thirty had fallen out that day on the road, though many of these afterwards were well enough to rejoin their regiment.

The bakers of the Army Service Corps were pushed forward across the Prah to get their oven up, and thus issue a part ration of bread when the troops advanced. The butchers were also with the troops, but beyond two wretched African sheep, when skinned, little larger than rabbits, there was no fresh meat obtainable.

There was much stir in camp among the men one morning. Going to the door of the hut I was told a spy had been captured. "Oh, a spy, eh?" "Why, yes; a spy!—an Ashanti spy, caught lurking in the bush!"

The startling intelligence did not seem very important, as the Ansah princes had got all the information the Ashantis wanted, when they openly passed through our lines, but my informant evidently thought I was mad, or struck dumb by the news, for he again yelled, "A spy, man!" and passed on breathlessly to impart the thrilling tidings.

In the centre of the camp, bound between West Indian soldiers, was the spy. One glance was enough for me to recognise him as the native whom I met so mysteriously in the forest at the last camp;

A WEST INDIAN SOLDIER.

## AN ASHANTI SPY. 105

there was the same big hat and strings of charms, and a soldier was carrying his spear. He was a fine fellow, made of very different stuff to the cowardly coast nigger, and was looking round fearlessly, though inwardly ill at ease with all his apparent *sang-froid*. One Ashanti of that stamp would be far preferable to a dozen of the Fanti men, who, with an air of superiority, inform every white man they meet, "Shantee man, no good, sah! Big coward him, sah!" Give the Ashanti people the same chances our own coast tribes have had, and they would be allies worth having, and reliable authorities seem very sanguine as to the successful result of British rule in Ashanti, when once the bloody rites of fetish are stopped.

It was amusing to see the faces of some of the group, eyeing the captive as if he were a wild beast, and evidently expecting a startling *dénouement* ending in hanging or shooting. There was an audible sigh of relief, or disappointment, when some of the Staff arrived, and Sir Francis, after exchanging a dozen words with the spy, ordered his immediate release. His capture might have divulged some useful information of intentions in Kumassi if they were needed, but as the man was this side of our outposts, it is far more likely he was an Ashanti who had been on a hunting or trading expedition, and was home-ward bound when he found the way blocked by the troops, so was hiding till he could slip through the barrier and reach his own country.

At Prahsu there was an improvised mosque in the Houssa lines, and a Mohammedan priest in attendance. At five every morning the chanting of the *Muezzin* might regularly be heard; for these splendid allies of ours are devout followers of the great Prophet.

It is a striking fact that on the West Coast of Africa the Mohammedan negroes are far better than those who profess to have adopted Christianity. The Mohammedan is always polite; he is usually dressed in clean white flowing robes, and he has a certain dignity of character rarely found in the other class. Why this should be so it is difficult to say. The christianized negro is noted for cheating and lying all the week, and as assiduously singing hymns on Sunday. He has usually received some sort of an education, and knows smatterings of English, and this gives him an advantage over his more ignorant brethren which he is not slow to use. He feels he is a very superior person, and could not demean himself with low work, so starts to live by his wits as much as possible. In their eagerness to prove their usefulness and swell their report, some missionaries are only too ready to induce the negro to embrace Christianity, and will even go as far as to buy converts at the rate of 5s. a head when new members are scarce. The result of this state of affairs is obvious, and has spread its pernicious effect throughout Africa. It also makes things far more difficult for the true missionaries, but all the more honour is attached to their labours, and on the Gold Coast a good and steady work is going on, of which I have given particulars in a previous chapter.

The Arab blood gives the Houssas better and more refined features, and also an unselfish devotion seldom found in the pure negro, who seems ever to come under the ban of the curse of Ham. Another redeeming feature of a Mohammedan is that he seldom drinks.

Splendid fellows are these lithe active Houssas. They will follow their white officers with a courage and devotion equal to any of Her Majesty's troops. " Faithful unto death " is the true characteristic of the Mohammedan soldier, and he will go with his officer into Hades if needs be.

Volumes might be written of the struggles of the few Commissioners and other officers, who, with small detachments of Houssas, maintain order among thousands of savages along the frontier of British West African Dominions. They would add some very mournful pages to the history of our colonial possessions, and a long list would be required to publish all the names of officers and officials who have been killed, or died from sickness, among the dreary waste of forest and swamp, when enforcing a semblance of order among the savage inhabitants, who revel in battle, murder, cannibalism, and ju-ju or fetish worship with its horrible rites of human sacrifice.

The Special Service Corps crossed the Prah on January 5th, the Staff remaining for the arrival of the West Yorks, who came in at midday.

The previous evening a camp fire was arranged by the " Press," and a most successful concert was held under the leadership of Mr. Burleigh, the whole of the troops attending, and the officers also being present. A topical song, written and sung by Captain Ackland Hood, of the Rifle Brigade, appeared a general favourite. The words were adapted to the tune of "Tommy Atkins," the chorus being :—

"Oh Prempeh ! Prempeh ! Prempeh ! You had better mind your eye,
You'd better far be civil or, by Jove, you'll have to die,
And your kingdom of Ashanti, you'll never see it more,
If you fight the old West Yorkshire, and the Special Service Corps."

The same day, news of Jameson's invasion and defeat in the Transvaal, and also of the friction with America *re* Venezuela, was wired up from the coast. The whole message barely contained a dozen words, but it was quite enough to make everyone supremely anxious for further news, and there was much surmising among the troops. "Would Kumassi be invested, and the expedition on the coast again in time to be sent South to the Boers?" etc., etc. Next day, however, the idea of further war was dispelled by the brief but pithy telegram : " England disavows action Transvaal."

## CHAPTER VII.

OVER THE PRAH — LOATHSOME DISEASES — THE NATIVE LEVY — FLYING COLUMN TO BEKWAI — AKUSIREM — FUMSU — BRAFFU EADRU — NATIVE DISHES — LONG PIG CHOP OR IGUANA — A RIOT — THE ADANSIS — DEATH OF MAJOR FERGUSON — SNAKES.

On January the 6th the Staff crossed the Prah, having, unfortunately, to leave Major Ferguson in hospital with fever. He was walking with Prince Henry on the previous evening, apparently in the best of health, but next day signs of a chill were manifest, fever supervened, and he had to be removed at once to hospital. Prince Henry also contracted a slight cold, but no serious symptoms set in, and he had quite recovered when the march was resumed.

Once across the Prah, the whole aspect changed as the road entered the gloom of the true African forest. The official "Great North Road" was little better than a narrow sheep track, even after the path had been widened by the levies. The exuberance of the vegetation is almost incredible, and the track each side was walled in by a tangled mass of leaves, branches, creepers, and tree trunks, while gigantic cotton trees towered far above the other giants of the forest. The earth itself is covered with a thick layer of fallen leaves, out of which spring masses of ferns, moss and creepers; above these are shrubs, and luxuriant undergrowth, while long sinuous stems and adnascent creepers twine and interlace with the branches above, festooning the path in a hundred different curves till an unbroken network is formed, over which the branches of higher trees intermingle and form a perfect leafy canopy.

Many of these creepers hung within five feet of the path, often making it necessary to stoop, while the carriers, whose heads were protected by their loads, pushed their way through with little thought of those behind, and any unsuspecting person who followed too closely had a full benefit when the stems rebounded. The tortuous turnings of the road, which winds like a serpent through the forest, greatly add to the distance "as the crow flies." Huge trees lay across the track and much hindered the carriers, while the path often led through particularly damp and musty places. Here and there a large swamp had to be traversed, but gangs of natives were hard at work making long strips of corduroy of logs lashed together with monkey rope, thus spanning the vile patches of black fœtid mud.

The only breaks in the dense forest are the small clearings containing a few mud hovels. Atawasi Kwanta, a medium-sized village, had been visited by small-pox, so we passed through hurriedly and did not linger in the vicinity. This disease is very common, and makes terrible havoc among negroes, and both men and women are constantly met fearfully pitted. There are many loathsome diseases peculiar to West Africa, and disgusting sights have to be viewed daily. Children suffering from vile hereditary diseases; men and women with suppurating ulcers, while at one village a woman, with nose and eyes completely eaten away, was pushed forward in full view of everyone. The poor creature was a horrible sight, and no one could repress an involuntary shudder at the disgusting object. Elephantiasis is also very common on the coast, and women may be frequently seen with one or both legs the size of a young elephant, and only just the tips of the toes showing from the festering mass. African leprosy is found in various forms, but is not particularly repulsive, though the victims are covered with white patches, which gradually spread.

A terrible pest among the niggers is the Guinea worm, which infests the pools. It is a long parasitic worm which burrows in the cellular tissue, especially of the legs, and causes the utmost distress. There is also the jigger or chigoe, a vile little insect, scarcely larger than a pin's head. It burrows under the skin of the foot and, luckily, soon makes its presence known by itching and pain. Woe to the man, white or black, who does not remove it at once with a sharp-pointed knife, for delay is disastrous. It speedily lays eggs, and a multitude of young follow the footsteps of their parent. When once the eggs are laid, it is difficult to remove all traces of the pest, and if it goes on unchecked the foot will rot away and mortify.

Tobiassi was reached at ten a.m., and a strong stockade and rough sheds had been built near the village by the native levy. The rest camps were necessarily much rougher north of the Prah, and after Kwisa the advance party of natives under the Engineers could not be pushed forward ahead of the troops to construct camps in readiness. Beyond Tobiassi, the road was obstructed every few yards by huge trunks lying directly across the path, and the size of some of these may be judged by it being necessary, in some cases, to build rough steps to surmount the obstacles. The road goes across two narrow ravines, the ascents of these dips being steep and difficult; in fact, one of them was so near the perpendicular, that it would have been impossible to climb it had not the gnarled roots of the trees, laid bare in many places, given a secure foothold.

We reached Esiaman Kuma at midday, and though the village is small, the water supply was splendid and plantains very plentiful. This camp was also formed and stockaded by the native levy.

Prince Christian and Major Piggott had pushed forward to the outposts. The native levies were doing much useful work in the advance. They had been assembled under Major Baden-Powell at Cape Coast on December 16th, and consisted of three hundred Krobos under Chief Malikoli, one hundred Mumfords under Chief Crew, and a company of Elminas under Chief Ando, a fine old warrior who did good service as an ally in 1874. The Krobos are a fairly warlike tribe; but the Mumfords, though finely developed fishermen, have no great aptitude for war. At Prahsu they were joined by one hundred Adansis who were very useful in scouting and gleaning information from the front. The pay of the levy was less than that of the carriers:—sixpence a day, and threepence for subsistence, the latter sum being ample for the purchase of yams and plantains upon which they usually live. Some of the men had Sniders; many were armed only with the long Dane flint-lock guns; but this despised weapon can do much execution in the bush, when loaded with a handful of buck-shots or rough potleg.

With Major Baden-Powell was Captain Graham, 5th Lancers, and Captains Aplin, Middlemas, Houston, Mitchell and Green were with the Houssas. Major Gordon afterwards took command of the right flank.

When the news arrived from Bekwai, it was evident that a sharp advance would be necessary to save the King from reprisals from Kumassi. There was little doubt that Prempeh would take speedy vengeance when he heard of the Bekwai chief's treason, as his disaffection would be likely to spread among other Ashanti tribes, who were heartily sick of the constant wars and executions carried on by the despotic ring of chiefs in Kumassi. A small flying column was therefore at once organized and ordered to proceed from our outposts to the Bekwai capital, twenty miles distant. The column had with them supplies for a week and that involved the employment of a large force of unarmed carriers who could only march in single file through the bush.

At Essian Kwanta there was a strong picket of Ashantis, and as the only road led past their outposts they would have, probably, laid in ambush till the carriers came up, and then opened fire, which would have caused the greatest confusion in the native ranks. Major Baden-Powell therefore determined to make a forced night march past this outpost, and having gained his position, to attack the Ashantis with his armed force unencumbered with carriers. The column was made up of the levies and two companies of Houssas, great secrecy being observed as to the movements on hand. The troops fell in at nine o'clock and none of the natives knew of the operations till they were fallen in and furnished with ammunition, so there was no risk of chance traitors warning the Ashantis, a contingency always to be guarded against when dealing with negroes. The levies seemed fairly ready for a fight, and it was difficult to restrain the war-loving Houssas, ever spoiling for a brush with the Ashantis despite the odds. The march by a side path was difficult in the darkness, and the scouts in front had their suspicions aroused several times, and hurled suddenly lighted brands into the thicket, but all the draws proved blanks, and the little column reached Bekwai country safely, having now got in rear of the outpost on the main road. They halted at Heman, about half way to the Bekwai capital, and heard there that so far the King had not been attacked from Kumassi. After a brief rest the carriers and a company of Houssas resumed their march to the capital, while the remainder of the force marched down the main path to drive the Ashantis from Essian Kwanta. Officers and men alike eagerly pushed forward, but reached their destination only to find the wily Ashantis had made tracks. No doubt their scouts had visited the camp occupied by the troops the afternoon before, and finding to their dismay they were outflanked, they did not wait long, but set off full pelt for Kumassi, leaving their smouldering fires as the only evidence of occupation.

The little force was disappointed to find their birds had flown; yet there was nothing for it but to turn back again and follow the remainder of the column to Bekwai. They were received there by the King and all his councillors, and the Bekwai monarch accepted the British flag, much relieved for his prompt succour; for he had been in mortal fear of being captured and beheaded by Prempeh before the English arrived.

The King and a vast retinue assembled to receive the force. The Union Jack was tied to the flagstaff in a ball, and the King, advancing, pulled the halyard, unfurling the flag. The fifes and drums of the Houssas immediately struck up "God save the Queen," while the Bekwai monarch feigned sleep, saying that he would remain under the flag till he died. He then shook hands with the officers, pouring such effusive compliments on Major Baden-Powell's head, calling him friend, protector and deliverer, that the gallant Major blushed. The King finished the palaver by executing a few steps of the fetish dance for the edification of the assembled officers.

Next day they came to business, and then the dusky monarch at once showed real true African gratitude. He was asked, as a small return, if he would provide some of his subjects, who were idling in the villages, to form an armed levy, and others to act as carriers, for which they were all to be paid 1/- per day a head.

Ah, yes! He would provide the thousand fighting men asked for, but he could get no more for carriers. All right, send the thousand fighting men and we will use them as carriers; which were the more needed. He had not reckoned on this, and at once began a long yarn that they could not carry loads, and would also take a long time to collect and get ready. When, however, he was threatened with the withdrawal of the force, he soon came round, afterwards furnishing all the men first asked for.

Meantime, the main body was steadily moving up country. On January 7th, *reveillé* sounded in camp at Esiaman Kuma at 4.30, and the whole place was soon a scene of bustle and confusion, till, everything ready, the Headquarter Staff moved off shortly after 5 a.m., for the longest march on the whole advance.

Progress at first was very slow, the path being narrow and washed away on one side into a rugged gully. It rose gradually, winding along the edge of a deep and thickly-wooded valley which was almost indistinguishable, so thick was the bush rising on all sides. The surroundings were very pleasant on this high ground, and the path beautifully dry. The forest resounded with the calls of birds, a clear prolonged cuckoo predominating, while gorgeous little sun-birds and cardinals flitted from tree to tree,

IN THE FOREST.

and groups of parrots flew to and fro with hoarse cries. The track led through glorious scenery, and many splendid patches of plantains, with their enormous leaves of brilliant green, and clusters of fruit which form the staple food, not only of the natives, who roast them green as a substitute for bread, but also of the parrots and monkeys, who feed on the pulpy way-bread when ripe and yellow.

The road greatly improved as we reached the next camp, Fumsu, where the Special Service Corps had halted. The river Fum was very low, and the channel completely choked with large masses of rock. Crossing the bridge and again entering the bush, we found Colonel Stopford with his men in the woods in skirmishing order.

Passing through the long line of out-posts, we reached a very swampy district, the whole road reeking with the vile fœtid vapour oozing from the sticky mass of rotting vegetation. Yet in these horrible marshes beautiful butterflies flutter round in myriads over the sea of mud; crane-flies and many brilliant little insects abound, while enormous dragon-flies, with their reticulated wings, gaily flit from pool to pool among all the steaming mugginess.

In some places the road was only made passable by the corded chain of logs thrown over, while in others the booted individual had the choice of wading knee deep across a strip of sticky morass, or "dashing"* a carrier for the loan of his broad back, while his naked legs splashed through the mire. In this district, close to the village, one of Captain Donald Stewart's Houssa Escort, named Dawudu Moshi, was shot dead by an Ashanti ambush. The miscreants escaped in the forest, and there is little doubt that they were lying in wait to kill either Captain Stewart or Mr. Vroom, the District Commissioner; probably the latter gentleman, who had incurred the hate of the Ansahs and others in Kumassi, for the spirited action he had displayed, on various occasions, during the previous negotiations.

Leaving these swamps and passing through Braffo Eadru, the path became firmer and wider. The bush was much less dense, and the sun blazed down with terrific force on the road leading into Akusirem. A camp had been prepared here, and the Army Service Corps had pushed forward stores, and formed a supply depôt in the village. However, the *Lancet* Correspondent, Dr. Cunninghame, who had gone on ahead of the Staff, tested the water, and found it very bad, and close behind the village a large

*Paying.

rotting patch of decaying plantains was also found. He immediately reported this to Surgeon-Colonel Taylor, who pushed on and inspected the place, which he found so unsatisfactory that the camp was condemned at once. For once, at any rate, one of the War Correspondents, opprobriously termed the "curse of modern Armies," has proved a blessing in disguise, as his report just arrived in time to prevent the Special Service Corps advancing to Akusirem, and the effect might have proved disastrous if they had been quartered in the camp. Instructions were given them to halt at Fumsu and march the two stages, a matter of sixteen miles, into Braffu Eadru on the following day.

Captain Benson, R.H.A., the popular commandant of the Artillery, was attacked with fever here and was seriously ill. Captain Curtiss had also succumbed to the ravages of malaria, which had attacked, more or less severely, those officers and men who were active in pushing forward supplies, or bridge building, camp making and laying the telegraph. They had all had long turns of arduous duty, and Africa requires a heavy penalty from those who over-work themselves, on her West Coast at least.

Luckily the weather was very favourable, being a particularly dry and hot season. Had there been rain, the dampness caused thereby would have brought a much larger amount of sickness in its train. There seemed every chance of getting the affair settled, and the troops back to the coast before the rains started, for death would stalk freely among the Europeans exposed during those wet months.

Malaria is a tricky thing, and it is attributed to half a dozen causes, which probably all, more or less, combine in producing it. The chief cause no doubt is the poison exhaling from the ground. The system becomes saturated with malaria, as it is inhaled at every breath, and everything reeks with it. No precautions will ward it off for ever, though they may do much in rendering the attacks less frequent; but carelessness will surely be fatal. It may be kept off for a time, perhaps several weeks, but it spares no man for long, and everyone in its sphere will be attacked sooner or later. A sudden chill or slight cold is just enough to bring it on. First cold pain, then frequent shiverings and burnings; the temperature flies up as the fever increases, delirium supervenes, and the life or death struggle begins. If the first attack prove slight, and a profuse perspiration relieves the fever, a second attack may be postponed for some time to come, but the awful chain of British graves right down to the coast, and the appalling mortality among white people, should be seriously reflected on by anyone who thinks of casting in his lot with darkest West Africa.

Quinine is supposed to be the only remedy for malaria, and is universally taken, but the effect of that alkaloid is harmful in many ways, though it has held supreme sway for want of a better substitute. This has now, however, been supplied by "Kreat Halviva," which entirely supersedes quinine in its therapeutic value, and has none of the baneful after-effects, as deafness, drumming in the head, lapses of memory, dizziness, and other well-known allies to cinchona bark. There were many officers and men who escaped the malaria, and attributed it to the fact of their taking "Kreat Halviva," being high in their praise of the same. Many residents on the Gold Coast swear by it as a wonderful preventive, and I add these remarks at the risk of puffing the tonic, as the great question of antidotes is of vital importance to Europeans in malarious climes. This view has also been advocated by Surgeon-General Sir W. Moore, K.C.E.I., Brigade-Surgeon Geo. Neates Hunter, and many other authorities on malaria who have had unusual opportunities of testing it.

The road from Akusirem to Sheramasi was very rough, with many big obstacles to block the way. In one place on the road a curious natural archway had been formed. A huge cotton tree, probably struck by lightning, had fallen from the bank right across the track, snapping in its fall a rather smaller tree of the same species, some twelve feet from the ground. The roots of the first tree rested on the bank, and the other end, lodging fairly on the stump of the second, was firmly fastened by yards of intertwining creeper, Nature thus forming a magnificent triumphal arch.

Passing on we reached the Kiribu river, a tributary to the Fum, and which flows in a straight silver streak through thick overhanging foliage, forming one of the loveliest pieces of tropical scenery to be seen on the road. Crossing the river the bush becomes singularly open on each side, and is only short scrub in many places, with a few higher trees here and there. This gave the sun full play, which proved the last straw that almost broke the camel's back. Everyone felt it severely, and after the long and fatiguing march Brafu Eadru proved a welcome sight. This village was quite deserted, as were the other villages on the road from the Prah. The people had removed themselves and all their belongings into the bush, and out of reach of pending hostilities.

The houses of these people, though of similar build, are far more substantial and cleaner than those on the other side of the Prah, and with a little judicious cleaning and disinfecting, they made very fair quarters, though in wet weather they would be hardly tenable. In many ways they resemble the houses of the ancient Romans of the first century, which may be seen in the remains of Pompeii and Herculaneum.

Outwardly, each house represents four houses, all standing corner to corner, enclosing a quadrangle with an entrance way in one corner. The walls are formed of wattle, smoothly plastered with mud, or rather clay, and the roofs thatched. Inside the courtyard you find the houses have outer walls only, and the sides facing the enclosure are left open. The lower half of the walls is stuccoed with a brilliant red clay which dries in the sun a smooth glazed surface. This clay was used by the troops to coat their helmets and straps in place of pipe clay. On the straps, especially, it looked well, and at a little distance, the equipment thus treated had the appearance of highly polished tan leather.

The roofs of these places were infested with lizards and other more loathsome creatures that occasionally dropped squarely on a sleeping face; but the dwellings were airy, and yet kept off the dew. The mud floor also, being smoothed and hardened, and often raised a few inches from the ground, made a safe, if hard, spot to lay our blankets and sleep in peace, even though the improvised pillow consisted of a box of ammunition or case of meat.

Wandering in the vicinity of the village, I came across a few suspicious bundles tied in dried palm leaves and laid across a frame-work of bamboo. This place formed a sort of necropolis for defunct chiefs; but such a method of disposing of dead bodies, chiefs or no chiefs, cannot be recommended, though these corpses were as dried and shrivelled as any Egyptian mummy. As interment in the ordinary way is usually practised, these remains may have been bodies of deceased fetish priests, kept above ground to enable their living colleagues to make good use of the various offerings placed round for the benefit of the dead. Food and drink is always provided in large quantities for deceased persons; in some cases a hollow bamboo being inserted in the mouth of the corpse, leads up to the surface, and at regular intervals particles of food and drink are put down. The fetish gods are also regaled with offerings of the best meat and drink, and the credulous niggers are delighted to find the god has accepted their gift, which of course has either been appropriated by the crafty priests, or the food devoured by ants and the drink evaporated in the sun.

Near each village is the medicine heap, consisting of a raised platform of bamboo or a hollowed tree stump, and piles of broken crockery, small bones, bits of metal and rag, placed indiscriminately together, and supposed to be a constant source of gratification to the fetish gods.

At this village I screwed up my courage to try a native dish that is often eaten on the coast. The dish consisted of an oleaginous stew made of the "achatina variegata," which, I may add for the benefit of readers unlearned in malacology, are immense land snails, often measuring nine or ten inches when crawling. No wonder then that gourmet curiosity and squeamishness had a struggle, but the former was victorious, and with a final effort, I started the attack. It tasted like dambake when particularly rank seaweed has been used in the preparation, and was just passable, though certainly not a dish one would choose again. In Cape Coast large quantities of these Titanic molluscs are collected and sold in the market. A brawny Jack Tar observed, as he turned away with evident disgust from some tempting piles of these helical dainties offered for sale at threepence each :—" The cussed niggers are every bit as bad as them French Johnnies," a comparison that our across channel neighbours would think odious. I must admit, however, that the niggers' stew appealed to me far more than a most carefully prepared dish that I tasted in Boulogne, where the animals had been carefully reared and selected, at least so said the *garçon*.

Continuing with native dishes, the favourite food of many of the natives is kankee, a mixture of pounded corn and water, and "fou-fou" made of cassada plant, which the women laboriously beat out in a hollowed tree-stump with a heavy wooden pestal. The first time I tasted kankee was in a village near the coast, where some balls were prepared specially for me by the small, but not fair, hands of a real live, if dusky, young princess. I devoured a few of them with a good grace, but it was like eating sour dough, though I managed to surreptitiously sprinkle over them a tiny pinch of saccharine, a bottle of which is always carried in case of emergency. This same stuff I afterwards tried boiled in a stew with a little bouilli-beef and plenty of the vegetable pepper, and in that case it resembled boiled damper, but the dish was so highly seasoned that relief had immediately to be sought by copious draughts of demulcent cocoanut milk.

*Apropos* of native dishes, the tale is told of a well-known Government official dining with a native chief. He managed to get through one dish, and was attacking another with avidity, when, from the bottom of the vessel, a delicious morsel was fished up, like a small human hand. The dinner was spoiled, and the unfortunate official was seized with a terrible organic working. Cannibalism at last, and he had partaken of it. When he had recovered sufficiently to move, he seized the negro by the shoulder and pointing to the ghastly fragment, gasped, "baby child, you scoundrel" and the inward groaning started again. A broad grin overspread the sable features of the chief. "Him no piccan you fool! Him iguana chop; dats him flipper." It was a stewed iguana.

Kola nuts are eaten by many of the natives habitually, and they are said to be very sustaining for a long march, and also to contain valuable medicinal qualities. The natives, especially the women, chew them like tobacco and expectorate as freely as any enlightened Boer.

The cable was run into Brafu Eadru during the afternoon, and taken over the Adansi hills the next day, while the Staff halted to allow the troops to close up before they crossed to Kwisa. Fortunately the cable is always looked on in reverential awe by these natives, and nothing is more wonderful, to their idea, than to hear the sounders at work. Its fame has spread, and no nigger would dare cut or injure what they call the " fetish cord." During the last war, the Ashantis, fearing to be overcome by the powers of this fetish string, fastened a long line of cotton on the opposite side of the road for a considerable distance, hoping thus to counteract the white man's fetish.

The carriers were all done up after the long march, and the leisure day following, was greatly appreciated by them; but the old adage about Satan and idle hands again proved true.

Camped by the side of the stream were a large party of Winnebahs. A couple of Sierra Leone hammock-men went on a foraging expedition, and stole some plantains cooking on a fire. The owners retaliated, and there was a petty squabble, after which the Modenas of Sierra Leone raided the Winnebahs' camp. Though the latter were more numerous, the Modenas were the more resolute, and a splendid faction fight started. Sticks, clubs, stones, were speedily brought into play, and Donnybrook Fair was for once surpassed, though the niggers religiously followed the maxim of the "bould Irish buoys": "If you see a head—hit it." Some familiar whacks were exchanged with a force that would have cracked the skull of any Irishman, and the niggers on both sides, with their blood thoroughly up, fought like demons. The sturdy Modenas forced the Winnebahs to retire, but every step was fiercely contested, and they again rallied on the bridge and attempted to hold it. Thrice the Modenas dashed up, and thrice they were repulsed, many of the combatants being hurled from the bridge into the water which soon cooled their passion.

A few of the natives had matchets and slashed right and left, happily with little serious effect. Mr. Bennett Burleigh was the first white man on the spot, and armed with nothing more formidable than his white sunshade, he rushed in the midst of the combatants. It was almost ludicrous to see his broad form used as a shelter for many a hard pressed black, and showers of blows were dealt all round him, while he, I think, rather enjoyed the fun. Perhaps he thought of Trafalgar Square. One poor fugitive was cut off, and seeing the white man near, rushed to him for protection. He fell; and would soon have been dispatched by half a dozen men, who furiously started on him with heavy sticks, while one was about to make a clean cut on the fugitive's cranium with a matchet, when bang came the gamp, and with much difficulty and beating did Mr. Burleigh induce the maddened crew to let the poor fellow alone. Hostilities soon started on the other side of the water near the village, and as things were becoming serious, a message was sent to the camp, and the officers, hastily arming themselves with sticks, appeared on the scene. Prince Henry arrived first, and going into the thick of the fray with shirt sleeves rolled up, emerged a minute after with a lanky Winnebah, whom he had brought out of the fight in a sorry state, covered with blood. Both sides were fairly worn out, and the small party of white men had little difficulty in separating the rival factions. Thanks to their thick negro skulls, no one was seriously hurt, and they were mostly suffering from nothing worse than bruised or cut heads and bloody noses.

In the evening the thousand carriers from Bekwai arrived, and were dispatched down country to bring up supplies. They seemed greatly relieved to get through our lines, but whether their anxiety was caused by the desire to get beyond the camp, or joy at having some one between them and the Ashantis, it is difficult to say.

On January 9th, the Staff restarted for Kwisa, which is situated on the other side of the Adansi Hills. The road from Braffu Eadru runs through a low and marshy district with dense bush, till it starts to wind in zig-zag fashion up the thickly-wooded and steep sides of the Monsi Hill.

The track was very narrow, rugged and difficult, and though I started early, and had reached the hill by sunrise, the exertion of climbing brought out the perspiration in streams. Upward still, clambering over rocks, clinging to projecting roots and hanging creeper, with tongue furred, throat parched, till, hot and panting, the summit was gained. The top of these hills is 2,000 feet above sea-level, and a delightful breeze blows across them and cools the over-heated frame; but it comes as a deadly if welcome relief to those who linger to enjoy it.

I was disappointed, yet pleased, with the view from the summit. Through a break in the trees, a cloudless sky was visible, and stretching away below, a vast white rolling sea of mist had risen above the trees, but was not yet dispelled by the sun. I had expected a glorious view of the green sea of vegetation, but that white expanse of cloud-land almost compensated for the loss of the former. Descending on the other side, we were tantalized by the refreshing sound of running water, but the bush was too impenetrable to reach the stream which flows in a hundred cascades down the rocky sides.

On the hill, large masses of iron-stone abound, and gold in small quantities is collected in the beds of the neighbouring streams. We read in one report of the expedition, "Gold sparkles in the auriferous sand," also "Specks of gold dust glitter in the clay walls of the houses." If this were true, the place must be a perfect El Dorado; but, alas ! "'tis not all gold that glitters," and these sparkling particles are nothing more precious than glistening pyrites.

Gold dust is, however, found in considerable quantities by the natives, who know where to seek for it, and it still forms the chief

MAJOR FERGUSON.
*From a photograph by Hospital Corporal-Major Saunders, Royal Horse Guards.*

currency of the Protectorate, though English silver coinage is becoming more common on the Coast proper.

Kwisa is the most salubrious camp on the road, while its reputation is further enhanced by a stream of beautiful limpid spring water flowing from the solid rock. The sparkling liquid was very acceptable after the water we had previously found, often as thick and coloured as the soup at a sixpenny dinner, while so-called streams were more often mere mud puddles.

Though Kwisa is undoubtedly a very healthy camp, several cases of fever occurred there. This is easily explained by the affected persons getting over-heated when crossing the hill, and afterwards taking a chill that at once brings on fever, and develops the malaria previously inhaled. Major Gordon was in charge of the camp, which was as beautifully clean and well laid out as his previous one at Prahsu.

Shortly after the Staff arrived, news was received from Prahsu announcing the death of Major Ferguson. Though he was as fine a specimen of manhood as ever donned uniform, malaria put its deadly grip on him, and he never rallied. His temperature rose to 110, and recourse was made to the cold pack with a possible view of lowering the fever, but every effort was unavailing, and he died the previous evening. His funeral took place on January 10th. The service, conducted by Major Wolfe Murray, was a very impressive one, and was attended by all the garrison at Prahsu. The remains were laid to rest next to the grave of Captain Huysh. The poor fellow was only thirty-one, and his loss came as a shock to every member of the Expedition; for he was generally beloved by all who knew him, and many an officer and man will mourn his loss at home and abroad.

Captain Graham was down with fever, and Major Gordon left Kwisa and temporarily took over his command with the scouts. Captain Benson had a relapse, and had to be sent to the coast, which was very disappointing to an officer who had worked so hard in getting his batteries efficient, only to be denied the honour of taking them to the front.

The Artillery were at Kwisa, and, happily, Sir Francis had a second efficient Artillery officer with the Expedition in the person of Captain Blunt, who pushed forward and took over the command when Captain Benson was first taken ill.

Sickness was beginning to make many gaps in the ranks of

both officers and men. There were, at this time, sixty cases on the sick list at the base alone, though only two deaths there, one of which was Sergeant-Major Stocker on the "Coromandel," and another a private soldier in the hospital at Cape Coast.

On January 16th the Staff halted for a day; the Special Service Corps crossed the hills to Kwisa, and the West Yorkshire Regiment advanced to Braffu Eadru.

Anxious to obtain a view from the summit of the hills, I again made the ascent at a later hour than on the previous day. This time I followed the course of the stream, which has its source among the rocks on the summit. The bed was so rocky that it was possible to follow the water right to the top by jumping and scrambling from boulder to boulder, with a little wading between. The bush closed right in to the edge of the water on both sides, the branches interlacing above, and forming a leafy avenue. Viewed from the top, this tunnel had a striking effect, as it was possible to see right down the whole length to the foot of the hill, the water flowing swiftly in smooth channels, then pouring in cascades over steep masses of rock, and glistening in places where the sun's rays penetrated the branches of the leafy canopy above.

The head of the spring proved to be some distance from the crest of the hill, and the tracts of the stream suddenly ended in a cul-de-sac of jungle. However, by dint of much struggling and laborious hacking with a jack knife, I struck the path close to the top. The noonday sun had dispelled every trace of mist, and through a break in the trees, as far as the eye could reach, there was a perfect flowing sea of leafage. Hills and hollows, ridges and lowland, all marked by waves of foliage; a vast expanse of heavy drifts of vegetation of every description. These hills form a crescent-shaped ridge, running from east to west, making a natural barrier for the Ashanti country proper, and with such a splendid line of defence, and also considering the difficulties of transport, Ashanti could be rendered practically unassailable in this direction by a little judicious generalship, even with a small force.

Snakes are very plentiful, but did not intrude much into the camps. In bush cutting many were disturbed, especially in the vicinity of bamboo clumps. The cobra is found, but chiefly in the long jungle grass and corn patches to the north. The deadly puff adder is sometimes in evidence, likewise the more harmless, but more formidable, python. They are of little nuisance, and it would be quite possible to travel for weeks without coming across a single snake, though, if search were made, no difficulty would be experienced in securing good specimens. I had a few hunts, and found many harmless reptiles not worth skinning. At Mansu, however, I bagged a fair-sized python, and at Kwisa a brilliant green snake, about five feet long, curled from the thatch of the hut and dropped close to our feet. Having dispatched and skinned the gentleman, whose bite, I am told, is fatal, I put the carcase on the fire to boil to extract the vertebra. A carrier seeing this, spread the report that a white man was cooking snake for chop, and an eager crowd assembled to watch my culinary operations. I dished up the dainty morsel in a split bamboo, and great was their disappointment when, after cutting out the backbone, I threw the rest away, instead of making a meal of it as they had anticipated.

The ants on the Gold Coast are ever a source of wonder and fear. They have wasp-like waists but jaws of iron, and for callous brutality, voracious cunning, defiant audacity, and unrelenting malevolence, give me the African ant. You find him in impenetrable woods, many parts under water and no other animals to be seen. In the inner recesses of the forest he is instantly found; in beautiful glades, cultivated patches, even in a town—the pertinaceous little brute is there; go where you will and he will follow you. White ants will attack a huge tree and reduce it to powder; they invade everything and everybody, and if they don't gnaw at your things for food, they will from sheer "cussedness."

I carefully treasured up a collection of various objects, but the ants got wind of it, and terrible havoc they made, devouring dried plants, entomological specimens, and a couple of small lemurs' skins into the bargain. If a swarm invaded a hut, little use was it disputing possession; you had to clear out bag and baggage, till they took their departure. The carnivorous little beast will crawl on you with unblushing effrontery, and coolly burrow his armoured head in your flesh as you are innocently watching him, and if you get in their toils, they are as painful, if not as poisonous, as any swarm of bees, and more difficult to get rid of, for each insect has to be hauled by main force from your body.

Their hills and houses are of various shapes and sizes, some making large mounds, while others are content with a smaller but far more elaborate dwelling, shaped like a three-storied Chinese Pagoda.

A more startling but innocent creature to be seen in the bush is the goliath beetle (Goliathus Drurii), which often grows to more than five inches in length, and he has an armour that requires considerable force to penetrate. The armoured little ant-eaters are also often found hiding away in some hollow tree waiting for their prey. These edentulous little animals are easily tamed, and pretty little creatures they are too, despite their somewhat dragon-like appearance. Tiger cats, sloths, lemurs and monkeys abound in the West African forest. Leopards and jackalls are common. A fair quantity of deer are found on the coast, while almost every animal that came from the Ark can be traced in the wide forest strip extending down the Guinea Coast.

At the foot of the hills there is a large track of sword grass about six feet high, with small clumps of trees dotted amongst it. These groves were loaded with bitter oranges, a juicy but tart fruit which makes a refreshing beverage, two being sufficient to make half a gallon of strong orangeade which can be sweetened to taste. These, and limes, might be well cultivated on the coast, and would pay, if shipped in sufficient quantities, as deck cargo, to England.

## CHAPTER VIII.

PRINCE HENRY ILL—FOMONAH—AN ALARM—ANNEXING OF BEKWAI AND ABADOOM—THE KINGS DESCRIBED—THE DRINK QUESTION IN AFRICA—NEWS OF PRINCE HENRY—THROUGH THE SWAMPS—A DASH FROM BEKWAI—NATIVE BEAUTY—DARWINISM—ADVANCE IN CLOSE COLUMNS—CAMPED IN THE FOREST—AN ASHANTI EMBASSY—AN UNFORTUNATE OCCURRENCE—NEAR THE GOAL—TORNADO IN THE FOREST.

ON Friday afternoon, January 10th, Prince Henry was not at all well, and though he made no complaint, everyone in camp noticed that he was not his usual cheery self. Naturally, he felt depressed at the news of Major Ferguson's death, for they were both walking together at Prahsu the evening before that gallant officer was taken ill. Towards evening, the Prince grew rapidly worse, and symptoms of malaria fever developed. Everyone hoped that as it was taken in its early stage, the Prince would recover sufficiently to resume the march. Surgeon-Colonel Taylor was in constant attendance, and everything done to relieve the fever; but malaria is a subtle enemy to deal with, and as the symptoms were serious, the doctors decided the Prince must return to the Coast without delay, and be removed to the "Coromandel."

The Royal sufferer was bitterly disappointed at this decision, and all ranks felt deeply for the brave officer who had entered into the campaign with such spirit, and who had uncomplainingly braved all the hardships, only to be invalided when the goal was almost in sight.

On Saturday morning, as we turned our faces Kumassi-wards, a little party, consisting of Prince Henry in a hammock, his attendant, George Butcher, and Surgeon-Captain Hilliard, who was in medical charge, started for the coast. The Prince cast longing eyes toward the troops already preparing to march, but he was much weaker, and realized that it would be useless to attempt to proceed further. Many expressions of deep sympathy for the poor fever-stricken patient went out from all members of the force : one could not but think that he, who, comparatively, a few hours before, had been in the best of health and spirits, was now paying Africa's penalty, whose malarious grip might demand even

K

life itself from its victim. We sorrowfully watched the hammock till it was lost in the gloom, as the bearers carefully wended their way up the steep sides of the Monsi Hill; and then we resumed our march.

Leaving Kwisa, the road descends rapidly, afterwards winding through a swampy district, infested with frogs of enormous proportions. The slimy batrachians, who infest these morasses, are held in religious horror by the natives, who refuse to touch them; and even the ominous croaking is the signal for absolute silence from the usually irrepressible carriers.

Having crossed the Adansis and entered Ashanti proper, the natives acted very differently on the march. There was no lagging behind or plumping down loads for "chop" at every half mile; and even their remarks were made in an undertone for fear of arousing the dreaded 'Shantiman. The one topic among the white men was the probable chance of fighting; for the Ashantis fell back on Kumassi before the advancing scouts without firing a shot. What could be the intentions of His Sable Majesty Kwaku Dua III.?

Several skulls were found in the vicinity of these swamps below Kwisa, which evidently marked the spot of a fierce battle in bygone days. This swampy district was trying, for the bush was so dense all round, that it completely cased in the narrow path. The air in those murky forest depths was also vitiated by the long lines of carriers, that it was scarcely possible to breathe. The road, after crossing some low sand hills, became dryer, however, and the undergrowth less dense, though the forest was as luxuriant as ever.

Fomonah was once a flourishing town, and the capital of the Adansi Kingdom, but it is now in ruins and has few inhabitants. Passing through the village clearing, we reached a broad but shallow brook which was easily forded. By the marks and excavations on the banks and in the bed of this river, the natives had evidently been prospecting for alluvial gold, which abounds in many of the West African streams. Crossing the water, we were refreshed by a fragrant smell from a clump of smallish trees covered with a white bloom resembling hawthorn blossom. Nature here seemed to have wilfully joined two extremes, for a few yards further on, a noxious creeper grew in abundance, emitting a vapid foul muskiness which got into the throat and nose, and gave a peculiar taste to the mouth.

THE ALARM.

*From a sketch by Mr. H. C. Seppings Wright, Artist Correspondent to "The Illustrated London News."*

## AN ALARM. 133

Dompiassi, another ruined town, is about four miles from Fomonah, and from there the road led direct into Essian Kwanta, where we arrived at 10.30, after a trying march of ten miles. Reports had reached Essian Kwanta that the piquet, who had evacuated the village and fallen back on Kumassi, had been reinforced, and 2,000 Ashantis were then within two miles of the camp bent on retaking their outpost.

The small company of Houssas turned out with an alacrity worthy of better results, and the native levy got under arms. The piles of cases of biscuit and meat were hastily thrown round as a barricade, and others packed to form a rude fort. I am afraid all were highly pleased with the prospect of a fight at last with the Ashantis, and Prince Christian bustled about looking eagerly forward for the brush. Everyone was disappointed when further news came in that the movement was not being proceeded with, and the Ashantis had withdrawn again. Thus nothing came of all the preparations and the wily foe did not show fight.

When the Special Service Corps and Artillery arrived, they marched through the village, and bivouacked in the bush about a mile ahead, while the Staff took up their quarters in the village itself, which was deserted. The houses were superior dwellings, many having additional courtyards and out-houses for the use of the household slaves. The surroundings were also fairly clean; but there was a very bad smell, partly due to some plots of plantains rotting in the vicinity.

Large piles of stores were stacked in readiness for the advance, and Captain Donovan, of the Colonial Service, had pushed well ahead throughout the march with his carriers and supplies, entering Kwisa, and forming a camp there just behind the advanced scouts. Captain Swain, British Guiana Police, took the Bekwai carriers in hand, and he used these friendly Ashantis to the best possible advantage in getting necessaries to the front. Governor Maxwell was journeying from the coast to enter Kumassi when it had been invested.

Saturday afternoon, by the time we had settled into quarters at Essian Kwanta, a furious drumming announced the arrival of the young King of Abadoom, who was coming with the King of Bekwai to sign a treaty with the British. He seated himself on the outskirts of the town to await the time arranged for the palaver, and a little later, the King of Bekwai arrived in the vicinity of the camp, resting his royal bones on a stool in the forest.

Punctually at five o'clock, the guard of honour, furnished by the Special Service Corps, marched in, and was drawn up in line outside headquarters. The Kings then came on the scene; the Bekwai monarch in great state. Immense war drums thundered, tom-toms were thumped, big metal bells hammered on continuously, while a hideous tooting on elephants' tusks completed his noisy if inharmonic arrangements for wooing the gentle muse. Behind these raucous melodists marched the Fetish priest and sacred executioner combined. With his appearance and rig, and enormous head-dress of leopard skin, surmounted with tusks and a high fringe of eagle's feathers, he could have taken his place among any Redskin chiefs of the Wild West, on the war path.

Then came his most sable Majesty of Bekwai, an intelligent but sensual looking negro of medium stature and apparently about forty-five years of age. A small black cap perched on the back of his cranium, and ornamented with gold filigree work, did duty for a crown; a long silken robe and sandals completed his outfit. His claw-like fingers were covered with massive gold rings finely worked, which were well displayed by a paw bearer on either side, holding a bunched-up silken cloth on which the royal hands rested. Several gold fetish ornaments were hung on his wrists and suspended round his neck, while his royal toes were also adorned with gold work. In fact his Majesty was a veritable walking jeweller's shop.

Over his head rose the mighty folds of a gorgeous umbrella of plush and silk, which the attendant kept on a continuous hop and twirl for no apparent reason except it were to circulate the air about the King, but it seemed a clumsy and laborious method of fanning. Immediately behind his Kingship walked a prime minister, who placed his hands round the royal waist as a support to the monarch as he walked in majestic state.

The Lord Chamberlain followed, with a fine collection of rusty keys of every description hung in bunches on his body as an insignia of office; and bringing up the rear were a motley crew of minor chiefs, fetish men, soldiers with flintlocks, ladies in waiting and slaves with fly whisks, or bearing their master's stools, chairs and litters.

The King of Abadoom had a very different gathering. He was a gentle lad of fourteen, of pleasing countenance, and very nervous throughout the proceedings, though any lack on his part was amply made up by his two chief advisers; one, a cunning,

## A KINGDOM ANNEXED. 135

white-headed old rascal, the other a younger but no less crafty-looking negro. Many of the King's retainers were boys younger than their master, but there were also older chiefs, sheltering their sacred heads from the sun under common cotton umbrellas sent up from the coast, and all much the worse for wear. The bearers of these sorry gamps were quite young boys, some not more than five or six years of age. The poor little fellows are doomed to stand behind their master's chair for hours, with arms stretched upward to the utmost extent, in order to shade the lazy negro sitting at his ease, while his poor little slave is ready to drop with exhaustion.

When the Kings were seated on their respective thrones (otherwise brass-studded kitchen chairs), and the followers had grouped themselves round, the "General Salute" was sounded, the troops presenting arms as Sir Francis Scott and his Staff appeared on the scene. In the centre of the gathering stood a small camp table, with papers, pen and ink duly arrayed thereon, also a short end of candle (a valuable commodity in the bush) for use in sealing the treaty.

Captain Donald Stewart officiated; and, after asking if they had signed a treaty with any other foreign power, and being answered in the negative, he read the articles of the treaty between "Her Most Gracious Majesty Queen Victoria and the Kings of Bekwai and Abadoom." Each article was translated by a native interpreter, the terms being as follows :—

"That Her Most Gracious Majesty would accord her protection over their countries, the same to be part of the Jurisdiction of the Gold Coast, provided that,—

The respective countries of Bekwai and Abadoom should be always kept open for trade; every facility being offered to traders; the roads kept open, and in good repair.

That capital punishment must be abolished for all crimes except murder, and no slaves to be kept, bought, or traded with.

They were to enter into no contracts with other Foreign Powers.

The King not to enter into any act of aggression or war, but must refer all disputes to the Governor of the Gold Coast.

Great Britain would respect, and not interfere in any way with the customs and habits of the country not enumerated in the above, and no levy or tax would be imposed on them. The King's methods of collecting the revenue remaining the same.

Human sacrifices must be abolished and kept down with a strong hand."

The young King listened attentively, but the more skilled diplomatist of Bekwai did not want to appear too eager to accept British terms. He was in frequent conference with his chiefs, and having craved permission to speak, began to raise salient points of order and law.

The High Chamberlain wished to know what was to be done if a man committed a murder?

Captain Stewart replied that he would be tried under British law, and, if found guilty, be put to death.

That only half satisfied the contumacious old wretch.

"The King had a number of young slave girls that he was now going to give to his young men as wives; if one ran away might not she be killed, if caught?"

It was pointed out that slavery must be abolished, and they would therefore be no longer slaves, but free.

We were then favoured with a few different phases of breaking the Seventh Commandment. It appears that in Ashanti, Sir Francis Jeune had a counterpart in the Executioner, who dealt summary justice to the offending parties; but the Bekwais had previously been told that no man or woman must be put to death except for murder, so that all these questions of moral law-breaking, involving death to the guilty parties, had been answered in that one stipulation.

More caviling was in course of preparation, and king and ministers were in close conference; but as the proceedings were getting unduly protracted, Sir Francis remarked to the interpreter, "Tell him I am not here to be made a fool of, and if he has any more to say, he must say it quickly." Then, finding the King of Abadoom was quite ready to sign the articles, he gave the signal for him to advance.

The Bekwais were still deep in consultation on some learned subject, but it did not transpire. There was Bekwai prestige and precedent being rudely put aside, and the subordinate King of Abadoom signing first!

Their whole natures rebelled against such supersedure. The chiefs shouted; the court crier sprang to his feet and howled off some marvellous panegyric, informing us of the supreme dignity, nay, the cohabitation of the divine and mortal realized in their Lord and Master; while the King hastily gathered his rather

## THE DRINK QUESTION. 137

dirty robes around him, advancing to the table with more haste than dignity.

The seal was attached, and the royal finger nail touched it; Captain Stewart then held the pen, the King placed his digital extremities on it, "Yow Boatin" was duly written, and the treaty thus signed. The King of Abadoom, who had been rather disconcerted by the previous little scene, then went trembling through the same ceremony. The Union Jack was hoisted; the general salute sounded, as the troops sprang to attention and presented arms; thus annexing the Kingdoms of Bekwai and Abadoom under British rule and protection. After much shaking hands the Kings took their departure, and the troops hied away for tea and much needed repose.

As the King of Bekwai was leaving in state, he expectorated freely, and, to my disgust, there was a general scramble among the followers to secure the saliva; some youths actually applying their tongues to the spot, to obtain the last traces.

To the credit of the Bekwai Monarch, on one occasion when Prempeh required a number of victims for sacrifice, and sent to levy slaves from the dependent monarchs, he refused to send human beings, but substituted an offering of gold dust instead.

In this village I was offered a peculiar native spirit with a most pungent odour. One has heard of Europeans becoming addicted to drinking " stink-pot," but I doubt if any white man could have taken a nip of this vile concoction. I pushed the nigger and his jar away, but he took a deep draught, which made his eyes water, and then smacked his lips with evident relish.

There are certain people who are continually making an outcry against the drink traffic in Africa. These gentlemen are doubtlessly prompted by the best intentions, but they are sadly mistaken by attributing the whole evil to the white man. The general impression is, that the whole of the curse lies at the door of the white trader and his fire-water, and that if he were prohibited from supplying drink to the natives, the evil would be removed at one stroke. This is a pure fallacy; the natives much prefer European drink if they can afford to get it, which is not always, but they will have drink of some sort; if not proper spirits then Pombi, or some other vile mixture. Spirits are far beyond the reach of the majority of natives in the interior, so they freely drink their own liquors, which are nothing more or less than a fiery poison, far more terrible in effect than the most adulterated trade gin.

A trader once remarked that sending rum to the African at a high price was a blessing in disguise. He loses his taste for native drink, and can only afford occasional debauches on the less harmful spirit. This is a curious line of argument, but it only advocates the lesser of two evils.

Khama will undoubtedly be held up at once as an example in dealing with the evils of imported drink. Now Khama was a thorough prohibitionist from the first, and forbade the manufacture of all native drinks. He had hardly stamped them out when his country was invaded by traders who supplied bad spirits to his people, and the drink fiend again stalked throughout the land until he was able to get the second evil redressed. If Khama's legislation could be extended throughout Africa it would be a great blessing, but the only way to effectually stamp out the drink curse is to strike at the root of the matter, and not make a drastic removal of one evil and stimulate a greater one. On the coast towns, where cheap and common spirits are always obtainable, there are far too many mud liquor shanties licensed. Much greater care should be exercised by the proper authorities. They seem to grant a license to anyone who cares to pay for it, and the number of drink hovels in Cape Coast is a standing disgrace to the Colonial Government.

More news from Kumassi arrived by spies who stated that all the men were called into the capital, and the women were wailing in the villages for their husbands, who had gone to the *war*. News also came that every effort would be made to keep the white man from Kumassi, and envoys were on their way down to promise anything and everything, if only the troops would return to the coast. If the forces advanced on the city there might be no resistance unless the English fired the first shot, or injured or captured the King.

Telegrams arrived from the base concerning the sick. Captain Curtis, R.E., Lieutenants Mangan and Davies, who had all been dangerously ill, were now reported doing well. Everyone was hoping to hear Prince Henry had reached the Coast and had been safely removed to the "Coromandel," but his illness unfortunately proved even more serious than was at first anticipated. He arrived safely on the 12th at Prahsu, but had been much tried by the journey, the fever greatly increasing. The Medical Staff spoke of the great consideration shown by the Prince to all attending him. He was frequently bathed with warm water, with a view of inducing the skin to act. Though this water was well warmed, it seemed cool to the fever-stricken frame, and the Prince remarked " How refreshing that cold water is." The doctors were decidedly anxious about him, but he rallied enough to be moved to Mansu on the 14th and resumed the journey to the coast next day.

On Sunday, January 12th, the Staff remained at Essian Kwanta to enable the Ammunition Column and Bearer Company to close up, in readiness for the final advance into Kumassi.

Several hundreds of carriers were encamped in the forest just below the village. The thick undergrowth had been cut away, leaving the high trees alone standing. At night the flickering light of the numerous camp fires throwing a red glare on the surrounding foliage; hundreds of black naked forms moving about under the trees, or lying round the blazing fires in every conceivable position; a perfect babel of voices jabbering and shouting in unknown tongues, and you have the weird picture that requires far more than a pen to portray.

At half-past five the sun is just rising, the birds give a few preliminary whistles, flocks of parrots fly overhead, the crickets have ceased their chorus, while the sloths also stop their child-like screams, that render sleep impossible to the bush novice. He constantly awakes during the night, startled from his doze with dim visions of murder and violence, till he suddenly remembers it is only the sloth, an African substitute for our feline tribe in their nocturnal choruses. Monkeys are not as common as is generally supposed, though at night they often come round the camp for a midnight chatter, while jackals occasionally give a short interlude by a series of mournful howls.

At sunrise, on January 13th, we resumed our march and experienced one of the worst strips of road on the whole advance. Progress was painfully slow, as the track was narrow, and a very large body of troops and carriers were on the move, the column wending its way over tree trunks and through vile patches of foul-smelling swamp, happily now rendered passable by furlongs of corduroy thrown across by the native levy. Passing slowly onward through Adawassi, now in ruins, we went through Kuraman and reached Ejinassi at midday.

The Special Service Corps marched on through the village and pitched camp in Amoaful, once a large and important town, but now little better than a heap of ruins. This place was the scene of a sanguinary conflict with the Ashantis during the '74 war, when fighting raged between Amoaful and Ejinassi all day, the natives being repulsed at nightfall.

The Headquarter Staff again halted for a day, remaining in Ejinassi on the 14th to enable the forces in the rear to close up. The Special Service Corps advanced to Esumeja, their late camp being occupied by the West Yorkshire Regiment, who arrived from Essian Kwanta at eleven o'clock, and they marched into camp in splendid style, despite the drawbacks they were still suffering from.

The day passed very quietly, though the necessary delay was chafing, with Kumassi so near; and yet the force were in a state of absolute uncertainty as to the probable issue of the expedition. The water in all the adjoining villages was very bad, the only available supply being from a muddy gutter streamlet. There was one trivial incident; a hammock-bearer was caught robbing an Ashanti woman, so a parade of natives took place in the morning, while a Houssa Corporal administered twelve strokes on the thief, who was deeply impressed by the ceremony, as were the other natives, though in a different way.

In the afternoon the Bekwai Prime Minister arrived from the capital, bringing a "dash" for the white Chief. The "dash" consisted of a long string of natives, loaded with yams, plantains, fowls, and eggs, a present of gold dust, and last, but not least, a bullock, which was, perhaps, the most acceptable present of the batch, for no fresh meat had been procurable on the road. Major Piggott volunteered to shoot it, as none of the natives were capable of properly slaughtering the beast. Immediately fire-arms came on the scene, the cowardly Fantis bolted to a safe place in the bush; a splendid shot in the forehead brought the animal down, and it was soon skinned and cut up, making an agreeable change after the long spell of preserved meat.

In connection with this beef, a curious incident occurred which caused much discussion and rumour in camp. Major Piggott cut off a joint of beef, and sent it ahead to the commander of the advanced scouts by a runner, with a scrap of paper attached, "Major Gordon. Killed 14th inst." Major Gordon received the meat safely, and as paper was scarce, he scribbled a note of receipt on the back and returned it by the messenger, who duly delivered the same. The front script alone was an ominous missive to those out of the ken, and naturally the worst conclusion was jumped at, and the startling news spread. Poor Gordon! Killed! How terrible! Excitement ran high; fighting was imminent now, and bitterly was his death to be avenged. Then some far-seeing person turned the paper over, and found on the back a note of acknowledgment written by the defunct officer himself, and the matter was cleared up.

The Bekwai people had opened a market as requested, and a plentiful stock of bananas, plantains, yams, and paw-paws were offered for sale. So high a value did these bush people put on an English three-penny bit, that sufficient fruit could be purchased with it to last a week if you thought the load worth the carrying. The market women were all very ugly, but probably that was intentional, for fear if more comely Bekwai maids were sent they might be turning the heads or capturing the hearts of the white men. At any rate, Darwin could never have been to Ashanti, or he would assuredly have found his missing link; and the evolutionary theory seems borne out in Africa by types of startling reliability.

With all due respect to these ladies, as some of them waddled about, it required a distinct stretch of imagination to realize that they were human beings, and not belonging to a race of the quadrumanous gorillas; and their shaved heads, a sign of slavery, did not add to their beauty. Many prevalent fashions among West African women are as cruel as those practised by their more enlightened European sisters; though the facial disfigurements are not as common on the Gold Coast as in surrounding districts, where the upper lip is slit and widened by pegs till a large ring is inserted to keep the orifice extended.

Though barbarism has its dark side, these bush people, quite cut off from every trace of civilisation, and out of the reach of missionaries, lead a very contented existence. " Ignorance is bliss," and the few requirements they have, are easily supplied : they have no luxury and no wants, few yearnings and few aspirations ; a pointed stick makes them a spear, and a few sticks plastered with mud, a house, while an abundance of fruit springs up around for food which requires little preparation. Undoubtedly their great curse is the pernicious form of government and fetish, though this, of course, has more effect on the chief towns and immediate surroundings, than on the small scattered bush villages. With their cheeks for bellows, a stone for a hammer, a hard tree stump for an anvil, and tongs made of a split piece of green wood, they can turn out work of a sort that would really compare favourably with that of an English blacksmith. Unfortunately, at first, civilisation spoils all this, they begin to covet; and once give them an education they lose their simplicity, becoming proud and arrogant; considering themselves quite equal to a white man.

The black brotherhood is all very well in its place, but the negro cannot be treated as an equal by a white man. He must first be taught to regenerate his character, quit habits of brutish sloth, and abandon the practice of most degrading crimes and filthy ways. Speke says, "I do not deem the African negro capable of raising himself from the degradation in which he lives," and there is a great amount of truth in the assertion. Centuries of barbarism cannot be changed in a moment, though it may be hid under a thin veneer of civilisation, and, at present, it is doubtful if the invasion of the white man has been a great blessing to the African. That is more the fault of the European than the negro. With patient teaching, and wise legislation only, will the savage be taught self-respect, and gradually emerge from his age of darkness and hereditary paganism with all its incumbent horrors.

A white man has much influence over an uncivilised black by his superior moral power, and even the ordinary things of every-day life of a European seem supernatural to the savage mind; but this influence is only too often abused. The native wants a certain number of kicks, but also a certain number of "ha'pence"; and strict justice and impartial treatment will go a long way with a nigger. If the justice is too much tempered with mercy, he is not slow to take advantage of it; and on the other hand, too harsh a discipline will brutalize him.

The fresh arrival in Africa who starts by making friendly overtures to natives usually turns into one of the hardest men when dealing with them, because he is so often taken in and has his clemency abused at every turn. The negro may become as faithful as a dog with proper treatment, but he will need as strict a breaking in as a colt, who is either made or marred by early training. He won't follow his teachers into civilisation, neither will he be driven to it, but he must be firmly led.

The natives have few games, the most universal being Po, which is played in most of the villages. The game takes place on a board containing twelve round holes, each containing four men.

## BUSH ETHICS. 143

On making inquiry as to the rules, the answer was always the same, "No savey, sah!" but they get very excited when playing, and will gamble the very wraps from their bodies. Apparently it is not unlike the Indian "Pachisi"; at least, they have similar methods of reckoning.

Funerals are attended by scenes of disgraceful orgie, especially if a chief or big man has died. His remains are closed over by some dozens of his progeny, who, with his faithful wives, are all as drunk as they can afford to be. In cases of war, the dead enemies are never buried, but the bodies are sometimes eaten, or thrown into the bush to be devoured by wild beasts.

The birth of a child gives no pleasure to the Ashanti, with his plurality of wives; the woman is often banished to the bush, and never remains in the husband's house during confinement. The female offspring is sold as a wife-slave, at a tender age, to some neighbouring chief. Who can wonder that pudicity is unknown among these women, whatever other virtues they may possess, when wives are looked on in the same light as a farmer in England regards cattle. They all work for their lord; do everything for him, and their numbers are a standard of his wealth. There, indeed, Marie Corelli would have ample scope to dilate on, and anathematize the supreme egotism of man; and there is certainly an opening for a branch of the "Women's Rights Association." Perhaps some of our more advanced sisters of civilization will turn their wasted energies in this direction. "The Society for the Emancipation of African Womanhood" would sound even better than the "League for Supplying the Blacks with Flannel Petticoats and Pocket Handkerchiefs," or similar *société de bienfaisance*.

There was a great difficulty in keeping shaved in the bush; some let their hirsute appendages flourish, others shaved clean every day, but the climate played havoc with razors, and shaving was an ordeal. I had one of the finely-ground "Mabs," however, and that kept in splendid condition, often shaving half-a-dozen in one day; for no one is particular in those things in the wilds. "He that hath, lendeth," is a universal maxim there.

On the 15th instant, preparations were made for the final advance, as the force had practically closed up. The order of march behind the scouts was :—

The Advance Guard of the Special Service Corps, under Major Northcote.
Houssa Artillery, with maxim and two seven-pounders, ammunition, and two rocket tubes.

The Special Service Corps, under Colonel Stopford, accompanied by Captain Blunt and Artillery.

The baggage and part of the Medical Staff Bearer Company with sick hammocks.

The Head-quarter Staff.

The West Yorkshire Regiment.

Remainder of the Bearer Company.

Baggage column.

Company of the West India Regiment.

Houssa Artillery.

Away in the rear The Supply and Ammunition Columns and Field Hospital.

Progress was painfully slow, the pace being reduced to a regular crawl, with frequent halts. The road at first was moderately clear, but plunged into a thick bush tunnel with the branches interwoven above, only just allowing free passage. The smell in the leafy avenue was unbearable as we followed in rear of hundreds of carriers. The numerous obstructions soon also caused straggling, and the long line of troops and bearers extended for some miles.

Crossing three streams in succession, which join about two miles down, and form the River Suberri, the road passes two sharp ridges with sides approaching the perpendicular, but once having cleared these, the path widened into an open and fairly smooth track right into Esumeja, being the best and widest piece of road after the Prah.

From the top of the ridges a splendid view was obtained. The long straggling line of the column could be seen winding in and out, patches of scarlet showing the position of the troops moving through the trees, with streaks of white, caused by the light robes of the carriers.

At Esumeja we found the Bekwai King drawn up in state, with his band well to the fore, to play us from his dominions. They made a terrible din, monotonously uttering a peculiar war chant, which was almost drowned by the infernal drumming and jangling of the musicians. We sighed in vain for wax to stop our ears, like the companions of Ulysses, when they rowed past the sirens and their delusive melodies. This music, however, would have rather caused one to die in agony than in ecstacy of delight. Judging from their faces they derived a considerable amount of gratification from the display, but we were much relieved to get out of earshot.

After leaving Esumeja the forest archway was again apparent, while the rough and swampy track reduced the advance to a snail's pace, and there were frequent stoppages. The fœtid smell caused by the narrow air space, vitiated by hundreds of carriers, and the stench from the swamp was really filthy. Everything comes to an end at last, but the trying march had its effect on the troops, many of whom fell by the wayside, thoroughly exhausted, and the numerous sick severely taxed the resources of the Bearer Company. We reached Edunku at three o'clock, the Special Service Corps advancing to Dede Siwa, and bivouacking on the banks of the Adra; but it was almost sunset before the end of the long straggling column came in and had settled down. The troops pitched their *tentes d'abri* where practicable, and these useful and portable little shelters, which are just large enough for three men to snuggle inside, can be easily put up in any situation.

Some of the miserable hovels in the village were turned into temporary hospital wards, and the remainder only afforded accommodation for a few officers of the Staff. Several of us bivouacked in the forest, hastily rigging up rough shelters of bamboo poles, with creepers twined above, and palm leaves laid over for a roof. Fires were soon burning, and we had settled down fairly comfortably before the chilly night came on. An encampment in the bush is soon made, as the material is near at hand. Some search for young trees or bamboos for uprights; others lop down plantains and palm leaves, and thus rough shelters are easily formed.

Several Fanti servants and interpreters were grouped round a camp fire, each relating tales of their wonderful presence of mind and their prowess, and what they would do if the 'Shantiman came across the river and attacked our camp that night. Crack! bang! bang! went some fresh bamboos, thrown on the next fire. 'Shantiman had come at last, and they were off helter skelter to the bush, without waiting to see the cause.

These explosions, when burning bamboos, are very common, as the cavities between the joints are often filled with water, and when put on the fire steam is generated, blowing up the section before the wood is burnt through. This water is often drunk by the natives, who select a likely-looking reed, and obtain a pint or more from a single cavity; though it would not be fit for European consumption except in a case of dire extremity.

There were various howlings and roarings from the different

animals prowling round in the forest; but after making big fires by the shanty, for comfort's sake, I had dropped off to sleep in spite of this mournful nocturnal chorus, when suddenly despairing screams of mortal agony, followed by a fearful hub-bub, and more cries, harrowed every soul as they were startled from their sleep. The attack had come at last, and the wily foe had crept through the bush and was upon us, was the first thought. To spring up and get outside was the work of a moment, and two other pyjamed figures came rushing on the scene shortly after, while the startled natives sat half dazed on their mats, which they had spread near the fires.

Hastening in the direction of the noise there was a gang of hammock bearers with a Fanti in the midst, who was yelling and screaming madly, for no apparent cause, while the others shouted to drown his yells. Our slumbers had thus been disturbed, and our small camp alarmed, for nothing more serious than some horseplay of the niggers, who speedily retired at the end of a good thick stick.

Morning dawned, and everyone was up betimes to resume the march. Still no signs of the Ashantis, and only four hours' sharp travelling from Kumassi. The road was good, but the column made a short advance only, ready to invest the capital on the morrow. Passing down a broad well-cleared track we passed Adwabin, which place was quite deserted save for a hideous old hag, who sat in one of the houses, left, apparently, with the hope that the English would make off with her.

After an easy march Dede Siwa was reached, the West Yorks camping on the site occupied the previous day by the Special Service Corps, who crossed the Adra and halted on the other bank. The Headquarter Staff took up their quarters in the village, which boasted of several very fair houses, the inhabitants having cleared out stick and stone. Officers and men were fretting with the slow advance, and all would have preferred a quick dash into Kumassi, but that would have entailed possible risk, with no gain beyond the few hours saved.

The Adra river was then a shallow stream about one hundred and fifty feet wide, and it was easily and quickly bridged over in a rough fashion, though the Engineer officers and men who were directing operations, had to stand up to their middle in slush and water for some hours. Stockades were also thrown up, so that the bridge could easily have been held.

## AN UNFORTUNATE RIOT.

Both the Engineers and Army Service Corps were decidedly undermanned, especially the former. There were only sufficient men sent out to meet the bare exigencies of the Expedition, and when fever made many gaps in the ranks, the remainder of the sappers were very hard pressed, especially the Telegraph Section. They had lost the services of their commander, Captain Curtiss, and several men, though Lieutenant McInnes, with a mere handful of assistants, pluckily pushed ahead with the cable.

Envoys came down to the outposts bringing as hostages, boys bedecked with gold, and said to be Prempeh's sons. They were only two poor slave children of no value to Prempeh or anyone else. Major Baden-Powell instructed them to return to Kumassi and tell the King that it was not the intention of the British to force the fighting, or depose Prempeh if he agreed to come to terms, but they had better hurry to Kumassi and await the Governor's arrival, for the Expedition must enter the capital, and the treaty would be arranged there.

Prempeh, still hoping to delay the advance, again sent down Kwaku Fukoo, Boatin, and a number of subsidiary chiefs to treat with the white man and promise anything and everything if they could only stop the troops investing Kumassi.

The envoys came down to Ordasum, where the advanced party of Houssas and native levies were camped, and they also brought a numerous following; attendants and slaves bearing stools, umbrellas, litters, state swords, and many emblems of office.

An unfortunate occurrence followed this visit; and though the Ashantis were themselves greatly to blame, it was none the less to be regretted, as it was contrary to the British methods of treating negotiators of an armistice. The Ashantis, huddled together waiting palaver, were obstructing the Houssa quarters. Three times they were asked to move by the interpreters, but they seemed to think it derogatory to their dignity, and would not budge an inch. The Houssas, always ready for a little fun, thereupon started to move the offending niggers, who were still stubborn, till canes were seized and freely used. The Ashantis moved then; the followers, dropping umbrellas and stools, bolted into the forest, leaving their belongings behind. The native levies, seeing a chance of "getting their own back" for years of aggression, then rushed at the Ashantis, whom they freely hustled and cuffed, till the officers came on the scene and stopped the row. In the confusion the envoys had been driven for a considerable distance, dropping even their smallest articles in the ignominious flight, and some of these things were stolen by our levies, who looked on Ashanti goods as lawful spoil.

The Ashantis soon regained confidence, and after retailing their grievances, returned to camp, where a short search revealed most of the lost property, which was restored to the owners. Three delinquents were then tied to a tree, and had half-a-dozen lashes apiece, in sight of the Ashantis, who saw strict justice had been done; but they took advantage of this by trebling the previous stated amount of their losses to Captain Donald Stewart, when the palaver started.

Captain Stewart, through the interpreter, first said he was very sorry for what had happened. It was an accident, and they must tell the King so.

They had complained about their losses, but most of the things had been recovered and returned, yet they now gave a finely exaggerated tale of missing property, but he would tell the Governor, and see what could be done. Chief Assufu first said he had lost £60 worth of gold dust, and now he has added £100 to that. The Ashantis were fond of doing such things. Every man who had lost anything during the last twenty years put it down, but the Governor would see they got justice. He was now ready to hear their message from the King.

The lanky Kwaku Fukoo, after a long preamble, replied that they had taken the letter to the King, and Ansah had read it; but the voluble linguist then went on with such a jumbled speech that no one could quite grasp the gist of his remarks.

Captain Stewart answered that they did not seem to understand the letter, which said that it was not the intention of Her Majesty's Forces to depose King Prempeh if he fully submitted and paid a war indemnity, and would agree to the demands of the British Government, namely, the appointment of a Resident. Also he must send hostages to be held till the indemnity was paid.

Kwaku Fukoo interrupted: "You want hostages! Why, I brought you two, and you refused to take them." Captain Stewart rejoined: "Thank you! We shall choose the hostages, not you, and the two children you brought were not royal personages, and not worth anything. You know that!" (A broad grin of acknowledgment illuminated three hundred dusky

A TORNADO. 149

faces.) "We shall come to Kumassi, and the King must submit in proper fashion to the Governor."

Boatin sprang to his feet: "I am the eye of Kumassi, and the people agree to submit. Lo ! I say so ! We are here to settle the whole matter for the King, and you need not come further. I am a big chief, yet your people have robbed me. Perhaps we shall be treated thus if we let you come to Kumassi."

Captain Stewart rejoined that the palaver about their losses was settled, and they had punished the guilty. The Governor would agree about compensation. Things had gone too far, and the Expedition must go to Kumassi and nowhere else. The Chiefs begged and pleaded that the treaty might be drawn up there and then, and they would touch the British flag in token of submission, so the white men could then march back to the coast. Finding that their entreaties met with no response, and that the terms would be discussed in Kumassi alone, the envoys returned with sad hearts to the capital. The visit of these messengers still further reduced the chances of fighting, but in the last Expedition the same tactics were adopted in the earlier stages of the advance, when the sole efforts of the Ashantis were also to keep the troops out of Kumassi, and when the British General steadily advanced, the foe resisted and made a desperate stand outside the town.

There seemed now two probable courses; either Prempeh would bolt, or a stand would be made at the gates of the city when they found the occupation of the capital inevitable.

The night of the 16th the whole force was encamped on the banks of the Adra, and everyone turned in, eagerly looking forward to the final march on the morrow, and the solving of the Ashanti enigma, which was a difficult one. It was a glorious night for Ashanti, and little mist, so all settled down to sleep in eager expectation of the morrow, and what it would bring forth.

About midnight, without any previous warning, a fearful clap of thunder awakened everyone with a start. The lightning flashed incessantly, and the rain suddenly poured down in torrents. The rough roofs of plantain-leaf thatch were washed away in a second, and everyone was drenched to the skin. It was a copious shower bath which would have been pleasant in the heat of the day, if we could have stripped, and put clothes and effects in a dry place. The flashes of lightning were vivid and incessant, followed immediately by the deafening roar of thunder reverberating through the trees. The forest was lit up as brightly as at noonday, the electric fluid playing dangerously over the tree tops, and bringing many a giant of the forest down with a crash. In one case a huge cotton tree was struck, and fell, crushing to jelly a group of native carriers who were clustering, affrighted, round its ample roots. The tornado raged without cessation for over two hours, and then the clouds dispersed as suddenly as they had gathered.

Everything was in a deplorable state of dampness, with water, inches deep, flowing around; but, when the rain ceased, soldiers and carriers turned out to cut down wood for bonfires, and, before long, cheery piles were blazing for all to warm and dry themselves by. During the storm the officers moved about freely among the troops, administering rum to those who needed a stimulant, and the surgeons were up all night doing what they could to the poor fever-stricken patients in their charge.

Things were getting more comfortable, when the storm started again, extinguishing the fires and swamping everything; but, luckily, tea and cocoa had been prepared by the men before the rain began. At 4.30 *reveillé* sounded, ending a strange and dreadful night; and, after a hasty breakfast had been swallowed in the rain, the column re-formed to wend its bedraggled steps into Kumassi.

Captain Birch, R.A.; Captain Bain, Royal Irish Constabulary; Lieutenant Straubenzee, R.A.; and Lieutenant Vesey, R.E., disembarked at Cape Coast on January 12th to reinforce the Departmental Corps. They travelled up country almost night and day, with relays of hammock bearers, and reached the main body near the Adra, making a record journey through the bush.

## CHAPTER IX.

KUMASSI—KING PREMPEH—THE QUEEN MOTHER—COURTIERS—A STATE RECEPTION IN KUMASSI—A PROCESSION BY TORCHLIGHT — THE GOLGOTHA—THE ROYAL PALACE—SACRIFICES—SUNDAY IN ASHANTI— THE LAST SCENE—PREMPEH'S DOWNFALL—THE LOOT.

THE rain poured down steadily till eight o'clock, but when it ceased things were as bad for some time afterwards, sundry small streams of water still dropping from every tree as we passed beneath.

The men of the Special Service Corps led the way, followed closely by the Headquarter Staff; the remainder of the column stretching far in the rear.

The path, turned into a veritable quagmire with the rains, made marching anything but pleasant. The sun shone at last, and as it began to gain power, things became drier overhead, and our spirits rose accordingly. This was not altogether a blessing, however, for the fœtid vapours began to rise from the swamps by which Kumassi is insulated ; and the vile steamy mugginess was much increased by the surface-water of the previous night's storm.

The broken rest and general dampness affected the troops, though they stoically held out, determined to reach the long looked for goal, and not give in with their object in sight. Many, however, dropped by the way, thoroughly done, and the hammocks were crammed. Still others could not keep up, and staggered along, vainly trying not to fall out, while officers pluckily assisted their men by carrying accoutrements, and giving an arm when needed.

Surgeon-Lieutenant Spencer, though not well himself, relinquished his own hammock to a worn out sick one, and not content with that, loaded himself with the accoutrements of some of his men, who were just able to walk when thus relieved. That day's march was not the only occasion that this young officer acted in a similar way, and when the Medical Staff were reduced by sickness, he laboured day and night tending the patients in his charge. It is such acts of devotion and self-sacrifice as these that have ever made the British officer stand pre-eminent in the annals of civilization.

Other officers likewise showed the same self-sacrifice, and Surgeon-Captains Maher and Bevor, the medical officers with the West Yorks and Special Service Corps, had their hands very full, especially the former officer; and early and late they assiduously tended the lame and sick ones.

That march to Kumassi proved to be another fine exhibition of the stamina and national pluck which carries the Britisher through when other nations fail. Heavily equipped, the troops had tramped towards Kumassi; through sweltering heat and dank night fogs, and there was no malingering among them. Early and late the Tommies doggedly pressed on, defying the fever and not giving in till they dropped by the wayside, thoroughly overcome.

Kumassi at last! The proud and dreaded capital of Ashanti!

Major Baden-Powell's force had worked its way by different paths through the bush, capturing many armed Ashanti spies on the way. The main road into the town was narrow but fairly good, and led through a dense patch of high jungle grass, fringed with medicine heaps. There were also many graves strewn with fetish images, and rotting vultures tied by the neck to the head posts.

Suddenly a thunder of drums could be heard, but still the scouts warily advanced. Major Gordon and Captain Williams cut their way through the bush, and entered the town by the Kokofu road on the right flank, and a party of Bekwais forced a passage in the same way on the left. The main advance party consisted of the Political Officer, Captain Stewart, Major Piggott bearing the Union Jack on his Soudan Lance, Major Baden-Powell and Captain Graham with the scouts and levies, Captain Mitchell with a company of Houssas, and their drums and fifes. The levies were followed by a small party of four Engineers; Sergeant Lowe, Corporal Dale, and Sappers Richardson and Rubery, with the reel of cable, which they payed out and fixed as they marched. The wire was in and working at an early hour; a fresh feather in the cap of the smart telegraphists, who had slaved from morn till night in getting the cable laid from the coast.

Shortly after the scouts had arrived, the two flank parties appeared, and piquets were immediately posted on all the approaches to the Palaver Square, where the levies halted at 8.20 a.m., the flag being firmly planted in the centre of the market.

OCCUPATION OF KUMASSI BY BRITISH TROOPS.

*From a sketch by Mr. H. C. Seppings Wright, "Illustrated London News."*

The drumming increased, and at last King Prempeh, with his chiefs and hundreds of followers, was seen advancing. They made no show of resistance : the King seated himself on his throne, or raised dais, in one corner of the clearing, while the chiefs and followers ranged themselves in dense lines on the two sides of the square. Colonel Stopford's gallant boys heard the thunder of drums in the distance, and mistaking it for firing, eagerly pressed forward. Fatigue and fever were alike forgotten as they broke into a trot, eager for the fray, but the troops were doomed to disappointment when they drew nearer, and the true nature of the sounds was revealed.

Close behind the "Specials" came the Houssas with their seven-pounders, then Sir Francis Scott and his Staff, followed by the West Yorkshire Regiment and their carriers. As each company of troops arrived they were drawn up in the Palaver Square, and soon a long string of hammocks wended their way onward to the Field Hospital on the outskirts of the town, bearing many a poor fellow with aching head and burning frame. The baggage column then poured in with line after line of carriers, and it was three o'clock before the whole force was drawn up and dismissed to quarters.

The Houssa Band made an attempt to play the troops in, and among other appropriate airs, the strains of "Home, Sweet Home," floated through the trees, as if in irony at the dirty surroundings.

Viewed from a distance, the long rows of enormous coloured umbrellas resembled the line of round-abouts in Barnet pleasure fair, with far more infernal din than in that English orgie. The chiefs and petty kings were arranged in rotation, from the King himself, ranging gradually downward according to rank, till the minor chiefs took up their position by the side of the road leading into the town. The least powerful chief had one big umbrella and a small group of dependents and slaves, with a couple or so of drums and tom-toms ; but higher up the line, the followings grew with the importance of their master, and the number of musicians likewise increased.

Near Prempeh, the Kings of the surrounding Ashanti dependencies were placed, with their swords of state and fetish dancers ; but little attention beyond a passing glance was paid to these groups, for on the built throne sat Prempeh and all his royal gathering in choice barbaric array.

Was *that* oily, peevish-looking object the monarch whose name alone made the surrounding tribes tremble? It seemed impossible, but it was he, and in a state of ludicrous funk.

He was sitting with his back half turned to the square, but now and again he glanced round furtively at the troops formed up there. He wore a black crown, heavily worked with gold, a silken robe and sandals. Suspended from his body and wrists were various fetish charms, while behind him hung a dried lemur as a special fetish. He was seated on an ordinary brass-studded chair, which was placed on the top of the tier of baked clay forming the throne. The fabled stool of solid gold was not to be found, and had been removed to a safe distance, long before the troops entered the capital.

Seated on the left of King Prempeh, was the Queen Mother, smiling and jabbering, with an air of nonchalance that contrasted strongly with the marked concern exhibited by her puny-hearted son. Though her face wore a hard, cruel expression, she had regular features, and would have been good looking had her appearance been less sinister. Round her were perched a numerous train of women, decently and cleanly dressed, but their shaved heads and flat oily faces gave them a most repulsive look. Prempeh's Aunt, swathed in a gaudy wrapper of silk, sat among them, enjoying a gnaw of chew-stick, and grinning at the white men who approached the throne. Like the Queen Mother, the demeanour of these women was one of absolute indifference, though the faces of the sterner sex were livid with fear.

The lower parts of the throne were filled by prime ministers, advisers, sword bearers, executioners, and criers, in every description of barbaric apparel. On the outside of the circle, slaves bearing huge plaited fans, kept a constant current of air directed toward the King. The throne, with its numerous occupants, was sheltered by immense and gaudy umbrellas held aloft by gigantic Swefis, captured in a raid by Samory, or some other manhunter, and sent to slavery in Kumassi.

Grouped in a large circle round the throne were some hundreds of Prempeh's minions, under-executioners, lesser ministers of the household, and slaves. In the centre of the circle, three hideous fetish dwarfs, in little red shirts, capered about, while seated in a group on the right were Prempeh's own personal attendants. These boys and men were protected by various fetish laws, and wore as a badge, a small hair cap surmounted with a mortar board of gold, resembling one of Spratt's dog biscuits. They seemed to enjoy their position immensely, but as their paramount privilege consisted in being sacrificed on the death of the King, to accompany him to the next world, the honour of such a post was highly enigmatical.

Surrounding the royal circle were the musicians, and the din was absolutely ear-splitting. Enormous war drums, bedecked with skulls, dried eyes, ears and other portions of the body, boomed out in deafening thunder as they were vigorously hammered by perspiring slaves, tom-toms were untiringly thumped, a continuous clanging was kept up by means of iron rings, and hollow metallic vessels knocked together, while a separate band of slaves added to the infernal din by monotonous roars from elephants' tusks, carefully graded to play two alternate notes. Each lusty tooter could have put a steam siren in the shade, the first deep roar resembling a hundred hoarse steam-boat whistles, followed by the shriller shrieking of an army of tugboats in mortal agony.

Drawn up in line were the native levies, with their long guns, every whit as proud as kings themselves. Major Baden-Powell had done wonders with these men, who in four weeks were transformed from a horde of savages into a disciplined force.

Right opposite Prempeh were his revolted subjects, the Bekwais, and many a glance of hate went across from those dusky ranks, to be returned by glances of envy from many of the petty Kings, who would gladly have thrown off Prempeh's rule in the same manner, had they dared.

Rushing about from King to chief in great perturbation of spirit, were the two Ansahs. They found playing at king-making very pleasant when masquerading in London, but fraught with considerable danger and anxiety in Ashanti.

The King had ascended his throne early in the morning, and sat right on till five o'clock, watching the arrival of the dreaded white men. The Royal family all seemed of a superior race to the remainder of their subjects; in fact, they bore little resemblance to the surrounding Ashantis, being better looking, and of a much lighter colour. The reason of this is not far to seek, for in Ashanti as in other countries in Africa, the Kings have as many wives as they like, picked from all classes of society; but blue blood is not the necessary qualification for a royal marriage; the indispensable endowment is good looks. The royal sons may marry pretty women, the royal ladies the best looking men they can find.

Prempeh's mother was very fickle in that respect; in fact, she was a veritable female Bluebeard. It is stated that at various times she had taken unto herself fifty husbands, all of whom were executed by her orders, until Prempeh's father came on the scene, and the offspring was considered comely enough to ascend the stool. The Kumassi eligibles must have, figuratively speaking, trembled in their shoes at an amorous glance from that female dragon. She so thoroughly turned the matrimonial market into a lottery, in which a blank meant death, though her speedy vengeance also would unerringly descend on those who failed to enter the lists when told.

The troops were quietly dismissed to their quarters, and still Prempeh held state reception in all barbaric pomp and splendour; but it was his last, though little did he realize how completely his power would be overthrown, without a chance on his part to fight for it. The Ashanti rulers may be skilled in wily statecraft, but they proved no match for European diplomacy with its far-reaching arms.

About one o'clock the reception had begun with a weird dance of executioners and dwarfs round the throne. Three dancers in long flowing robes twirled and leaped in a mazy serpentine fling, till they dropped thoroughly exhausted, to be followed by others. The chief executioner also gave a solo dance, accompanied by the most diabolical leers and suggestive gestures, as he furiously brandished his huge beheading knife, accompanying each wild flourish with a series of blood curdling whoops and yells.

The various kings and chiefs next approached to pay homage to the plenipotent monarch, while the din waxed louder than ever. Each chief advanced in turn, with all his followers, down a long lane formed through Prempeh's courtiers. The royal crier then sprang to his feet, and, in Ashanti epics, extolled his master's virtues and prowess. Other of the courtiers followed, and extending their arms towards Prempeh, vehemently yelled various adulatory but ridiculous effusions. These exaggerated encomiums were expressed in many ways.

"Oh, Prempeh, who is as powerful as thee!"

"Who is like unto thee!"

"Oh, King, thou art great and mighty!"

"All kings of the earth are but dirt before thy feet!"

"Thy wisdom and knowledge is revealed unto all nations!"

PREMPEH'S LAST STATE RECEPTION.
From a sketch by Mr. H. C. Seppings Wright, "Illustrated London News" Correspondent.

## A STATE RECEPTION.

"Who is like unto the King of the Ashantis!"

And much more in similar strain. The monarch, if he were flattered by these eulogies, could not fail to be wearied by their repetition hour after hour.

During this uproar, the headman of the visiting chief was also shouting and gesticulating, as if to call attention to the marvellous qualities of his own master, and when this pantomine had gone far enough, sudden silence fell on everyone; even the drums were hushed, while the chief advanced slowly, as if entranced, with his eyes glued on Prempeh's face, and prostrating himself on each step of the throne, he at last cringed full length at the monarch's feet. The King, after a mock show of deliberation, extended his hand, which the prostrate chief gingerly clasped between his own extended palms. Bowing his head, he shook with emotion, as if thoroughly overwhelmed by the ineffable bliss of holding the oily paw of the cruel nigger despot, and so great were the transports of joy that he could not let that hand go. Prempeh's prime minister pushed him with his foot, and his own headmen dragged at his robe. No! he could not tear himself away. The tugging grew more forcible, till, with mournful countenance and much rolling of eyes, he sorrowfully arose and prepared to descend. Then the silence was broken as suddenly as it commenced, and the din started again with redoubled vigour.

The Chief moved down one step, and stopped again. The wrench was too great! He hesitated, then advanced a stage lower, stopped undecided, while his waiting attendants beckoned and howled for him to come. It was impossible, and he sorrowfully shook his head from side to side; but, with a vigorous and unceremonious shove, the prime minister sent him flying off the step into the outstretched arms of his people.

The hypocritical old wretch dragged his robe securely round his shoulders, heaved a great sigh of relief at having got through his part of the business, and marched off with his followers. Another immediately took his place, and exactly the same ceremony was gone through, and kings and chiefs succeeded each other in this performance, in all its details; though, at heart, those cringing negroes were cursing the very existence of the monarch they were professing to revere.

After seeing a dozen or more go through the same form I turned to inspect the city; I say "city" advisedly, but mud heap would have been better. It certainly boasted of many regular and wide streets with fairly built wattle houses on each side; but the very roads were defiled, and the place was a mass of festering pollution. The much vaunted capital was a combined filth heap and charnel house.

The town stands in a large clearing at the foot of a hill, and appears to have been larger than at present, notably on the east side, which was once an extensive suburb, but now is deserted. It is almost surrounded by a swamp; but under proper sanitary conditions the place might be made fairly inhabitable, though the misty exhalations from the marshes envelop the town at night in a thick fog which is not conducive to health.

Disgusted with the filthy hole, I turned into quarters in one of the clay bedaubed dwellings. Outside they are substantially built, but once inside, the compound was a quagmire of polluted mud and filth, round which the veranda-like chambers opened; and in that state of foul squalor had the Ashantis lived like pigs. Heaps of this accumulated offal had to be carted away before the places were fit for European occupation, and then only with abundant disinfectant was existence possible. Everyone suffered more or less from sore throat, which was due to the vile smell and dampness.

Lieutenant Pritchard, R.E., was indefatigable in his endeavours to make things pleasant. This young Engineer had exhibited great tact and energy throughout the march, and had been right forward with the advance; done a full share of duty when his superiors were stricken with fever, and came through with flying colours, though, unfortunately, he was seized with malaria after Kumassi was invested and his work practically done.

Captain Blunt ranged his guns so to have full sweep across the Palaver Square and its approaches, and Major Baden-Powell pushed through the town to Bantama, and held all the roads from that direction. The Special Service Corps and West Yorks were quartered in two of the many separate districts into which the town was divided by stretches of dense elephant grass and corn patches.

At five o'clock, Sir Francis Scott and all the officers of the Expeditionary Force seated themselves in a semi-circle on the square, while Captain Stewart and his interpreter went to tell the King that the Commander was ready to see him. Some of the chiefs blustered a little after Captain Stewart had gone, but the Ansahs finally persuaded Prempeh to pluck up his failing spirits and comply, which he did with a bad grace.

The huge umbrellas began to bob and twist, and drums were beaten as the whole of that vast assemblage got into motion, and came slowly across the square toward the Commander-in-chief. The two Ansahs acted as prompters, going through the motions in dumb show, while the lesser chiefs passed, salaaming with outstretched hand to each Officer in succession down the line.

These chiefs were succeeded by the more important men and their followers, and finally Prempeh himself, with a large nut in his mouth, as a special fetish charm to guard against the wiles of the white man, was half dragged past between two attendants. He looked remarkably like a fat over-grown youngster, sucking a bull's-eye, but ready for a good cry at being taken to school.

A more abject picture of pusillanimity could never be painted than of that despot as he passed, cringing and trembling, down the line. He afterwards advanced and shook hands with Sir Francis Scott and Major Piggott, who must have both felt overwhelmed by the honour. Sir Francis then addressed a few words to him through the interpreter :—

" Tell him, I am glad to see him here, and that there has been no fighting. I think he and his people have shown very good sense in not resisting the advance of the Queen's forces. I don't want any of those noises and disturbances at night, as we had when I was here twenty-two years ago in the last war. He must tell his people to bring things and form a market, and everything will be paid for. The town must be kept clean. White men cannot live in such filth, and the long grass will have to be cut down.

"We want good order, and I have told my people that they must not plunder anyone. The Governor, who is Her Majesty's representative, will be here to-morrow. He will arrange a day for palaver, and you must make your submission to him in native custom. That is all. I wish you a good evening."

The white troops were respectfully standing in a line behind the officers to witness the proceedings, but the native carriers, with less deference, clustered round the Staff, obstructing the view of the soldiers behind. Little notice was taken of this until Prempeh approached, when curiosity overcame other scruples, and there was a rush to get a closer view of the King. The Ashantis instantly divined treachery, and were panic stricken; for a moment the utmost confusion reigned. Their black hearts, imputing their own methods to others, suspected a ruse; they thought they had been betrayed, and the men were going to fall upon them; but their apprehensions were soon quieted when the troops stopped on the edge of the crowd, where they could feast their eyes on that flabby, yellow, but royal countenance.

When the palaver was over, Prempeh again resumed his seat on the throne, but many chiefs had taken their departure, eager to get clear away. Evidently Prempeh thought he was well out of the wood, and nothing would now be done by the force except to instal a Resident, and march away satisfied with any amount of flimsy promises, which the Ashantis could as easily break as heretofore.

Most of the officers and men had retired to the European side of the town when the royal litter arrived, and the King descended from his perch to be borne in triumph to the Palace. In tropical regions there is no twilight; the sun had set, and sudden darkness descended when the royal procession was formed. The King and many of his adherents had been fortifying their nerves, and were fairly on the way of being "beastly drunk," as a "cockney" West Yorkshireman remarked.

There were only three white men in the vicinity, but Prempeh insisted on shaking hands with all; I can feel the grip of that clammy paw again, as I write.

A start was then made for the Palace, and the weird appearance of that barbaric state procession by torchlight, baffles description. The musicians marched first, some of the enormous drums being carried between four slaves, and beaten by drummers in rear. Hundreds of torches were lit, while the crowd of nobles, courtiers, captains, citizens, and slaves, went mad with transports of joy, excitement, and rum.

The purport of all this enthusiasm was echoed in their cry: "Prempeh! Prempeh! Your fetish has proved too strong for the white man! No power on earth can prevail against thee!"

They leaped, they squirmed, shouted and screamed, directing all their frenzied motions to the royal litter, from which little could be seen except a crowned head; and a puny hand waving in acknowledgment to the roaring plaudits.

Wearing European costume, and patent boots fit for Bond Street, were the two Ansah *Princes*. They squirmed and shouted with the rest, looking perfectly ridiculous in their civilized attire. Prince Christian and Major Piggott appeared on a bank watching the proceedings: both Ansahs danced furiously to the rear of the litter, and then walked quietly behind with the greatest nonchalance; but directly the procession turned the corner, thinking they were free from European observation, they again danced and yelled with redoubled vigour:—the noble savages!

As soon as darkness fell, piquets were stationed in all directions, guarding every approach. Spies from Kumassi had entered the British lines the day before, and reported that the Ashantis did not want to fight, and would not resist if the English only wanted to establish a Church and a Resident; but if they interfered with Prempeh, soldiers were ready in the bush. Also that plenty of powder had been distributed in the town, and the spies thought they had undermined the Palace and Palaver Square in case of emergency. Ten thousand warriors also had been collected in the capital a few days before our entry.

No doubt exists that had not the Ansahs arrived with reports of the strength of the advancing English, which they greatly exaggerated, the Ashantis would have offered a spirited resistance at the entrance to Kumassi, when they found that no amount of subterfuge and false promise would keep back the invader. The wiser counsels of the Ansahs had prevailed, and the warriors were removed to the bush, still ready to answer to the calls of their chiefs if needed.

Everyone retired early, thoroughly worn out with the previous night's broken rest and the long trying day that followed, and all slept soundly despite the strange and wretched surroundings.

On Saturday, the 18th, Governor Maxwell arrived, and he was accorded an official reception. The troops were paraded, and as His Excellency entered the Square, a salute was fired by the Artillery. He addressed a few words to the force, complimenting them on the excellent way they had surmounted all obstacles and gained their object.

Strict orders had been issued against looting, and also to respect the sacred fetish temples or hovels, which were all marked by white cards so that no one should unwittingly enter and defile the sanctity of mud and sticks. The town was littered with fetish heaps, shrines, images, clay pans, bottles, and other symbolic fetish tokens, and many a sly kick was given by the Houssas to these charm pots.

The water at first was very bad, and all endeavours to draw

the Ashantis on the subject proved futile, till by accident the royal springs were discovered, and a fairly decent supply was the result.

Many of the houses in the principal street were highly embellished, the walls being stuccoed in red, and finished in white; but with all this decoration there was still the filth and stench, and the hundreds of carriers were at once set to work to thoroughly cleanse and clear the end of the town occupied by the troops. Beyond an occasional drumming, all was quiet in the native quarter, and the streets were thronged as usual by the proletarian Ashantis and slaves, though the upper classes did not show themselves much.

One of the first objects I visited in the capital was the famous Fetish Grove called Samanpon, or spirit house. In this grove the decapitated bodies were thrown after sacrifice. Kumassi means literally "the place of bloody death," and well its name described it. This grove stood at the edge of the Palaver Square, on which many a poor slave, both male and female, had been barbarously tortured and executed, the bodies being dragged across and thrown among the trees in the sacred grove, to form food for the hundreds of vultures that circled among the trees, disturbed from their gruesome feast by the approach of any bold spirit who dared to venture into those sacred precincts, and risk the displeasure of the fetish gods of the Ashanti Nation.

This horrible Golgotha, of which Bowditch speaks in 1817, is piled with the remains of hundreds of miserable creatures, executed simply to please the Ashanti rulers' insatiable lust for human blood. Huge cotton trees had their buttresses piled with bones and skulls; human remains were littered about in every direction, while the whole of that terrible place reeked with pestilential odours.

Every step I took in that rank grass revealed hidden human bones mouldering there, while fat, contented-looking vultures, battened and gorged with human carrion, swarmed the trees above in hundreds.

On Saturday evening I strolled down to the King's Palace, which occupies a considerable space in the centre of the town. The palatial residence destroyed in the last campaign has been replaced by a heterogeneous collection of well-built wattle huts of enormous proportions and barn-like appearance. Large courtyards, alleys, and small quadrangles succeeded each other, with

THE KUMASSI GOLGOTHA.

## THE ROYAL PALACE. 169

quarters for the numerous wives and slaves, and storerooms; all built with little design, either architectural or beautiful. In some places the foundations of the old palace were still to be seen. The buildings stood in a large enclosure, surrounded by a fence of tall bamboo, and containing a fetish grove and private place of execution for any person it was thought expedient to decapitate on the quiet. Passing up a broad avenue with a companion, the chief entrance to the Palace was reached, a large gateway hung with enormous wooden doors. One door was immediately swung back to admit us, but the dusky janitors nearly dropped with astonishment when two presumptuous white men entered.

We stood in a large courtyard just inside, with spacious thatched alcoves opening all round, in which a couple of hundred slaves and attendants lay in silent rows, resting on their mats. Large earthen ewers of water stood in the enclosure, palms occupied the corners, and on a balcony higher than the rest were the huge bloodstained war drums, decorated with ghastly human remains *ad lib.*

There was another doorway leading to the private apartments of the uxorious King, with two naked daggers hung above on the lintel. As we paused at this entrance the Ashantis started up in horror, expecting to see those suspended swords of Damocles fall on our sacrilegious heads; but military regulations forbade a further investigation, and we retired, to the evident relief of the hundreds of attendants, who immediately barred the outer door, behind us and in the face of two approaching officers on exploring bent.

Prempeh's numerous wives were all safely transferred to the bush, so we had little opportunity of seeing any Ashanti beauties, unless the Gorgonian attendants of the Queen Mother were analogous types.

Polygamy is a very distinctive feature among these African tribes, and the natives religiously follow the precepts of the Book of Mormon, even if it has never been revealed to them, or expounded by a Joseph Smith or Brigham Young.

Ashanti ethics are curious and manifold. There are king's ethics and subjects' ethics; king's psychics and subjects' psychics; but individual influence and rank greatly determine the rules and laws of life; for they are promulgated by the fetish priests, who naturally know on which side their "bread is buttered," and grant dispensation accordingly.

The King of Ashanti was accredited in the English Press as having 3,333 wives granted him by law. Though there were no means of testing the accuracy of this statement, it must be accepted with the proverbial grain of salt. Any numbers derived from native sources are to be looked on with suspicion; for they have no true idea of numeration, the word "many" being used for all large amounts, and may as equally signify hundreds as thousands. The King could marry whomsoever he pleased, the more the merrier. Certain death fell on any man who looked on one of the King's wives, and instances are also known in which young lovers have been ruthlessly parted for the maiden to be placed in the royal harem, and afterwards, being discovered secretly renewing their vows, they have both been barbarously tortured and executed.

When Prempeh ascended the throne, he proclaimed, as a punishment to the family, that any man who should cohabit with the sisters of Prince Yao Atchereboanda of Kumassi should be put to death. A few months ago, just before the Ansahs started to England, Kwasie Adjaye, Captain of the Royal Hammockmen, and commanding one thousand guns, was accused of familiarity with one of these sisters, Princess Akosia Bereyna, and he was publicly put to death on this flimsy pretext.

On one occasion, Prempeh is said to have caused a public execution of four hundred young virgins, their blood being used for the stucco on the Palace walls. Even if the numbers are exaggerated, the information is probably true in the main, as virgin's blood is supposed to contain very sacred properties, and much of the Ju-ju or fetish medicine of the West Africans must be obtained from different parts of a young girl immediately after slaughter.

The royal wives were carefully guarded by eunuchs, but were often executed for a fancied offence; if they were *passé*, or had been denounced as unfaithful, by some evil-disposed person, though they had little chance of infidelity.

The Ashanti subjects who could not rely on the good services of the executioner to dispose of old wives, whose beauty had faded or who were too old to work, could easily rid themselves of the encumbrance. They had only to bring an accusation of unfaithfulness against the poor wretch and she had to undergo the ordeal of poison.

The fetish priest, on being consulted, arrived with an elaborate apparatus of skins, idols, etc., and seated himself in front of the victim, who knew she was innocent, and had perfect confidence in facing the ordeal. The crafty fetishman then made a poisonous mixture, and poured it down her throat. He shrieked and wailed, while numerous interested spectators chanted a weird chorus. He is a clever conjuror, and manipulated his paraphernalia cleverly, but greeted every movement with a well-feigned astonishment, not lost on the people. Excitement grew to fever pitch as he muttered mysterious incantations; but at last, the poison beginning to act, the poor woman screamed in fearful agony as the pains seized her.

The priest paused in his mummeries to frantically clutch the air as one possessed, while the victim lay writhing in the last throes of mortal agony. When he saw the poison had successfully done its work, he sprang up denouncing the dying woman. Her agony was then speedily ended by the infuriated spectators rushing in, and beating the remaining life from the pulsating body with their clubs. By this means this wonderful fetish priest had consulted the Spirits, and the Gods had devoured the life from the wicked woman whose only offence, most probably, was that her husband was tired of her. This ordeal by poison was not confined to Ashanti alone; but was, and is still, practised in many places in the interior. Another more inquisitorial form of torture was to bury a man to his neck in a colony of white ants, who slowly devoured the flesh off the living body.

I have no wish to dwell unduly on these horrors; but in order to give a faithful account of the habits of the people of West Africa it is necessary to recount many gruesome details in speaking of their devilish fetish worship. English people have no idea of the fearful enormities constantly practised in darkest Africa, and it is just as well that their eyes should be opened, so that they will be in a better position to judge the difficulties to be encountered in civilizing these people, and why it seems impossible for them to be made respectable members of society. In the apparently most civilized districts, all manner of diabolical crimes are committed under the very nose of the authorities; and so superstitious are the people, and so powerful the influence of the fetish priests, that the greatest difficulty is experienced in tracing these acts to their source. In many places the tenth child in every family is slain at birth as an offering. I could not find out for what supposed reason the gods require this sacrifice, but as the offspring of most African women exceeds this number, many hundreds of innocent babes must be yearly killed. Even on the Gold Coast itself, in well-populated districts, the moment the tenth child is born in many families, it is either buried alive or taken to the shore and thrown into the sea. It is difficult to advise any course for the Government to stop such practices, as most stringent legislation is of little use in restraining accepted traditions, which the people are bound to follow by a superstitious dread of fearful penalties. It would be a good plan to keep a more watchful eye on these wretched priests, who do much to counteract the missionaries' efforts to teach the people better things. One day, perhaps, the Authorities will remove some of these wretches to safe quarters in the Castle; for though it is undoubtedly a dangerous precedent to take drastic measures in dealing with the religion of a fanatical people, numbers of these priests have earned enough rope to rig the gallows for themselves. This is digressing somewhat, so to resume.

On Sunday, at 7 a.m., a church parade was held, at which all the Garrison attended. The service was a combined one, conducted by Canon Taylor Smith, the Church of England Chaplain, and the Reverend William Somerville, the Wesleyan Missionary who was with the force.

It was an impressive sight with the sombre forest surroundings, the grey mists hanging over the tree tops, the long lines of red coats, and a sprinkling of the dark uniforms and faces of the West India Regiment. Behind stretched a long sea of dusky faces and naked bodies of hundreds of wondering savages, carriers, levies, and Ashantis looking on, the latter wondering what strange fetish ceremony was being gone through by those assembled white soldiers.

One could not but be struck with the conduct of the three Chaplains accompanying the force. There was no bigoted intolerance and no friction; but the Church of England, Methodist and Roman Catholic all joined in visiting the sick, ministering to their flock, and working together for the general good. Many instances could be quoted of the two Protestant Chaplains, and Father Wade, who was attending the Roman Catholics, relinquishing their hammocks to aid some fallen wayfarer on the road, and generally assisting the sick when practicable. A small, practical illustration of prejudice laid aside for the common good. A pity it is, that there cannot be more instances of it, in these days, when, despite the cry for the reunion

## A MEMORABLE SUNDAY.

of Christendom, many rabid "Stiggins" of all denominations are occupied with riotous controversy over small points of doctrine, upon which no two men can think the same. These unseemly contentions have no effect beyond sowing seeds of dissension and doubt, broad-cast throughout the land. It would be a good day for England if these men would combine in their duty to the cause of humanity, in place of wasting energy on petty bickerings over theological differences; though the latter gives these self-seekers a chance for ostentatious but cheap advertisement, and turns the pulpit into a mere rostrum for pressing individual ideas and subjective idealism.

Captain Stewart had intimated to Prempeh that he must tender his submission on Monday, January 20th.

Occasionally on Sunday there was a distant desultory drumming, but Ashantis became more scarce in the town, and it was evident that some movement was in the air.

On Sunday evening, a palaver was held in the palace, the chiefs being hastily summoned, and it was thought that this was a ruse to get them together to endeavour to slip away in the night, get clear, collect their forces and attempt an attack on Kumassi when most of the troops had been withdrawn. They well knew that the white soldiers would have to leave before the rains set in, and may have thought that eventually they would be left in peace to return to Kumassi, and resume their life, in the old sweet way, as in 1874, when all troops, both white and coloured, were withdrawn.

To guard against any escape, the jungle was cleared right round the palace, and a cordon of the native levy drawn round after dark. The Palace Garden joined the bush at the back, and a secret footpath led through the swamp beyond. The piquets soon secured many prisoners, who emerged from the palace to reconnoitre on the various roads, only to find each was barred. The palace people grew anxious when the various spies did not return, and one of the Ansahs came out to see what was in the wind, and was found on the secret pathway.

About three o'clock the Queen Mother emerged from the palace with torches, and a long train of attendants, and passed unconsciously right through the outposts, but she was not stopped. She and her people went to her own private residence, which was quietly surrounded as soon as she was domiciled. Several chiefs were also captured during the night, trying to slip away; but Prempeh had either got an inkling of affairs, or did not mean to bolt, as he did not attempt to leave in person. The various prisoners were released at daylight, when everything was in readiness for the final act to take place.

The King had been told to appear at six o'clock, with all his chiefs, on the palaver ground. The white troops formed up on the square at 7 a.m.; and the Houssas, followed by the long lines of levies, had arrived from their quarters just before. After a weary wait, it seemed that Prempeh did not mean to come, so Captain Stewart and the interpreter went to fetch him. Major Barker also took a company of the Special Service Corps to strengthen the cordon round the palace, making escape impossible. Captain Stewart went in alone and told the King he must come at once, or he would take him by force.

There was a beating of one solitary drum, as the King entered his litter, and with a little delay, the Queen Mother joined the royal procession, which slowly wended its way across the clearing, into the square formed by the troops. Prempeh was accompanied by his chiefs, and followed by a large procession of guards, soldiers, slaves and attendants; but with a quick flank movement the Houssas cut this crowd away from their leaders, and umbrellas and stools, bearers and attendants, were soon flying in every direction.

The Queen Mother took a seat on her son's left; the chiefs and a few select servants ranging themselves in a long line facing Governor Maxwell, Sir Francis Scott, and Colonel Kempster. These officers were seated on an improvised dais of biscuit boxes, surrounded by the remaining officers of the Staff.

One chief was still absent, but presently the disobedient old rascal came in sight with his followers, escorted by a body of Houssas, sent to fetch him. These troops moved along at a quick rate; an undignified and unceremonious way for his chiefship to make his debut, and one which he bitterly resented. He was pushed and jostled by his followers pressed in rear by the gallant little Houssas; and then his attendants were all turned roughly aside, and he had to walk into the square unattended. He turned indignantly to expostulate, but a muscular sergeant added insult to injury, by seizing a stool and squatting him forcibly down upon it. The palaver then commenced.

THE PALAVER.
*From a sketch by Mr. H. C. Seppings Wright, Artist Correspondent to "The Illustrated London News."*

1, HIS EXCELLENCY (GOVERNOR MAXWELL. 2, SIR FRANCIS SCOTT. 3, COLONEL KEMPSTER. 4, LIEUT.-COL. BELFIELD. 5, SURG.-COL. TAYLOR. 6, COL. WARD. 7, MAJOR PIGGOTT. 8, PRINCE CHRISTIAN. 9, CAPT. DONALD STEWART. 10, MR. HADDON SMITH. 11, SURG.-COL HENDERSON. 12, MR. BENNETT BURLEIGH. 13, CAPT. LARKYMORE. 14, SURG.-MAJ. HUGHES. 15, CANON TAYLOR SMITH. 16, LIEUT. FABER, R.E. 17, LIEUT. PRITCHARD, R.E. 18, MR. GWYNNE (Reuter's). 19, FATHER WADE. 20, MR. VROOM (Native Commissioner). 21, KING PREMPEH. 22, QUEEN MOTHER. 24, STATE UMBRELLAS

Mr. Vroom, the Native Commissioner, acted as interpreter, and through him the conditions of the treaty were given to the Ashantis; but it had to be again repeated by the royal linguist to Prempeh, who could not bemean himself by listening to the stranger's voice.

Governor Maxwell reminded the King of his direct refusal to the ultimatums dispatched to him; further, that he sent Envoys to England, in direct opposition to orders; for they were told that all negotiations must be made to the Governor on the coast.

His Excellency went on to say that no article of our last treaty with Ashanti had been kept. They had made no attempt to pay the war indemnity, and it was still owing. Human sacrifices were to have been abolished, but they had still gone on. No road had been kept clear through the bush to the coast, which was another express stipulation of that treaty. However, the British Government had no wish to depose Prempeh if he would agree to the following conditions :—

He must make his submission in native fashion; and pay an indemnity of 50,000 ounces of gold dust.

He was now ready to receive the submission of the King and the Queen Mother.

Prempeh hesitated.—It was a terrible blow to the prestige of that haughty despot, to whom "all the princes of the earth bowed down," to thus humiliate himself in the presence of those white men and his own people.

He looked sheepish, toying with his fetish ornaments, and ready to cry with mortification. Albert Ansah stepped up and held a whispered consultation with him. Then, quietly slipping off his sandals, the King arose, removed his circlet, and he and the Queen Mother reluctantly walked over to prostrate themselves before the Governor, and embrace his feet.

The scene was a most striking one. The heavy masses of foliage, that solid square of red coats and glistening bayonets, the Artillery drawn up ready for any emergency, the black bodies of the native levies, resting on their long guns in the background, while inside the square the Ashantis sat as if turned to stone, as Mother and Son, whose word was a matter of life and death, and whose slightest move constituted a command which all obeyed, were thus forced to humble themselves in sight of the assembled thousands.

It was indeed a fall to the pride of that plenipotent monarch and his royal mother, to whom many a tortured victim had pleaded in vain for life, and at whose feet the very chiefs had to prostrate themselves, before they dared speak.

A perfect hush fell on the assembled multitude, and even the irrepressible natives were silenced as the King and his royal mother knelt, and tendered their submission; then rose to their feet, thoroughly humiliated and confounded, and returned to their people.

Prempeh collected himself, and being prompted by the Ansahs, again rose, exclaiming in a clear voice, "I now claim the protection of the Queen of England." The chiefs seconded this remark with a resonant cry of "Yeo! Yeo! Yeo!" *i.e.*, "Good! Good! Good!"

The Governor reminded him that only one of the conditions had been fulfilled. He was now ready to receive the indemnity which had been promised.

Oh, yes! The King knew that quite well and he would be most pleased to pay it. Unfortunately, the treasury was not full just then, so he would pay 340 bendas, *i.e.*, 680 ounces of gold, and pay the rest by instalments.

The Governor replied: "It is absurd to think that a man able to send envoys to England, has only that small amount in his treasury. Ashanti shall have British protection, but first British demands must be complied with. The King has been told that he must pay the indemnity, and he must provide the whole or a large part of the amount at once. The Ashantis have proved that their word cannot be trusted, and they have repeatedly promised to pay the last indemnity, but had never fulfilled that promise. The King must this time give me ample security."

Prempeh, with a deprecatory gesture, said he would pay in time.

The Governor rejoined: "The King, the Queen Mother, the King's father, his two uncles, his brother, the two War Chiefs, and the Kings of Mampon, Ejesu, and Ofesu, will be taken as prisoners to the Coast. They will be treated with due respect."

Had a thunderbolt burst in their midst, the Ashantis could not have been more amazed. Consternation was depicted on every countenance, and all sat transfixed for a moment, then leaping to their feet, the chiefs begged that Prempeh should not be taken from them.

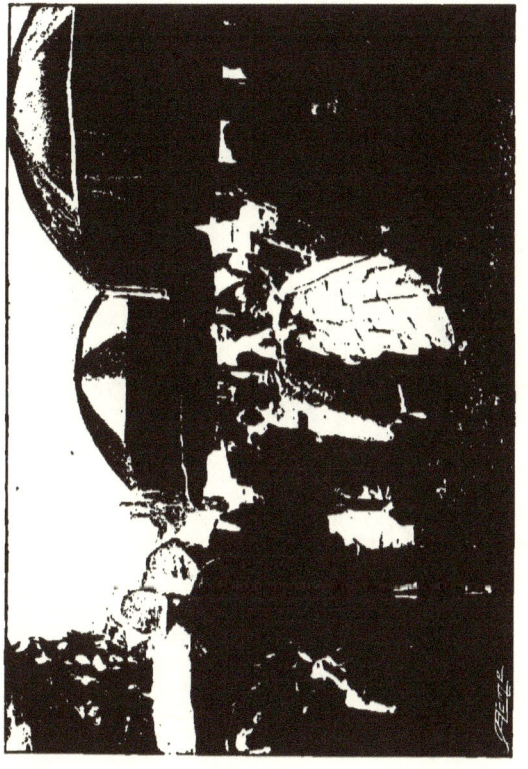

PREMPEH AND THE QUEEN MOTHER RISE TO TENDER THEIR SUBMISSION.

## A SMART COUP.

Kokofuku, pointing to the Ansahs, who stood by, looking half amused, half astonished, shouted angrily, " And what about those men, who have brought this trouble upon our heads ? "

The Governor replied: " The Ansahs will be arrested as criminals and taken to the coast on a charge of forgery."

The signal was instantly given; Captain Donovan of the Colonial Service stepped out and handcuffed the two Princes; several officers and warrant officers, previously appointed, drew their swords and formed up as escort to the Ashanti King and Chiefs.

The *dénouement* was startling and complete, and one almost expected to see the curtain fall on that dramatic scene, amid the plaudits of the audience and hammering from the *gods*.

The captives were marched, shortly after, to a house prepared for their reception, and the Ansahs were incarcerated in the Houssas' Guard room. The Princes were struck dumb at their reception. Words cannot describe John's expression of mingled hate, fear, rage and astonishment. Thus was the crafty negro foiled ; a man of undoubted talent, whose cleverness and education, if directed properly, might have made him a leading light on the Gold Coast. Born in Kumassi, he was taken as a babe to Cape Coast Castle. He was well educated, took an oath of allegiance, and entered the Gold Coast Rifle Corps. As a youth he fought for the English against his own country in 1874, and obtaining a medal. Then he constantly had intrigues with Kumassi, and was dismissed from the Public Service of the Gold Coast Colony. With his younger brother Albert, who had returned to Kumassi, he worked hard for his own ends, and these two educated princes finely duped their more ignorant Ashanti countrymen. When they, as envoys, arrived in England, they immediately began to work in their own interests, selling concessions to which they had no right, and forging documents purporting to come from King Prempeh himself. As a specimen of their cool effrontery, they wrote the following letter in London, and forwarded it to the Queen, but needless to add, their character and fame had gone before, and they were not received.

(Seal.)
To THE MOST GRACIOUS AND ILLUSTRIOUS SOVEREIGN, VICTORIA,
QUEEN OF GREAT BRITAIN AND IRELAND.

Kwaku Dua III., King of Ashanti, wisheth health and prosperity.

We pray Your Most Gracious Majesty to know that we have appointed our trusty and well-beloved grandson, Prince John Ossoo Ansah, son of the late Prince Ansah, of Ashanti, on our behalf to lay before your Majesty divers matters affecting the good estate of our kingdom and the well-being of our subjects, with full power for the said Prince Ansah as our ambassador extraordinary and minister plenipotentiary to negotiate and conclude all such treaties relating to the furtherance of trade and all matters therewith connected as your Majesty shall be pleased to entertain.

We therefore pray that your Majesty will be pleased to receive the said Prince Ansah on our behalf and to accord to him your Majesty's most royal favour.

Given at our Court at Kumassi this 8th day of September, 1894.    my
KWAKU DUA III.,                X
King of Ashanti.    mark.

Two companies of the West Yorkshire Regiment, under Captain H. Walker, immediately took possession of the Palace. The cordon had not been withdrawn, so no one could leave. All the doors were barred, however, on the inside, and there was a hum of many voices to be heard as the troops approached. One company, therefore, formed round to strengthen the cordon of levies, while the others, under the guidance of Major Baden-Powell, proceeded to make an entrance by a side door. Owing to the rumour that the Palace was undermined, the main entrance was not selected. The side door was burst in, and opened into a large deserted courtyard. Another painted door was then broken down, and the troops dashed in among some hundreds of natives. No resistance, however, was offered, and they were taken prisoners, disarmed, and placed under escort outside.

The work of collecting the valuables in the palace was next proceeded with. Looting the palace of a king of great reputed opulence was tempting work ; but though a great many valuables were seized, there was no fabulous wealth discovered as in the palaces looted in India and China. The treasure collected, only consisted of the richly worked head-dress of the King, also rings, gold trinkets and charms, gold hilted swords, etc., etc., with hundreds of articles of small value.

The celebrated Golden Stool of Ashanti, the solid gold crown, and many other almost historical relics of great intrinsic worth, had been previously removed to a place of safety, and secretly hidden where, perhaps, no eye will ever penetrate. An Ashanti custom was to bury the treasure in the bush in time of war, the slaves occupied in the task being then beheaded. From reports, this had been done just before the troops invested this capital of mud and murder. The seized spoil was deposited in a heap outside Headquarters, and soon formed a pile of large dimensions,

## THE LOOT.

a great portion of the articles being of the most common-place description.

Gorgeous State umbrellas, enormous kinkassies or wardrums, brass-studded chairs, beautifully carved stools, European and native swords, native spears, Ashanti daggers and knives, executioners' blades and torture instruments, brass studded cases, leather fetish caps, silken and cotton cloths, execution stools with recent blood stains, valuable old English chinaware, common table knives, large glass vases, carved wooden sandals, silk and gingham pillows of down and soft cotton, a few tusks, ivory pieces for playing "po" and drafts, a few bottles of brandy, common blunderbusses, old flint locks, a few Sniders, and so on *ad infinitum*.

Fetish was represented by hundreds of charms of every size, shape, and description, from the common slaves' ju-ju of plaited straw to the elaborately worked charms of chased gold or leopard and lion skin, with human blood on the sacred inscription inside as a fancied panacea, of far-reaching power, to cure every disease, destroy an enemy, and grant the wearer a perfect immunity from any ills the flesh or spirit is heir to.

The writing in these charms is usually burnt or written on cloth or paper; but I saw one inscription beautifully branded on a dry strip of bamboo bark in Burmese style. The writing resembles that of the Sanscrit, the formation of the figures being identical, but as I am not an authority on the subject, I am unable to say if it is the same in every respect. Writing is unknown except among the fetish priests who have a written language of their own. Thus not only is the *bas bleu* unknown, but a very small percentage of the sterner sex ever learn what is looked upon as an occult accomplishment.

There was not a large number of guns discovered, in fact, few weapons of any description. The armed men had made off to the bush, and were no doubt only awaiting the call of their leaders, now safely ensconced, with a file or two of Houssa bayonets between them and their warriors.

Among the loot were some horrible cloths including a woman's robe, saturated with blood, and other evidences of very recent sacrifices were not wanting.

## CHAPTER X.

BANTAMA DESCRIBED—HUMAN SACRIFICES—THE FALL OF FETISHISM—AFRICA FOR THE AFRICANS—SAMORY—FETISH TREES DESTROYED—ENGLISH IMPRESSIONS—THE FUTURE OF ASHANTI—A MIDNIGHT RECONNAISSANCE—PREMPEH'S COUNTRY HOUSE.

IMMEDIATELY after the palaver, the native levy marched to Bantama and surrounded the Royal Mausoleum and fetish houses. When these were broken into, nothing was found except a row of empty brass coffins in the Mausoleum. The contents of the houses, which were of great value, had all been removed with the sacred bones of the Kings, before the capital was invested. The practice in Ashanti, when a person dies, is to bury all the personal belongings, that they may accompany the defunct to the next world. Before burial, each article has to be "killed," *i.e.*, broken, to enable its spirit to "shuffle off this mortal coil."

On the decease of an important personage, slaves have to be sacrificed, guns and spears snapped, bow strings carefully cut, arrows split, and the odd utensils, as plates, calabashes, &c., cracked; and thus the spirit of the departed native makes its exit in a manner befitting its rank, attended by the spirits of every needful commodity, from slaves to the deceased's dirty pipe. The Ashantis have no belief in award or punishment in the future state, though the fetish power looks sharply after its adherents in this life. Fetishism is a religion only in the literal sense of that word, which means "fearing the gods." There is no question of right or wrong in their creed, for the fetish is a spirit, or combination of spirits, manifested in material things, and which is ever ready to seriously injure unless handsomely propitiated. In short, by means of fetishism kings hold their despotic sway, and the priests draw large revenues, and exercise an enormous influence. In its tenets there is no question of doing good here and being rewarded in the next world, and in this respect, it differs greatly from the lowest forms of Hindoo idolatry, for even the Thugs professed to think they would reap a rich posthumous reward for every victim they secured with the sacred noose and pickaxe of Kāli.

These fetish houses at Bantama had doubtlessly contained rich treasure belonging to the defunct Ashanti monarchs, and this would be looked upon as sacred by the natives; but it was not to be found, having been previously removed. Outside the chief buildings were various food offerings placed for the refreshment of the departed chiefs, and the door was firmly cemented up. These offerings showed that the people were unaware of the sacrilege committed, and the villainous priests may have surreptitiously removed the valuables for their own use, months before the Expedition was thought of.

Near the buildings stood the sacred banyan tree, with a large metal basin fixed below. Beneath the shade of this tree, human fetish sacrifices took place on regular festivals, slaves being barbarously executed as offerings to the manes of departed kings. These festivals took place quarterly, when the King paid his periodical visit to show his respect to the deified shades of the departed, and also to satiate his real, and their imaginary, blood-lust, by the decapitation of twenty victims, whose blood was collected in the sacred bowl.

The fetish village was speedily set on fire, and the tree blown up, the bowl falling as trophy to the popular commander of the levy. The ground round the tree was saturated and fœtid with human blood, and the very roots were stained and impregnated with red corpuscles.

Some specially interested gentlemen, misled by the Ansahs, publicly stated that human sacrifice was unknown in Kumassi. The Princes *(par nobile fratrum !)* had serious thoughts, when in London, of bringing an action for slander against Governor Griffith and Sir Francis Scott, for stating that Prempeh indulged in the mild dissipation of occasional head-chopping; and thereby casting a reflection on the character and the integrity of the Ashanti *Embassy* then in London. The solicitor acting for these masquerading princes and forgers, found he could not weave a single mesh of the legal net required for a *prima facie* case, though he had twisted and contorted every clause of the laws relating to libel, and waded through briefs innumerable, in the hope of finding a precedent. He adopted, however, the moderately wise course of writing to the Press on the subject, and by a striking coincidence, the same week, abundant proof of recent sacrifice arrived by mail from Accra, the reports being voluntarily furnished by eyewitnesses.

Every day that we spent in Kumassi, also brought to light fresh evidences of the continuance of the practice, though the people had been warned, under pain of fearful penalties, not to give any information to the white men. By means of an interpreter I talked with many of them freely on other topics; but one had only to touch on anything connected with fetish or sacrifice, and they instantly glanced round much disturbed. "The priests are so wise and will tell the white man all he wishes to know, but we must not say words about it;" and the dark native minds fully believed the priest knew every thought they had, or word they uttered. There were fugitive Ashantis on the coast, however, who were not afraid to speak, and native traders who visited Kumassi with goods, and sometimes forfeited their lives for their temerity, have brought reports from time to time, of strange and bloody doings of Prempeh & Co. Much information was given me by an intelligent and well educated young captain or chief from Accra. He was in charge of his people serving as carriers to the Expedition, and proved to be a perfect mine of information respecting West African habits and customs.

There were two ways of evading sacrifice after a person had been selected for execution. One was to repeat the "King's Oath," a form of declaring allegiance to the sovereign; or the intended victim must break away from his captors and reach a certain spot on the outskirts of the town, which formed a sanctuary or place of refuge. Another subject would then have to be selected, and the escaped victim would be free for the time being. These seemingly merciful provisos were not available for those who were to be executed for an offence, real or imaginary, against the King, and if he wanted a victim, he had not far to look for an excuse. Even the person who unwittingly passed under the shade of a fetish tree was condemned to death. To prevent intended victims getting clear by either of the before-mentioned methods, the executioners sprang on the poor wretch from behind, and thrust a long stiletto through his cheeks and tongue to prevent him speaking. A long wooden skewer was then thrust through the muscles of his arms, fixing them behind, and in this horrible condition his legs were put in irons to keep him fast until he was wanted for execution.

On the death of any great personage, slaves were immediately sacrificed on the threshold. If a chief, male victims were selected; but if a great lady died, females were slaughtered, often young virgins of tender age. The burial was marked by another scene of bloodshed, and more victims were chosen and executed, one of the mourners being sometimes seized and killed, if it suited the priest's caprice to further amuse the crowd. Quite recently, Aframi, King of Gyeso died, and Prempeh had six men beheaded at the burial to "wash his grave," as the custom is called.

When the King or any of the royal family of Kumassi died, enormous sacrifices took place, and on the death of the King's

AN EXECUTIONER.

aunt, 400 slaves were tortured and executed for the supreme joy and edification of the people. In these large executions, the executioner in his frenzy would often seize an unsuspecting onlooker he had a grudge against, or had been bribed to remove, and the victim's head would be hacked off amid the plaudits of the onlookers. Fiendish tortures were also often resorted to, especially with prisoners of war, when the executioners vied with each other in devising fearful methods of torture, such as flaying alive, plucking out eyes, and even more original devices. When Prempeh ascended the throne enormous sacrifices also took place to celebrate the event.

Human sacrifices were offered to avert threatening calamities, and even as the troops invested the capital, two young slave girls had their throats quietly cut in the confines of the palace, their blood being poured out as a libation to the gods to act against the invading white man.

Sir Brandford Griffith closed his dispatch of February 19th, 1895, to the Marquis of Ripon, with these words :—

"I trust your Lordship will pardon me for placing this ghastly record of savage atrocity, barbarity and reckless sacrifice of human life before you for I know it will shock you, My Lord ; but all things considered it has appeared to me that under existing circumstances, it was my duty to place before your Lordship in a connected form, the account contained in this Dispatch, of the savage, cruel and ruthless conduct of the King of Kumassi, and of those supporting him in his atrocious and murderous career."

In these pages I have given accounts of a few atrocities gathered from various sources, and must apologize to my readers for the sickening details ; but so much talk was made at the time on this " totally uncalled for " Expedition, that it is well the true nature of the Kumassi Rulers be made known. The great wonder is that the bloody capital had remained so long. It has only been during the last few months that affairs in Ashanti excited comment ; but for a considerable time past, the Liverpool and Manchester Chambers of Commerce had urged on the Government the necessity for strong action. On the Gold Coast itself, also, public opinion had been expressing itself in both the missionary journal and the regular newspaper. The following extract from the *Gold Coast Chronicle* savours rather much of the editorial " We," and the style is a good specimen of the work of a coloured journalist. However, the pith of the remarks is true, and not out of place at this juncture when little more than a year had elapsed to see the fulfilment of the Editor's dearest wishes.

Extract from the *Gold Coast Chronicle*, Accra, Friday, 30th November, 1894 :—

" So many reports are afloat with regard to Ashanti at present, that one does not really know what he is to believe, although it is universally admitted that the public chest must suffer if something of a decisive character does not take place, as there have been no end of expeditions to the " bush " in late years, and no sooner does one expedition return from Cape Coast than another is sent to the same place, and still we have the greatest unrest conceivable in the interior. What are we all about? Can no one open his mouth and speak? If we were wise in our generation, we would just march our troops direct to Kumassi, and once and for all, put an end to fruitless missions to the interior. If after we reached Kumassi there was the slightest disposition on the part of the Ashantis to fight, we would then be afforded another opportunity of giving King Prempeh and his followers some adequate conception of the resources of civilisation. In plain words, we must go straight to Kumassi and occupy or annex it, declaring Ashanti a British protectorate. A District Commissioner with some 200 or 300 Houssas could be left in Kumassi to ensure the maintenance of order. This, surely, would not be a difficult task for us. In fact, it is almost impossible to understand the infatuation which has led the local Government so far into so many blunders with regard to Ashanti. To tell the truth, we appear to have been playing with the question of having a firm and vigorous policy in regard to Ashanti all along, and we must be ready to confess this.

We were told last week that Prince John Osoo Ansah was coming down to Cape Coast with some 500 followers on his way to London, but he has not reached the sea-board yet, from what we can gather, and the Governor is now waiting in Cape Coast for him, we believe; and if the information that we received a few days ago is to be relied upon, the Prince in question may suddenly alter his intentions, which would probably imply further waste of public money. There is no spectacle, hardly, more humiliating than this! Here we are being led about like pigs by Ashantis! The latter know full well our most vulnerable or weakest parts. When they wish us to pitch away a few thousands, they simply create some little row, and threaten to do this, that, and the other, and forthwith an expedition is sent to the "bush" to await the turn of events. Certainly we are being fought with weapons of a most amusing description by the Ashantis. The demands on our chest, in consequence of the constantly recurring expeditions, are getting so numerous that before long, at this rate, we shall have very little money left. Possibly the King of Ashanti thinks he can more conveniently injure us by placing us constantly under the necessity of sending expeditions to the interior; and thus contributing towards the ultimate exhaustion of our resources. If every expedition costs, say, £5,000, 10 must necessarily cost £50,000, and so on! It is time for us to see that we have not too much money to pitch away. We should like to hear of some demonstration of force which will be final. If there are 800 Houssas in this Colony, send them all to Ashanti with the Union Jack, and let the whole of that country be declared once and for all a British protectorate in spite of all opposition.

Our interior policy has been throughout a failure, and had the 1883 Administration possessed the good sense to avail itself of the offer that was made, the whole of Ashanti might now be under our flag, and during the past 11 years we should not have heard of fruitless missions and unnecessary expeditions to the "bush" so frequently, for in 1883 the Ashantis expressed a willingness to become British subjects, the King having sent down to the late Governor Rowe to ask whether Her Majesty's Government would effect some arrangements in the matter, and thus put an end to the quarrels, while avoiding all future misunderstanding or unpleasantness. In fact, we should not like to assume any responsibility for the acts of the Government in the year in question, for all round we had blunders; and it was just about the same time that Little Popo was also offered to us, but which the Germans, through our want of foresight and supineness, ultimately seized; it is difficult to see how we could have been very alive to our interests in those days, while manifesting so much indifference in matters pertaining to the extension of territory; but whatever we might have done in the past, it is obvious that we are being made now to suffer for it. But we can certainly atone for our past misdeeds by wiser action in the future. Every year has its lessons and they should not be forgotten. There is, however, a fair opportunity now to take Ashanti. Shall we avail ourselves of it, or shall we not? Are we for ever going to remain dead to our interests?

The traders who are living in the regions behind Ashanti would be glad to hear that our flag was in Kumassi, as they could then come right down to the sea-board to trade without any interruption, and be under no necessity to deal with us, as they have hitherto done, through the Ashantis, and the latter have heretofore occupied, commercially, the position of "middlemen." The Jebus were made to suffer for acting as "middlemen." And the Ashantis must certainly not be considered as saints when compared with the Jebus. It strikes us forcibly that when the inquiry is really made, there will be found some "balance" in favour of the Jebus, who have never been known to have been half so atrocious as the Ashantis. The Lagos trade was not injured so much as the Gold Coast trade has been by the Ashantis when war was declared against the King of Jebu. Is the British Government afraid of the Ashantis? If it is not, why should King Prempeh be permitted to do such things with impunity that no other monarch in Western Africa would be suffered to do? As middlemen, to continue the indictment, the Ashantis have almost ruined our trade. They are perpetually having wars, too, among themselves, and it comes to this, that they will not, whenever the civil wars break out, come to the Coast to trade or allow any of the people living in the regions behind their country to come down. It is a reproach, moreover, to the civilisation of this century, that any savage King should be suffered by the British Government to do what King Prempeh is daily doing. In a previous issue we also referred to the periodical slaughter of men, women, and children in Kumassi, and the constant sacrifices, and all notwithstanding the existence of the Treaty of Fomona!"

In the *Gold Coast Methodist Times* of the 31st of August, 1894, there was a statement under the head of "*Ashanti—(from a correspondent)—Coronation of Prempeh.—Magnificent Display of Royalty*"—that—

"On the 4th of June last, Prempeh, who had been elected to the Stool in 1888, was formally installed King of Ashanti and placed on the Golden Stool, amidst magnificent display of royalty at the Ashanti metropolis. The election of Prempeh, some six years ago, occasioned much serious contention and bloodshed in the kingdom, which led one of its principal Chiefs, Osai Esibey of Kokofu, to quit his district and flee to the Protectorate. Among the influential Chiefs present at Kumassi on the grand day mentioned, were Asafu Buakyi Bantuma Ewua, Etsia Yaw Buakyi of Bekwai, and Yaw Sapon of Dwabin, who turned up in state, making Kumassi look like on some memorable days gone by. After the coronation festivities, the Chiefs and King with his Counsellors are said to have devoted full two weeks to deliberations as to how order and peace could be restored in the kingdom, and Ashanti regain its past glory and renown. The assembly dispersed about the 24th of June; it having been agreed to levy from the nation an amount of money to send to the

British Government for the giving back to the Kingdom of Esibey of Kokofu and Nkansa of Adansi, Chiefs who have taken refuge in the Protectorate. To this end 40 pereguins (£324) was to be raised by each of the great Chiefs in their various districts."

The next paragraph, headed: "DREADFUL SLAUGHTER OF HUMAN BEINGS," ran as follows :—

"It being customary with the new King of Ashanti on his enthronement to observe a general funeral custom for royal relatives deceased, Prempeh also being now installed, kept the hereditary custom by slaying some 400 human beings in cold blood in honour of the royal dead, each of his Chiefs bringing him presents of human victims from their provinces except the Chief of Bekwai, who brought gold dust instead of human victims, stating his intention to conform to British custom and practice, for, said he, 'My ancestors did not prosper by their human sacrifices, and I am determined not to follow their practices.'"

A trader also gives a fearful account of a "custom" he saw in Kumassi in the previous November. It was held by General Amanquanta of Ashanti in memory of General Awan, killed in the civil war with Asibi and Kumassi. To celebrate the anniversary, eight Nkoranza male captives, and one unfortunate Princess, daughter of the late King Kari, were slaughtered in cold blood. Prempeh attended this blood feast in person.

The following is an account given by Mahama Dankawrah, a young Houssa, who joined the force with his friend Bapio, when they reached British territory, after escaping from Ashanti. He states :—

"About 12 years ago I came from my country (Kawrah) to Attabubu to trade. While there Chief Ali caught me and sold me as a slave to one Kwadjo Mensah at Nsuta. I was there only two days when my master sold me for a pereguin (£8) to one Cucoe Tumfo at Agogo. I was employed by Cucoe trading with the Coast, and out of the money I earned, my master was able to buy Bapio Grunshi (who is here with me) at Mampon for £8, about four years ago. After the soldiers came—about three weeks or so—our master asked us to go to Quarmin with him to bring some of his sheep which were at Quarmin back here. We went with him there. When we arrived he took us to the King's house and sold us for £7 each to the King. After the King bought us he put me in irons, but not Bapio, for 12 days. I tried all I could to break the irons, and managed to do so after some time, when I ran away with Bapio to Agogo to Mr. Harri Tenuha. About two years ago the present Nsuta King's mother died at Konkrompe (near Attabubu), but they did not bring the remains back to Nsuta till a fortnight ago. The day that the remains arrived at the town we heard the beating of the great drum (Tumpang). I was at Quarmin in irons, but Bapio had been sent to Nsuta to bring meat, and was going to see what the matter was, when a man told him that the King would kill him if he went to look on, as he was a stranger, so he did not go. A man told Bapio that it was slaves who were sacrificed on this occasion. He does not know how many, but whenever the Ashantis beat Tumpang, it means that there is to be sacrificing. While I was lying in irons I overheard the executioner in the next room tell a friend that he had just killed seven slaves. The same night I broke my irons, and Bapio and I ran away. Some time ago a Kumassi man died at Quarmin. His family came about 16 days ago to Quarmin to get the remains. The same day they bought an old female slave and sacrificed her there; we saw the headless body of this woman lying in the street the same day, the head having been taken by the family above-mentioned to Kumassi, as the custom is."

After Prempeh's capture, the streets were filled with flying Ashantis, taking what they could carry, to the bush. A group of priests and fetish men crowded together in anxious deliberation in a *temple*, on the north side of the town. Vile wretches, murderers, capable of any deed of cowardly cunning. Were these low-looking creatures real humanity? The humanity which God created? Surely not! They were more like apes than human beings. The very leers and contortions of those lean faces, as their owners wildly gesticulated, resembled the grin of the skulls that we kicked into light when we walked through the dank grass of the horrible fetish grove. Their palaver did not last long, and priests and executioners cleared to the bush, though in strict justice, it seemed a pity some at least were not hung to the adjoining fetish trees, as carrion for the vultures they could provide food for no longer. Some of these "Ju Ju" men, trained from childhood in the mystery and ways of the forest, and taught carefully all that has been handed down in their profession for generations, are not altogether imposters, and know secrets which are not known in the Western World of Science; but all that counts as nothing against their bloody and devilish rites.

The immense fetish trees were blown up one after another, and the sacred houses and temples set on fire, or razed to the ground, and a cry of despair went up from the miserable creatures watching from the surrounding forest. "Our fetish is gone and our gods have deserted us!" In a few hours they had a practical lesson on the fallacy of fetishism that years of patient missionary labour could not have taught them. The day before, they would have declared that no power on earth could prevail against the gods of Ashanti; but when they saw Prempeh, the natural head of fetish, forced to humble himself and afterwards be taken prisoner, when the sacred houses and blood-washed trees, the very abode of the spirits, were destroyed by the white man's powder, and still the gods availed them nothing, their faith was shaken. It was a trial of orthodoxy that even the negro mind could not stand.

## AFRICA FOR AFRICANS. 193

A mission is being founded again in Kumassi by the Wesleyans, under the personal direction of Revs. Dennis Kemp and Somerville. This mission is to embrace Ashanti, and will not be confined to the capital alone; but a large sum is needed to put it on a firm and satisfactory basis. I have referred to the splendid work done by Methodists on the Gold Coast, and as this is simply an extension of the work there, I trust among the large amounts annually subscribed for Foreign Missions, ample funds will find their way into these channels, where, I am convinced, good use will be made of the money subscribed. The native mind has never been so ripe for instruction, and with their belief in fetish shaken to the very foundation, the mission will be a great blessing and success.

The Ashantis, with all their blood lust and cruelty, are a superior race to the Fanti, and much of the Ashanti savagery and butchery lay at the door of the rulers and priests. When the people have regained confidence, with judicious government and wise teaching, the Ashantis will be creditable allies to Great Britain, and the country a valuable acquisition.

Mr. Labouchere may say "Africa for the Africans," and plead the cause of the negroes being robbed of their land. Let him ask any reliable native resident, where British rule has been firmly established, if he would prefer his own ruler or the present administration, and ninety-nine cases out of a hundred I guarantee the answer would be for a civilized government.

Think for a moment of Kumassi under the bloody rule of a despotic tyrant like Prempeh, the people ground down and degraded with slavery and every other dark form of barbarism, the country in a state of perpetual civil war, and trade—*nil.*

Under British rule, trade will flourish, slavery and bloodshed are abolished, the people also being instructed in schools, and taught habits of self-respect and cleanliness. Thousands of the natives are rejoicing even now at the downfall of Prempeh.

No doubt in the Congo Free State things are in a most disgraceful condition in the interior, and I heard some heartrending tales from a hammock bearer, who had previously been pressed into the service of the State by Belgian agents in Sierra Leone. As his statements only bear out reports from other sources, they are no doubt true. The natives in this place, so aptly called "King Leopold's White Elephant," are ground down and wickedly oppressed and tortured by the officials of a civilized government. It is time that strong measures were taken to alter the unsatisfactory state of affairs, mainly brought about by young and inexperienced Belgian officers, whose sole aim seems to be extorting goods from the natives, and making money. The poor negroes in those districts have indeed found the rule of the white man anything but a blessing, and one can imagine the sort of oppression under the *gallant* Major Lothaire and others of his kin.

Ashanti had stood as the great barrier to the development of our West African Colony, and the Expedition had been a brilliant success in fully accomplishing its object, in spite of Mr. Regan's prophecy, published on December 23rd, 1895, and which reached us by the mail that arrived on the same day that the whole thing was satisfactorily settled, and Prempeh captured.

It was interesting to learn that everything had been muddled from the start; also that a Resident might have been fixed and the question permanently settled for a couple of thousand pounds; but happily for the prestige of England, she has not descended to settling State affairs by "Whiteley," or by "Regan" either. If that gentleman had only waited a few weeks, he would have found the means justified the end. There was also much talk of Samory and his intentions, but how the Alamany could attack us at Kumassi it is difficult to say, for their army is chiefly cavalry, who would be useless in the forest, for bush fighting. It is far more likely that Samory will be only too glad to be able to trade extensively with the English. This will naturally take away the monopoly from the firm who now send their agents to trade with the great Mohammedan chief in the Hinterland, as the whole country will be opened up to the traders on the coast. A railway line is to be built from Saltpond which will be joined to Accra and Cape Coast Castle by a coast line. The main line will lead through the valley round the Adansi Hills, across the Ashanti country to the Hinterland beyond.

The limit of the forest is reached 70 miles north of Kumassi, and the country is then healthy and open. Large herds of cattle and horses are owned by the Mohammedan Houssa tribes. The country is rich, the inhabitants a fine race, intelligent and industrious. Samory will no doubt be affected, as one of his best slave markets is now closed in Kumassi; but with fair treatment, judging from his present attitude, he will be rather willing to assist than hinder the British.

# FALL OF FETISHISM.

The forest land will for ever remain much as it is. The coast tribes are far too indolent to clear, and the climate is too deadly for white men to attempt to work even as overseers, but when a good road has been made from the coast, the timber trade may be greatly developed, as it is now only hindered by the difficulties of transport. There is much gold in the forest, but the climate forbids the white man to disturb the surface of the earth, and stir up the malaria germs; for it is certain death for the European to attempt to prospect.

The gathered loot was sold by auction outside Headquarters, and fancy prices were realized for specially interesting articles, though much of the stuff was not worth picking up.

Everyone in camp turned out to see the enormous fetish tree, facing the market place, destroyed. Charges were inserted all round the massive trunk, the cable was attached, and when everyone had withdrawn to a safe distance, the lever was pressed. There was a dull roar; a complete section about a foot wide was blown away as cleanly as if cut, and the mighty trunk rearing its lofty branches over 150 feet in the air, poised itself for a second, and fell to the earth with a thunder and force that shook the ground, crushing down large trees and part of the sacred grove in its fall, and badly injuring some natives who had gone too close after they had been warned. The enormous stump with its buttresses and gnarled roots was afterwards set on fire, and when darkness fell on the capital the blazing fetish houses and heaps of rubbish, with the black bodies of the levies as they rushed hither and thither, demolishing walls and throwing fresh fuel on the blazing piles, made a weird and striking scene, that will be long imprinted on the minds of those who witnessed it. The public square was turned into a temporary Gehenna, and tons of filth and rubbish there destroyed.

There were many trivial but exciting episodes during the day with Ashantis being mobbed and robbed by carriers, or natives being disarmed by the Houssas, but a few of our niggers were tied up and thrashed for robbing Ashantis, and things quieted down by night, and the proud capital was left desolate and deserted.

Strong piquets were stationed right round the place, as it was thought probable that an attempt might be made to rescue Prempeh, but the night passed quietly, broken only by the challenges of the native sentries—" Halt dere! who come up dat dare road?"

"Hullo! did you take me for Shanti man?" "Oh no, sah! Shanti man him bad tink, sah! You no smell like Shanti, sah! Good night, sah!" and the cheery little Houssas resumed their watch.

The Governor's smart coup in arresting all the chief men, had robbed the warriors of their leaders; and the open failure of the fetish power had demoralized them thoroughly, but every precaution had to be taken. A popular tradition was that if the King died at Kumassi, his fetish power remained, being transmitted to the next ruler; but if he crossed the boundary, the power departed with him from the capital, never to return. If Prempeh had acted up to his acknowledged principles he should have committed suicide rather than be removed; but he was too great a coward to do that, simply to bestow his evanescent power on his successor. There were many who would have been glad to save his Royal Highness the trouble, by assassinating him; for thus the fetish would remain with them for ever; but they lacked opportunity as a careful watch was kept on the King, till he was transferred to a safe region.

On January 21st, a report reached Kumassi of Ashanti warriors massing in a village near Mampon. Major Baden-Powell took charge of a flying column, consisting of the levies under Major Gordon, two companies of Houssas under Captain Mitchell and a Maxim gun under Armourer-Sergeant Williams. They started at midnight, and after a toilsome march through thick bush and reeking swamp, reached the village, only to find the 400 armed Ashantis had heard of their coming, and made off, leaving smouldering camp fires as evidence of their recent presence.

When this column returned to camp, the main body was just preparing to set out on the return march to the coast. They had fresh orders to reconnoitre Prempeh's summer residence where much valuable property had been stored. On arrival at this palace it was found to be deserted and looted. It subsequently transpired that Prempeh's head slave had been placed in charge, and other slaves, freed from bondage in Kumassi, had flown there with the news of Prempeh's downfall. They had then all systematically plundered the store rooms, securing the valuables, shaking the dust of Ashanti off their feet, returning to their own tribes with a recompense for their forced sojourn in the King's service. A large number of these slaves were taken during the war with Mampon, who opposed Prempeh's enstoolment. Over a thousand prisoners of war were then dragged into slavery to Kumassi, and many of the chiefs, beside the old and infirm, were bound together and burned alive by the savage army of Prempeh. Prempeh afterwards placed Osuche on the Mampon Stool, where he had reigned as right-hand man of the Kumassi rulers. His capture by the British will be hailed with joy by his people, whom report says he has kept down with an iron hand, and an ever-ready beheading knife. Many a home in this district would rejoice in the restoration of a long-lost son, father or husband, freed after, perhaps, years of bondage.

While in Kumassi the number of sick swelled to rather an alarming extent, and the Medical Officers anxiously looked forward to the day the mud of Ashanti should be shaken off. Every white man, paradoxical as it may read, was a sickly yellow, for the malaria was upon all in a slight or severe form, and a fever bred of the grisly and horrible surroundings. It was always pretty hot, though not so glaring as on the coast, where you lay an egg aside, and if you wait long enough, find a chicken in its place. Then there were the tortures of prickly heat to contend with, and a longing for a draught of water a few degrees below 90°. At midday clothes might go; the natives were to be envied; and the *noblesse oblige* of civilization, in dress at least, was to be lamented. Then as night came on, the falling dew chilled you to the bone; yet when rolled in a blanket the perspiration would drop from the forehead while alternate shiverings and burnings succeeded each other in painful monotony. Darkest West Africa indeed is no ideal spot; and as to those would-be journalists, sitting in the snug security of their Fleet Street attics, and writing on the Ashanti Picnic—well, they ought to be made to partake of a similar picnic. The West African medal may well be hung on a ribbon of yellow and black —fever and death stalk hand in hand in effective combination.

The Field Hospital was as well arranged as possible, and everything was done to relieve the numbers of sick, who were in a pitiful state with the dreaded fever. It was also a case of "physician heal thyself," for malaria is no respecter of persons, and attacked the Medical Staff as freely as other corps. Many a fine lad lay suffering in the Hospital tent, dreaming in a hazy delirium, of the home and dear ones far over the sea, which some of the poor fellows were destined to never see again.

Close behind the town the forest rose in a dense, gloomy wall.

One day I ventured to explore this unknown waste. In half an hour I could not have got more than two hundred yards. The ground was a complete quagmire, and my journeying was from root to root, and leaping on to fallen trunks and branches. A miserable silence was over everything; and around, as far as the eye could reach, stretched the dreary mangrove swamps, dark brownish green foliage above, and a mass of twisted roots rearing their pale stems above the mud and water below. The muddy stream gleamed in the fierce sunlight, while here and there among the trees the white fever mist hung in thin wreaths, of which, if the white man breathe, he shall surely die. Emerging from a narrow tunnel-like waterway under the trees, which I had traversed for the last hour, winding in and out among the mangrove roots, amid the semi-darkness made by the dense foliage overhead, with its stifling, steam-like atmosphere, heavy with the foul smell of putrifying mud and rotting vegetation, I reached drier ground.

The forest was still as dense as ever and there were many curious trees, and low shrubs of graceful palm-like leaves, forming a huge crown over the top of the branches, high palms, with their smooth columnar stems and finely pinnated leaves interlocked above, forming arches and woven canopies of varied shape. Then high above them rose the taller forest trees, whose giant branches formed a second canopy from the sun. Immense creepers clung around them, some stretching obliquely from their summits like mast-stays, others spirally twisted around each other and winding round the trunks like huge serpents ready for their prey. Many of the trees were covered with parasitic plants, and creepers climbing over each other in one vast struggle for existence. Moralists would no doubt liken this scene to the clamorous fight of humanity in the hopeless struggle of man to lift himself to the vague unattainable ideal of life, as shown in the picture of M. Rochegrosse, "Angoisse Humaine," recently exhibited in the Paris Salon; and their simile would not be out of place.

Looking upward, the finely divided foliage was strongly defined against a cloudless sky. There were few flowers, and the ground was deeply covered with dead leaves and rotten wood, through which low-creeping plants thrust their heads. Here and there huge trunks lay rotting on the ground, forming a playground for hundreds of lively lizards, with red heads and brilliant green tails, which are the prettiest creatures to be seen in the bush, though rather alarming at first, when they dash over your sleeping body, and the thought of a venomous bite crosses your mind. They are, however, perfectly harmless, and though the larger species could inflict a nasty wound, their fangs are not poisonous.

This forest land and the savage inhabitants who dwell in its recesses, amid a chaos of slave-raiding and village-burning, which goes on ceaselessly in the wild country that lies between the north of the European colonies and the little-known Soudan, is indeed a place of weird and interesting memories, and weeks might be spent in exploring the forest and the hinterland beyond, finding fresh interest day by day in the study of the features of the country, both animal and vegetable. A lengthy account of the information that I was able to glean, would hardly be in keeping with this work, which is dealing with the campaign, and not an exploring expedition, scientific or otherwise; but this short description of the flora and fauna seen near Kumassi may be of interest.

Pushing through the forest there were few animals to be seen; occasionally a rustling among the bushes announced some lordly snake on the prowl, or a chatter and cracking overhead denoted that a solemn palaver of monkeys had been disturbed. Then birds there were in plenty, parrots of large size, a few aasvogels or vultures also clattered affrighted through the trees, leaving their meal off some dead creature in the bush. In one place near a narrow streamlet were nests of the passerine weaver birds, some hanging from fine branches along which even the bamboo snake would not have the temerity to crawl in search of the luscious eggs. The nests were composed of twigs and fibre, with a cunningly made exit at the bottom of the carefully-woven chamber. There were many brilliant birds, including gorgeous copper-coloured pigeons, but these had been found lower down the road, where Prince Henry had shot a fine specimen.

After coming off second best in a patch of prickly pear, a cactus which is happily not common in the bush, I suddenly reached swampy ground again, while in places the trees cleared, opening out on large sticky patches of arundineous mud, which would have made a capital ground for sportsmen. The green canes made a refuge for numbers of small animals, and if properly taken in hand, would probably have provided some lord of the forest to add to the spoils. On the outskirts of one of these swamps an animal of the peccary species broke cover, but disappeared with a whisk of his tusks before I had time to pot him. There was soon more sport on hand, for a buzzing hum and a stinging sensation on the cheek localized the swampy haunt of the tsetse fly, which fortunately had not worried us much on the upward march, and had left one or two donkeys that travelled with the force unmolested. My face was soon in a pickle, and in West Africa, where any little bite or cut becomes a festering sore which will not heal, such things are to be dreaded.

The tsetse is much more active than the mosquito. In its flight it moves with such intense rapidity, that the eye cannot follow it, and when it settles it alights so quietly that the victim does not feel it. When it considers itself secure it thrusts in its weapon and sucks the blood. It is only while its needle-like proboscis is embedded in the flesh that the fly can be caught. Even when distended with blood it escapes by a rapid flight sideways. To man the bite is as unpleasant as that of the mosquito; and that is saying a great deal; for anyone who has been forced to give his body as a prey to these little pests knows how painful are the wounds which they inflict. Horses, cows, sheep, asses, and dogs, with other animals useful to man, are destroyed by the tsetse; and so deadly is its poison, that if a cow is only bitten once by a fly it will die of the effects, although wild animals are quite safe. It is on them chiefly that the tsetse feeds, and they are apparently inoculated and do not suffer any evil effects.

Needless to say, the ants also were everywhere apparent, both the cannibal black, who takes a fiendish delight in burrowing his head into your flesh and feasting to his heart's content, and also his vegetarian but more destructive white brother, who chaws up every article of clothing or equipment he can lay his jaws on. In the rainy season the young ants, who have wings, rise in the air, but they return to mother earth as soon as dry weather sets in and the wings then drop off. It is said that so prolific are they, that a single female deposits as many as fifteen thousand eggs in twenty-four hours. . Many an African traveller has had to fall back upon a colony of white ants for food. Hunger is a good sauce, and the creatures are collected, and a handful or two thrown into a fry-pan with a little fat, and though I did not try this tempting dish, they are said to be just passable, will keep a long time, and can be easily prepared. Of course, in size the insects are like young shrimps; to the English idea of ants, cooking them would seem impossible.

Another African insect that should be mentioned is an enormous spider which the niggers call Boui. According to M. Foâ, a famous French traveller, the natives pin much faith in the revelations of this curious-looking creature. He was engaged once on a very long chase after elephants, and his followers were becoming impatient, when at last they found the home of one of these spiders. "Now," said one of his men, "we shall know whether or no we shall find the elephants."

M. Foâ and his men placed themselves in a circle round the hole, but at some distance. In the middle the oldest negro crouched near the hole and commenced his invocation.

"Boui," he said, "behold for three weeks we have travelled through the woods from dawn till sunset. We can travel no farther, and we have seen no ivory. Tell us : Must we return to our village? If such be the case, return quickly into your mansion. But if we shall have ivory and food, come out and take the air."

At the last words he threw a little water into the hole. Four velvet paws, joined like the fingers of a monkey's hand, showed themselves immediately near the orifice. The men stood in silence, their eyes fixed on the insect. If it withdrew, the negroes would at once abandon the chase.

After a moment's hesitation the yellow velvety spider, as large as a pigeon's egg, came forth. There was no more talk about going back. The Boui had foretold success, and, as results proved, foretold correctly, for they got two fine elephants.

On my return to the town, the natives were cutting down a large patch of elephant grass to clear the environs. Unfortunately, most of the officers were busily engaged preparing for the coastward march, as sport in plenty was provided, this grass being full of animals. Several fair-sized pythons also came to light, and were dispatched by the niggers, who so battered the carcases that skinning was out of the question. At intervals, a loud cry would announce the discovery of some fresh animal, chiefly of the wild pig species; but, as a rule, after an exciting chase, the four-legged brutes had the best of it, and got clear into the forest. With organised beaters a good day's shooting might have been organized. The only animal of importance killed was a not overbig leopard, which was so battered about the head by the eager natives that it was completely spoiled, the skin falling a trophy to a Sergeant-Major of the Supply, who gave it the first blow with a heavy stick as it ran.

## CHAPTER XI.

COASTWARD MARCH—PEACE SOCIETY PRECEPTS—DEATH OF PRINCE HENRY —EATING DEAD BODIES—A CIVILIZED NEGRO—THE COAST—ARRIVAL OF PREMPEH—CONCLUSION.

ON Wednesday, January 22nd, the column slowly wended its way from Kumassi through the swamps, and before evening the white troops were encamped safely at Dede Siwa, leaving Governor Maxwell and Captain Stewart in Kumassi with a large force of Houssas, and the West India contingent.

The royal prisoners travelled in hammocks, the Queen Mother being carried in a long basket on the heads of two niggers, from whence she looked round muttering and chewing or smoking. The first day she was rather given to spit at any white men who approached, but under the tender care of Mr. Knollys, of the Colonial Service, who had charge of the prisoners, she calmed down and soon began to enjoy the novelty of the journey.

The West Yorkshire regiment guarded the royal captives and the Ansahs, who marched down handcuffed to Prahsu, where they remained, awaiting their trial on the coast.

The Special Service Corps held the rear; and sick at heart and worn out, the white troops plodded homeward: the Expedition had ended without their firing a shot. No doubt everyone ought to have been deeply gratified that there had been no bloodshed. Humanitarians sigh and exclaim " What a mercy ! " Well, it was a mercy, but terribly disheartening to the officers and men. They had braved the hardships and climatic dangers, and toiled steadily onward, warming to their work as the king remained defiant, and made a show of holding out to the bitter end ; but it was only to find a craven braggart monarch, who hoped, by double dealing and temporizing, to defeat the ends of justice, and when that failed, did not hesitate to cringe and crave for pardon.

The troops had been buoyed up with the prospect of a stiff struggle at the end, and a chance of distinguishing themselves, and it seemed, by the abject surrender, that they had marched and endured for nothing. There is not the slightest doubt that

## DEATH OF PRINCE HENRY.

if the Expedition had been left to the Houssas and native levies, the Ashantis would have resisted to the last; for it was only on the arrival of the Ansahs in Kumassi, with highly coloured reports of the rapid advance of thousands of white troops, that Prempeh decided not to fight unless it were forced on him, or he was molested. The prompt action of Governor Maxwell at the final palaver settled the matter—diplomacy had conquered brute force and cunning.

The flag had hardly been unfurled outside the temporary Headquarters when it was suddenly hoisted to half-mast. Prince Henry was dead!

The brief notice, wired up from the coast, came as a fearful shock to all members of the force when they arrived in camp. It seemed impossible to realise that the gallant Prince, who had been amongst us in the best of health and spirits, cheerfully enduring the hardships of the campaign only a few short days before, should have fallen a victim to the dreaded malaria. But it was too true. He had rallied on his arrival at the coast, and earnestly desired to remain till he heard the Expedition had reached its goal; but he submitted to the doctor's advice, and went on board Her Majesty's Ship "Blonde," which left Cape Coast on the afternoon of the 17th; at the same time Kumassi was being peacefully invested. The "Blonde" set out at once for Madeira, but on Sunday, the 19th, a change for the worse occurred, and His Royal Highness expired peacefully on Monday evening at twenty minutes to nine o'clock, off Sierra Leone.

Prince Henry Maurice of Battenberg was the third son of Prince Alexander, and he was born on October 5th, 1858, being in his thirty-eighth year when he died. On July 23rd, 1885, he married Her Royal Highness Princess Beatrice, at Whippingham Church, in the Isle of Wight, and there are three sons and one daughter of the marriage, the eldest of whom was only nine years old on his father's sad decease. Mr. Gladstone, speaking in Parliament before the wedding, in 1885, said: "I believe everything connected with this young Prince is what the country would wish, and that his future life will be the same."

Prince and Princess Henry of Battenberg have lived in constant companionship with Our Queen, greatly comforting and aiding her in her solitude. In times of national rejoicing, they have been at her side; in days of sorrow and affliction, they have mourned with Her Majesty and shared her grief. The Prince had a handsome and gallant bearing, and had endeared himself to every member of the expeditionary force with whom he had come in contact.

Born of a family of soldiers, Prince Henry was naturally anxious to identify himself with the military service of his adopted country, and availed himself of the opportunity when the Ashanti Expedition was decided upon. There he fell in the midst of faithful service, meeting a soldier's death, if not on the battlefield; and that reflection must afford a slight measure of consolation to our noble Queen, and the afflicted widow and her children. The Prince knew the risks and bravely accepted them, to sink exhausted in the service of his Sovereign and adopted country. Though he died sadly, he died well and nobly!

There is little more of interest to add. The downward journey was more depressing than the advance, though everyone was anxiously looking forward to returning home again. The levies scoured the bush in advance of the prisoners in case there should be any attempt to assassinate the King, and several times disturbed waiting Ashantis, who were lurking in the trees to obtain a last glimpse of Prempeh, rather than lying in wait to kill him. Passing through Bekwai dominions the same watchful care was necessary, as many of the inhabitants there would gladly have killed him, but in hate rather than fetish fanaticism. A brutal but natural longing for revenge for past wrongs, rather than a re-echo from Seneca :—

> "There can be slain
> No sacrifice to God more acceptable
> Than an unjust and wicked king."

Leaving the main body, Prince Christian, Major Piggott, and others pushed ahead by forced marches to the coast.

This coastward march was not devoid of interest, especially the journey from Essian Kwanta over the Adansis to Fumsu. This one march covered the distance of four ordinary daily marches. There were no hammocks available, being all taken up for the sick; my kit was ahead, so there was nothing for it but to push forward on foot. I set off early with a few natives, and found everything quiet, the villages still being deserted. Occasionally small groups of niggers, escaped slaves from Kumassi, peered cautiously through the trees.

# THE ADANSI TREATY.

Leaving Bekwai country, the old Adansi kingdom was reached. The dread of Ashanti being removed, ths Adansis will return to their own territory, and the ruined capital Fomonah will again flourish, under the rule of the King: a fine old man who had offered every facility to the Expedition, and with whom a treaty had been drawn up a few weeks before the march started. The text of this treaty may be of interest:—

TREATY of Friendship and Protection made at Prahsu this eighteenth day of October one thousand eight hundred and ninety-five between Her Most Gracious Majesty Victoria, Queen of Great Britain and Ireland, Empress of India, &c., &c., Her heirs and successors, by her subject, Captain Donald William Stewart, an officer in the Civil Service of the Gold Coast Colony, acting under instructions received from His Excellency William Edward Maxwell, also a subject of Her Majesty, Companion of the Most Distinguished Order of Saint Michael and Saint George, Governor and Commander-in-Chief of the Gold Coast Colony, on the one part, and the King, Chiefs and principal headmen of the Country of Adansi on the other part.

Whereas Kweku Lukansa, King of the country of Adansi, and the Chiefs and principal headmen of that country, for and on behalf of themselves, their heirs, successors and people have presented to the Governor of the Gold Coast Colony a request that their country should be placed under the protection of Great Britain, and have agreed to enter into a treaty with Her Majesty the Queen of Great Britain and Ireland, Empress of India, &c., &c., her heirs and successors, by the said Captain Donald William Stewart acting for that purpose for the said Governor.

Now, therefore, Kweku Lukansa, King of Adansi, and the Chiefs, and principal men of that country, whose names are hereinafter signed to this treaty, for themselves, their heirs and successors and the people of Adansi on the one part, and his Excellency William Edward Maxwell, Companion of the Most Distinguished Order of Saint Michael and Saint George, Governor and Commander-in-Chief of the Gold Coast Colony, a subject of and representing Her Most Gracious Majesty Victoria, Queen of the United Kingdom of Great Britain and Ireland, Empress of India, &c., &c., her heirs and successors, by Captain Donald William Stewart, a subject of Her Majesty (acting for the Governor), on the other part, do hereby enter into this treaty containing the following Articles:—

ARTICLE I.—The King of the country of Adansi for himself and his lawful successors, together with the Chiefs and principal men of the country of Adansi, whose names are hereinafter signed and seals affixed, for and on behalf of themselves and their successors and people of Adansi hereby place themselves under the protection of Great Britain, declaring that they have not entered into any treaty with any other foreign Power.

ARTICLE II.—Her Majesty's subject, the Governor of the Gold Coast Colony, for and on behalf of Her Majesty the Queen of Great Britain and Ireland, Empress of India, &c., &c., her heirs and successors, hereby takes the country of Adansi under the protection of Great Britain.

ARTICLE III.—It is hereby agreed that the King, Chiefs, and principal men, together with the other people of Adansi, will not enter into any war or commit any act of aggression on any of the Chiefs bordering on their country by which the trade of the country shall be interrupted, or the safety and property of the subjects of Her Majesty the Queen of England and Empress of India shall be lost, compromised, or endangered, and that the said King, Chiefs, and principal men of Adansi hereby undertake to refer to the Governor of the Gold Coast Colony, acting on behalf of Her Majesty, for friendly arbitration, any trade or other quarrels in which they may become involved before actually entering upon hostilities.

ARTICLE IV.—Should any difference or dispute accidentally arise between the King of Adansi or any of his Chiefs and principal headmen, or between any of the Chiefs and principal headmen, it shall be referred to the Governor of the Gold Coast Colony, or to the nearest British Authority, for the time being, whose decision shall be final and binding upon all parties concerned.

ARTICLE V.—British subjects shall have free access to all parts of Adansi, and shall have the right to build houses and possess property according to the law in force in the Gold Coast Colony : and they shall have full liberty to carry on such trade or manufacture as may be approved by any officer appointed for the purpose by Her Majesty's Government, and should any difference arise between the aforesaid British subjects and the King, Chiefs, and principal headmen of the country of Adansi as to the duties or customs to be paid to the said King, Chiefs, or the principal headmen of the towns in that country by such British subjects, or as to any other matter, that the dispute shall be referred to the officer mentioned in Article IV., whose decision in the matter shall be binding and final, and that the King, Chiefs, and principal headmen of Adansi will not extend the rights hereby guaranteed to British subjects to any other persons without the knowledge and consent of such officer.

ARTICLE VI.—In consideration of the protection guaranteed on the part of Great Britain to the King, Chiefs, and principal headmen and people of Adansi, they hereby bind themselves, their heirs and successors to keep their main roads in good order, that they will encourage trade, and give facilities to traders, and will not cede their territory to, or accept a protectorate from, or enter into any agreement, arrangement, or treaty with, any other foreign Power except through and with the consent of the Government of Her Majesty the Queen-Empress.

ARTICLE VII.—The Government of Her Majesty the Queen-Empress will not prevent the King of Adansi or his Chiefs and principal headmen and their lawful successors from levying customary revenues appertaining to them according to the laws and customs of their country, nor in the administration thereof ; and her Majesty's Government will respect the habits and customs of the country, but will not permit human sacrifices; and slave dealing when brought to the notice of the Government will be punished according to the laws of the Gold Coast Colony.

ARTICLE VIII.—This treaty shall come into force from the date hereof, but power is expressly reserved to Her Majesty the Queen-Empress to refuse to approve and ratify the same within one year from the date hereof. In witness whereof the parties to this treaty have hereunto set their hands and affixed their respective seals.

## A FUNERAL.

Done in triplicate at Prahsu, in the country of Assin, this 18th day of October in the year one thousand eight hundred and ninety-five, in the fifty-eighth year of the reign of Her Majesty the Queen-Empress.

Names of Signatories.　　　　　　　Their marks and Seals.
1. Kweku Inkansa, King of Adansi.　　　X　　(Seal.)
2. Kofi Kwedu, War Chief of Adansi.　　X　　　,,
3. Kojo Gimma, Chief of Ayowasi.　　　X　　　,,
4. Kweku Ashanti, Chief of Edubiasi.　　X　　　,,
5. Akwesi Fori, Chief of Dompoasi.　　　X　　　,,
6. Kweku Afuakwa. Chief of Ekrofrome, represented by Yow Yamua. } X　,,
7. Yaw Apia, Chief of Akrochire.　　　X　　　,,
8. Kwabina Kwantabisa, Chief of Odumasi.　X　,,
9. Kweku Wia, Chief of Kwisa.　　　X　　　,,
10. Kwami Iduo, Chief of Brobidiasi.　　X　　　,,
11. Kwami Essifi, Chief of Abejimu.　　X　　　,,
12. Kwami Apeajo, represented by Yow Simpon, of Adomemu. } X　,,
13. Kwabina Chiadi, Chief of Eginasi.　　X　　　,,
14. Kwesi Buabin, Chief of Medomma.　　X　　　,,
15. Kofi Ammua, represented by Se-Kojo of Kianbusu. } X　,,

DONALD WILLIAM STEWART, Captain,
　　　　　　　Travelling Commissioner,
　　　　　　　An officer in the Civil Service of the Gold Coast Colony, for and on behalf of William Edward Maxwell, Governor
(Seal.)　　　of the Gold Coast Colony.

Passing through Kwisa, where the little garrison were eagerly looking forward to the arrival of the troops, when they would strike camp and follow in rear of the returning column, the rugged sides of the Adansis were soon reached. On the top of the hill I halted and revelled in the glorious view, for the atmosphere was unusually clear, and the vast undulating sea of gloriously tinted foliage could be traced for miles. Then downward again, clambering with difficulty on the steep rugged track into Braffu Eadru.

A few miles past the village, a rolling of drums and a weird, monotonous chant issued from the depths of the forest. My carriers were behind, having halted indefinitely for "chop," so I went a short distance through the bush to see what the row meant. In a small forest clearing, a fetish man was dancing and shouting, the centre of a great crowd of men, women and children, who kept up a continuous *éloge*. Suspended on a pole in their midst, and carried by two men, was a corpse, which was being bumped and jolted in a very unceremonious fashion. I quietly watched the proceedings, undiscovered for some time, while the priest ever and anon approached the body and appeared to question it closely. Suddenly he stood transfixed, and muttered something, upon which a grey-haired patriarch was seized, in spite of his vigorous protestations, and rushed to the front. The priest started his incantations again with redoubled vigour, but a woman espied me watching, and the whole assembly were greatly disconcerted at the intrusion of a stranger, and a white man to boot.

I stood a few moments longer, but the burial was evidently not to be proceeded with in my presence, so I discreetly withdrew, followed by some niggers, who furtively watched me well down the road before returning to the grave side. On subsequent inquiry I found the fetish priest was asking the corpse "who has killed thee?" The spirit of the deceased is then supposed to reveal to the holy man the name of the one who has worked the evil. The wily priest always has a pre-selected victim named in the silent revelation; one who is either rich or unpopular, and though the dead man has probably died of colic and stomach-ache, the culprit may be put to death for witchcraft, or heavily fined, whichever is deemed expedient.

Passing Akusirem the sun set, and the rest of that day's journey had to be done in total darkness in the thick forest, though it was full moon, and there were occasional gleams through the trees. It was a dreary march, but Fumsu was at length reached, and crossing the river, I entered the village, thankful to have reached my destination after being on the road for over sixteen hours. The carriers all turned up shortly after, for though the African is slow, he is fairly sure, and you may generally rely on him to arrive at his destination, although he takes his own time to do so.

Close to the hovel in which I slept there was a curious fetish consisting of a large carved gourd, containing a few crocodiles teeth, and a raised crown-work over the whole, made of long strips of hippopotamus hide. I appropriated a couple of these strips as curios and placed them with my goods. At the next camp there was no trace of them; the hide would be of no value, intrinsic or otherwise, to the natives, and no doubt my carriers, with more conscience than I, had quietly replaced the strips on the sacred spot. I did not press the loss, but accepted the reproof. It was hardly fair that the sanctity of the spot should be disturbed, and the owner of the consecrated ground would have been much upset, had he found it marred. More than likely, to his pagan mind, it would have caused serious forebodings; for, probably, it had been raised to the fetish of some departed relation, and demanded respect in consequence. I am afraid we civilized beings are not always considerate in dealing with the belief of these heathen, and hardly realize what importance they attach to their god-worship.

Cannibalism is gradually dying out in Africa, but there are still tribes who keep up the abominable practice of eating their own dead. A few miles from Fumsu, the path was remarkably wide and clear, and in full light of the moon, and close to the road, I noticed a hole and the body of a negro at the bottom with a cloth over his face. A native, when ill and alone, will crawl into any nook, cover up his face and await death till he recovers or really does die. I debated a moment, wondering if this were a corpse partially buried, or a sick man, but as I looked, fancying I could see him breathing, I jumped down and pulled off the cloth. He was not only dead, but the flesh of both cheeks had been cleanly cut away and the mutilated face was plainly visible, though already a mass of flies and larvæ. It was a fearful sight, rendered more ghastly by the pale moonlight and silent forest; sickened and horrified, I clambered from the grave and resumed my journey.

With the carriers who came into Fumsu later, was an intelligent Houssa, and on my asking if he noticed the grave by the road, he at once replied in the affirmative, adding that three men were filling it when he passed. I told him of the mutilation and he at once said "O yes, sah, dat man then, sah, hab him face cut for chop, sah! Bush man make plenty chop long pig when he find man go die, sah!" Naturally, I was incredulous, but the Houssa's verdict may have been correct—that the negro had died, and being a stranger, the men who were burying him, had adjourned their task for a gruesome and disgusting feast. Certainly, if the deceased had belonged to any tribe in the vicinity, he would have been buried in state, with a crowd in attendance. It has since been suggested that slaves of some distant dead-eating tribe had escaped from Kumassi, and one of their number dying, his companions had simply acted up to their old principles. At any rate, the natives in that district are not usually given to eating their own dead.

The cultured enlightened negro from the coast was *en évidence* next day. Passing a small hamlet apparently deserted, I was hailed. " Hi! you white man, what you do here?" and from a shanty emerged a nigger in an old suit of white duck; evidently a discharged or deserted servant of some white officer.

"You speak English, do you?" I remarked.

"Corse I does! I'se Accra man, I is!"

"What are you doing here, then?"

"Well its like dis, de son of the chief of dis ere place he berry sick and I nuss him wid medecin I make. Dese people big fools dey is, my medecin ain't no little bit use, but den dey keep me here and de chief he gib me darter for wife cos I cure son." (The *lingua franca* of the West Coast.)

"Why, you have got a wife in Accra, haven't you?"

"In Accra, wall dat ain't here. I guess I want a wife while I'se in dis place, don't I? When I goes 'ome, get Accra wife again."

I went in to see his patient and found a young negro evidently suffering from fever and dysentery. I mixed him a little chlorodyne I had, gave him a dose, and telling the Accra nigger to give him the remainder, I left.

"Hi!" shouted the gentleman from Accra. "You stop and see my sick man an stop in his 'ouse. I charge you five shillin for dat:"—I was deaf and walked on. "Wat! you call self a gentman? You white rascal! You tief! You rob me you white liar! Heah, massa! dash me one shillin for luck an close palaver?"

Oh yes! he got his dash that time—half a dozen strokes judiciously applied!

Once in the Protectorate proper we were accorded a warm reception, for the villages had just heard of Prempeh's capture, and as we passed through, the women danced and shouted, clapping their hands in transports of joy at the Ashanti king's overthrow, and various offerings of palm wine, fou fou and plantains were always ready.

At Prahsu there were many sick, waiting their transport to the coast. Daily hammock trains plied between station and station clearing the hospital at the depôt there, but as one patient was moved, another victim took his place. As soon as possible they were taken down in stages to the coast, and placed on the

"Coromandel," out of the malarious zone. In the comfortable cots of the Hospital Ship, kept cool by punkahs, the sick quarters were indeed comfortable after the necessarily rough treatment in the bush. A man remarked that it seemed like heaven to lay his fever-worn frame in a comfortable berth, and to have decent food and treatment after the hardships on land. Much praise must be given to the brave Nursing Sisters who were unremitting in their care of the sick on the "Coromandel." There was a risk even when anchored right away from the deadly coast, and another tribute must go forth to the noble "Red Cross" Sisters.

Steps were being taken at the time to place the little cemetery on the banks of the Prah, in tolerable order. Poor Major Ferguson's body lay quite close to Captain Huyshe; and Major Piggott and Prince Christian spent some hours giving directions for the melancholy grave to be marked and fenced in, so that, at least, the sanctity of the spot might be respected, and a token made that the remains of a brave English officer rested there.

At Prahsu also, the garrison were eagerly looking forward to the day their work would be done, and the homeward march begun.

On the road we passed an intelligent-looking negro accompanied by a large train of attendants. It was King Asibi, Prempeh's rival for the stool, on his way from Accra, where he had been living in exile, to Kumassi; for now he could travel in safety to his native country.

Prince Christian was suffering from touches of Indian fever, Captain Williams was going down country very ill indeed, and Major Piggott was far from well, so all haste was made on the way.

On January 30th the first sight of the ocean was obtained, and spirits rose accordingly. On top of the hills a delightful breeze was blowing off the sea, the carriers stepped out gaily along the road, breaking into a merry song, and as we entered the dirty, smelly town of Cape Coast, it was a welcome sight, for it was the end of the dreary march, and anchored in the roads were the ships ready to take us home.

Man is supposed to become attached to the place he lives in for any length of time; but not on the West Coast of Africa, for there every day adds to the loathing of the surroundings, and the longing to leave them. Nostalgia, on the Gold Coast, is a universal and terrible complaint.

On February 1st, Sir Francis Scott and his Staff arrived at the Castle, all well but thoroughly worn out. Indeed every member of the force looked terribly jaded and ill, many being only just able to keep about at all. Major Piggott received the temporary appointment as Resident in Kumassi; and though he was very unwell, he returned a few days later with a force of Houssas to relieve the West India troops, who were already suffering very much from the climate, though they should be well seasoned from their previous training. Major Piggott was certainly the man to take over the reins in Ashanti. He has ever shown that fearlessness and force of character that were specially requisite for dealing with a half-subdued country, and demanding respect from the savage inhabitants.

Lieut. O'Donnell, who had been dispatched with Captain Cramer and Lieut. Armitage through the Koranza Country to advance on Kumassi from the North, with a large force of Houssas, arrived safely in the capital. He had made a treaty on the way, with the King of Juabin, an important ally of Kumassi. These plucky officers had arrived safely in the capital to find it peacefully occupied, but this fact must not detract any value from the service they rendered by this most trying and dangerous march. The officers and men of the Constabulary on the West Coast, have a continuous round of duties both arduous and exciting.

At the Castle the carriers were constantly returning in gangs, and being paid off; the rum shanties did a roaring trade. The work of paying off these natives was neither a small nor easy task, but one which was carried out with the utmost celerity. There was one officer, however, far too hasty when paying off these natives. They had worked hard, and worked well, and his treatment of them at the close was brutal and unworthy of an officer and a gentleman. Niggers are trying, and enough to spoil any person's temper, but there is reason and limit to all things, which this gentleman quite set aside. With this solitary exception at the close of the campaign, all the officers, from Sir Francis Scott downwards, had been most careful in their treatment of the natives serving with the expedition. There had been little flogging, and that only in flagrant cases; and in consequence of the respect generated by the white officers, there had been no desertion, and no disaffection among the thousands of men of various tribes employed as bearers, and in other capacities.

On February 4th, the West Yorkshire Regiment arrived at the

coast with Prempeh and the other captives. The King and Queen Mother had never left Kumassi before, and Prempeh especially seemed awed by the first sight of the mighty Ocean. The prisoners were at once put in surf boats and taken on board the "Racoon," which weighed anchor for Elmina Castle, where the King will be kept in captivity.

For some days thousands of natives had anxiously waited in eager expectancy, for a glimpse of that tyrant, whom they had dreaded so long. Men, women and children flocked in from all adjacent coast towns and bush villages, and lay at night in long silent rows on the sea front or along the sides of the houses. As each day passed, their excitement seemed rather to increase than their ardour to be damped by the weariness and discomforts to be endured. Then their patience was rewarded. The strains of a band could be heard in the distance, the regular roll of the approaching drums was unmistakable—it was the white troops at last.

Like a muffled roar did the cry travel from one end of the town to the other. "Prempeh is coming! He comes! He comes!" Thousands of people rushed in the direction of the Castle, and in a few seconds every inch of standing room was occupied by a black seething mass of expectant faces.

The regular tramp of marching feet drew nearer; there was the clash of arms as the entrance guard turned out and presented arms, a murmur of a thousand voices speaking in hushed tones, succeeded by one fearful yell of triumph and hate as the litters with the prisoners came in sight. Again and again was the yell repeated, drowning the loud tones of the band, which were re-echoing beneath the vaulted entrance to the Castle as the troops filed through into the courtyard. Small wonder that Prempeh was livid with fear, and trembling in every limb as he heard the furious cries, and saw the denunciatory gesticulations of the angry multitude that spread around him on every side. With fixed bayonets, his guard was formed strongly on either side, and had the wild passion of those frenzied people, kept back by the gleam of steel, been allowed full play, they would have wreaked a fearful vengeance on the unhappy occupants of the prisoners' litters.

Once in the compound of the Castle there was little delay. The postern opening to the shore was flung back; the West Yorkshire Regiment sallied forth and lined down to the water's edge. Right along the seashore, over the sand hills, up among the wretched Fanti mud hovels, clustering round on the sacred surf-beaten mass of rock forming the foundations of the Castle—there was the same sea of faces, and again did the frenzied cries and yells resound on all sides, as the prisoners issued forth, and passed down to the waiting surf boats.

Up on the Castle battlements all the European residents were crowded—Officers, Government officials and traders. As those Ashantis stood trembling, cowed and disheartened, looking one moment at the yelling crowd, then at the ever-rolling expanse of the vast Atlantic, a sight few of them had ever seen before, a thrill of pity must have gone through all the hearts of those white people there. But with those who had seen that king in his capital, the pity was only momentary. As a flash, all the horrors which lay at the door of those rulers, came to one's mind. That fearful " Golgotha," the slaves, and the terrible rites of human sacrifice: there was little room for pity; rather for thankfulness that the corrupt rule had come to an end at last; that Kumassi, henceforth, would not be a place to associate with deeds of cruelty and blood; and that in time, the thousands of Ashanti subjects would gain confidence, emerging from the cloud of a bloody fetish worship, to be taught a measure of self-respect by the presence of the English flag now floating over their head.

Mr. Knollys entered one of the captive-laden surf boats, and then with vigorous strokes, the boatmen reached the gun-boat, the prisoners were transferred and taken off to their exile; loved and regretted by very few, if by any. They will be well treated, and have fairly comfortable quarters, with good food. Their one craving will be for spirits, of which they are allowed little. Prempeh, especially, will miss his periodical debauches, in which he drowned dull care, for no doubt as with Cleomenes of old :—

"Consuming cares lay heavy on his mind :
In his black thoughts, revenge and slaughter roll,
And scenes of blood rise dreadful in his soul."

All day long in the streets of Cape Coast hundreds of the women danced and sang their songs of triumph. Their lords and masters were hourly returning in bodies and being paid off; and in the native quarter at least, everyone gave himself over to a somewhat riotous jollification. The spirit shanties, of course, did a roaring trade; but if drunkenness existed on all sides, it led only to scenes of uproarious joy; they were far too happy at being home again and all their troubles over, for any quarrelling amongst themselves. The white men also met with almost disquieting receptions if they ventured in the *Quartier Fanti*. Every other negro wished to shake hands, the women clapped their hands and shouted words of welcome, and the youngsters crowded round with their shrill little "Good hevenin, sah!" With the men who had been right to the front, the levies and others, a note of *bonne camaraderie* was at once struck up; but on every side there was a distinct and noticeable difference in the attitude of the people toward Europeans. When I first landed there was a respect shown to white men, but it was prompted by fear. Now it was entirely altered. The natives paid everyone the same respect; but there was in it both a difference and a distinction. The appearance of those regiments of white soldiers, the campaign in the interior, and capture of the King, had filled them with gratitude and wonder, and everyone was treated with a marked and deferential attention. Thus the Expedition will not be without its effect among our own friendly tribes and subjects on the coast.

His Excellency Governor Maxwell is a gentleman of tact and understanding; and since his tenure of office, he has taken in hand some much needed reforms, which he intends to bring about in the near future. Under his watchful guidance a new era of prosperity is assuredly dawning for the Gold Coast Colony. Much remains to be done, and advancement must necessarily be slow owing to the very nature of the country and climate; but a large increase of trade is looming in the near future. The initial cost of the Expedition cannot have been very large; and certainly not approaching the sum that the Government would be justified in expending to secure such advantages as are likely to accrue from the subjugation and annexation of Ashanti.\*

The troops had suffered terribly on the coastward march, and the subtle enemy, the fever, had thrown "Death" more victims for his own, beside laying its grip on very many more. The Field Hospital was crammed, and a few more days' delay in that fatal country, or bad management of the sick transport service, must have produced a calamitous result.

There was no hitch; the sick were speedily transferred to the "Coromandel," where the pure sea-air did much for them. Still litters poured into the base from the front, and as fast as the

---

\* Since writing the above, the hardly creditable debate respecting the Estimates has taken place in the House of Commons. The sum was comparatively small, and the proscriptive, not to say fatuitous, action of the Opposition is not worth commenting upon.

Hospital on Connor's Hill was cleared, fresh sick trains arrived, and the beds were again filled with the limp forms, and yellow drawn faces of suffering men, most of whom had landed a few weeks previously, perfectly fit, and in a glow of health and vigour.

The West Yorkshire Regiment, when their captives were safely transferred, at once embarked on the " Manilla." It was painful to see the thoroughly worn out condition of this fine regiment, a majority of which looked more fit for a hospital ward than anything else ; but the thought of Old England, after their long sojourn abroad, buoyed them up, and they pluckily did their work till the end, though numbers were forced to give in each day. The Special Service Corps marched into the Castle, travel stained and weary, and were to have embarked on board the " Coromandel." When they got down to Cape Coast, there was little room for any but sick on the Hospital ship, and one half of them had to be transferred to the " Manilla " before she sailed on the 6th. The Mail and Coasting Steamers were then requisitioned for by telegraph, from ports down the coast, and were used to carry drafts of officers and men, instead of coasting for cargo, and at length quarters were found for all.

On February 8th, the remaining sick from the hospital were carried to surf boats and swung on board the " Coromandel," making a total of nearly 250 sick officers and men, The Headquarters had embarked, and quietly and orderly the Expeditionary Force left for Old England, having brought to a close the most peaceful, but also the most successful and best managed campaign that has ever graced the annals of English History ; insignificant as the operations in Ashanti, 1895-6, may have seemed.

# INDEX OF ILLUSTRATIONS.

H.R.H. PRINCE HENRY OF BATTENBERG, K.G. (*Frontispiece*).

|  | PAGE |
|---|---|
| SKETCH MAP OF GOLD COAST | vii. |
| SCENE NEAR LAS PALMAS | 5 |
| SANTA CRUZ DE LA PALMA | 9 |
| CAVE DWELLINGS OF ATALAYA | 6 |
| CAPE COAST CASTLE | 29 |
| SIR FRANCIS SCOTT | 41 |
| GOLD COAST WOMEN | 63 |
| ARTILLERY CROSSING THE PRAH | 95 |
| A WEST INDIAN SOLDIER | 103 |
| IN THE FOREST | 113 |
| MAJOR FERGUSON | 123 |
| THE ALARM | 131 |
| OCCUPATION OF KUMASSI BY BRITISH TROOPS | 153 |
| PREMPEH'S LAST STATE RECEPTION | 159 |
| THE KUMASSI GOLGOTHA | 167 |
| THE PALAVER | 175 |
| PREMPEH AND THE QUEEN MOTHER RISE TO TENDER THEIR SUBMISSION | 179 |
| AN EXECUTIONER | 187 |

WIGHTMAN & Co., "The Westminster Press," Regency Street, London, S.W.

## GUNS, AMMUNITION, &c.
# WESTLEY RICHARDS'
## PERFECT PATENT HAMMERLESS EJECTOR GUNS

**OVER 10,000**      **IN USE.**

**SPECIALLY RECOMMENDED FOR ABROAD.**     **SPECIALLY RECOMMENDED FOR ABROAD.**

For fine workmanship, elegant form, durability, and Shooting, they cannot be surpassed. The simplest and most successful Ejector Gun yet invented. It has stood the test of eleven years' experience. Sixty thousand cartridges have been fired from one of these guns without failure or impairing the mechanism.

### IN THE MATTER OF THE WESTLEY RICHARDS' EJECTOR PATENT.

"We have defended our valuable Ejector Patent, and, after a protracted trial, the Patent has been held good and valid by the judgment of the Court of Appeal and the House of Lords. Proceedings will be taken against all infringers."

### A FEW TESTIMONIALS (*from a large number*).

"The three Hammerless Ejector Guns you made me in 1887 have given me every satisfaction, and have worked perfectly all the time."—EUSTON.

"Lord Egmont has pleasure in speaking highly of the pair of Ejector Guns supplied him by Messrs. Westley Richards and Co. They are beautifully balanced, shoot admirably, and the Ejector works easily and smoothly."

"I have given the gun supplied by you in August last a good trial, and I can only say it is as perfect as the pair I had from you in August, 1889. These guns have been in constant use, and the Ejectors work as well to-day as they did when they left your hands. I have never had the slightest trouble with the guns in any way. After such a trial as these have had, and have proved themselves so excellent, I think it only fair to tell you so."—H. M. UPCHER.

"I have just fired some 4,000 shots in twelve days, shooting from the last gun you made me, and nothing could have worked better than the Ejector."—E. C. (Major).

## WESTLEY RICHARDS' NEW DOUBLE '303 RIFLES
### FOR DEER STALKING AND OTHER SPORT.
SPECIALLY CONSTRUCTED WITH OUR SOLID STEEL PROJECTION TOP FASTENING.
The Safest and most mechanical in use for withstanding heavy charges.

Made with barrels of best Whitworth fluid compressed steel, and specially regulated with smokeless powder to give the greatest accuracy at short and long ranges.

**ACTUAL DIAGRAM.**
10 Consecutive Shots at 100 yards in 3½in. by 2½in.; 8 of these were in 1½in. by 2½in.

These accurate and powerful weapons combine New Features and Improvements, which we have carefully worked out, and which render them specially suitable for Sport.
**NEW SPECIAL SPORTING CARTRIDGE for Ditto.**

"Abundant living antelope targets shot at with the deadly Westley Richards Rifle made the Boers dead shots at 1,000 yards."—"South Africa," Dec. 27, 1890.

"Constant practice with the rifle (Westley Richards) made the Boers perfect shots, and they were the best riflemen in the world—and are out and out the best game shots in the world with a rifle."—"Tale of a Nomad" (Montagne).

## WESTLEY RICHARDS' Patent LONG RANGE LARGE GAME RIFLES '500
### Accurate from 100 to 500 yards.
**ACTUAL DIAGRAM.**
10 Consecutive Shots at 100 yards in 4½in. by 2½in. 8 shots in 3in. by 2½in.

These Single and Double Rifles shoot as accurately as a target rifle to 500 yards.

At 100 yards they give a force of impact 50% greater than the Lee-Metford '303 bore.

"We found it in every respect a splendid weapon. With the nickel-covered bullet the penetration was enormous.—Editor of "Field's" Report, June 23, 1894.

*Illustrated Price Lists of any description of Guns, Rifles, Revolvers, &c., sent free by post on application.* **178, NEW BOND STREET, LONDON;**
**128, Rue de Provence (Boulevard Haussmann), PARIS; & 12, Corporation St., BIRMINGHAM**

## West and South-West Coasts of Africa,
### THE CANARY ISLANDS, AND MADEIRA.

**THE ROYAL MAIL STEAMERS OF**

# THE AFRICAN STEAMSHIP Co.
(Incorporated 1852 by Royal Charter) AND THE

# British & African Steam Navigation Co.,
LIMITED,

*Sail*—Liverpool to West Africa ...Every Saturday & Alternate Wed.
Liverpool to South-West Africa...Every Four Weeks.
Hamburg to West Africa ...Every Ten Days.
Rotterdam to West Africa .. Every Ten Days.
Hamburg to South-West Africa...Every Month.
Antwerp to South-West Africa...Every Month.

TAKING PASSENGERS AT LOW RATES.

## TRIPS FOR HEALTH AND PLEASURE.
### THE CHEAPEST & BEST ROUTE TO MADEIRA & THE CANARY ISLANDS
IS BY THE STEAMERS OF THESE COMPANIES.

They have excellent accommodation for passengers, most being fitted with Electric Light, Electric Bells, Hot and Cold Water Baths, and other modern conveniences. Surgeon and Stewardess carried.

Grand Canary is recommended by the Faculty as one of the healthiest Islands, its climate being exceptionally mellow, dry and almost unvarying in its temperature all the year round.

**Saloon Fare (Single) £10. Return (Available for 12 Months) £15.**

Only Saloon Passengers taken. Tickets are available for Return by either Company's Steamers, and give passengers the option of breaking the journey, if the Steamers by which they travel call, at each or any of these three Islands. Option is also given to return from Grand Canary to Barcelona or Genoa by the magnificent Steamers of La Veloce Navigazione Italiana a Vapore.

**From Liverpool to Grand Canary every Saturday.**
**Liverpool to Madeira & Teneriffe every alternate Wednesday.**

*Full particulars may be obtained on application to—*

### ELDER, DEMPSTER & CO.,
**14, Castle Street, LIVERPOOL.**

Leadenhall Chambers, 4, St. Mary Axe, LONDON.
8, Commercial Buildings, Cross Street, MANCHESTER.
70, Queen Square, BRISTOL.
Luisenhof, Neue Groninger Strasse, HAMBURG.

# The Hotel Metropole
## GRAND CANARY.

THIS HOTEL, facing the sea, and situated in its own grounds, is the best and healthiest in the Islands, being away from the town, and having the full advantage of the sea ozone.

The Comfort of English visitors is made a speciality of.

The Hotel contains very large and beautifully furnished Reception Rooms, Dining, Billiard, and Smoking Rooms, Bath Rooms, Hot or Cold Water.

---

TERMS from 8s., 10s., 12s., and 15s. (according to position of Room) per Day each Person, inclusive.

---

*Two occupying one room, a reduction will be made.*
**CHILDREN AND SERVANTS, 5s. PER DAY EACH.**

---

Coffee after Dinner served in the large Patio or Verandahs.

---

DOCTOR AND TRAINED NURSE.

---

SANITATION EXCELLENT.

---

*Telegraphic Address:—*
### "METROPOLE, LASPALMAS."
A.B.C. CODE USED.

R. G. FALKNER, MANAGER.

| AGENTS IN LONDON: | AGENTS IN LIVERPOOL: |
|---|---|
| Messrs. ELDER, DEMPSTER & Co., Leadenhall Chambers, 4, St. Mary Axe. | Messrs. ELDER, DEMPSTER & Co., 14, Castle Street. |

ORIGINAL AND
ONLY GENUINE

## FOR
## COUGHS, COLDS, ASTHMA, BRONCHITIS.

# DR. J. COLLIS BROWNE'S
# CHLORODYNE.

D<sup>R.</sup> J. COLLIS BROWNE (late Army Medical Staff) DISCOVERED A REMEDY, to denote which he coined the word CHLORODYNE. Dr. Browne is the SOLE INVENTOR, and, as the composition of Chlorodyne cannot possibly be discovered by Analysis (organic substances defying elimination), and since the formula has never been published, it is evident that any statement to the effect that a compound is identical with Dr. Browne's Chlorodyne *must be false.*

D<sup>R.</sup> J. COLLIS BROWNE'S CHLORODYNE. —Vice-Chancellor Sir W. PAGE WOOD stated publicly in Court that Dr. J. COLLIS BROWNE was UNDOUBTEDLY the INVENTOR of CHLORODYNE, that the whole story of the defendant Freeman was deliberately untrue, and he regretted to say it had been sworn to.—See *Times,* July 13, 1864.

D<sup>R.</sup> J. COLLIS BROWNE'S CHLORODYNE is the TRUE PALLIATIVE in

N<sub>EURALGIA, GOUT, CANCER,
TOOTHACHE, RHEUMATISM.</sub>

T<sub>HE</sub> GREAT SPECIFIC FOR C<sub>HOLERA,</sub>

D<sub>IARRHŒA, DYSENTERY.</sub>

GENERAL BOARD of HEALTH, London, REPORT that it ACTS as a CHARM, one dose generally sufficient.

Dr. GIBBON, Army Medical Staff, Calcutta, states :—"2 DOSES COMPLETELY CURED ME of DIARRHŒA."

The *Illustrated London News* of Sept. 28, 1895, says :—
"If I were asked which single medicine I should prefer to take abroad with me, as likely to be most generally useful, to the exclusion of all others, I should say CHLORODYNE. I never travel without it, and its general applicability to the relief of a large number of simple ailments forms its best recommendation."

Royal Irish Fusiliers, Cork, Feb. 6, 1896.
DEAR SIR,—I wish to give public testimony to the infinite value which your remedy for Dysentery and Diarrhœa (DR. BROWNE'S CHLORODYNE) proved to several members of the Special Service Corps, in the recent Ashanti Expedition. I bought a small bottle just before leaving London for West Africa, and having used it myself with beneficial result, treated some of my comrades with equal success (though some of them were very bad). I should be very glad to recommend it to anyone about to travel in a treacherous climate, where they are so much exposed to this dangerous malady.—Gratefully yours,
G. SMITH, "Band," R.I.F.
To J. T. DAVENPORT.

D<sup>R.</sup> J. COLLIS BROWNE'S CHLORODYNE rapidly cuts short all attacks of

E<sub>PILEPSY, SPASMS, COLIC,
PALPITATION, HYSTERIA.</sub>

I<sub>MPORTANT</sub> CAUTION. — The IMMENSE SALE of this REMEDY has given rise to many UNSCRUPULOUS IMITATIONS. Be careful to observe Trade Mark. Of all Chemists, 1s. 1½d., 2s. 9d., and 4s. 6d.

Sole Manufacturer, J. T. DAVENPORT, 33, Great Russell St., W.C.

# BOVRIL.

## ITS ORIGIN.

**BOVRIL** is Beef, the entire lean of the best Beef procurable. Not the Forty Pounds Weight of Beef which would have to be eaten before the nourishment contained in one pound of Bovril could be imparted to the system, but Forty Pounds of the primest parts obtained from the finest selected cattle reared in Australia and South America, concentrated by a special process, rendering it the most perfect form of strengthening, stimulating, easily digestible nourishment in the smallest possible bulk.

## ITS USES.

**BOVRIL** is meat and drink at one draught, providing a perfect, warming, nourishing, invigorating beverage, which fortifies the system against Colds, Chills, and other Winter Ailments.

**BOVRIL** imparts fresh strength and renewed vitality to the healthy, and forms a true stimulative, recuperative food for Invalids, who relish it and retain it when other foods are rejected.

**BOVRIL** adds piquancy and nourishment to Soups, Sauces, Gravies, Ragout of Game or Poultry, Meat Pies or Puddings, Croquettes, Rissoles, and all Entrées, and is invaluable in every kitchen where economy and high-class cooking is desired.

**BOVRIL LTD.**, *Food Specialists*, **LONDON, E.C.**
Directors:—THE RIGHT HON. LORD PLAYFAIR, G.C.B., LL.D., Chairman;
DR. FARQUHARSON, M.P., and others.

---

### 'EASY SHAVING'
### WITH 'MAB' THE RAZOR

The Mab Razor is a revelation to those who have habitually used the big clumsy Razor of the period. The ease with which it is manipulated enables the user to shave in half the usual time. The blade is manufactured of the finest ENGLISH STEEL, and can be had either plain or hollow ground. At the great Shaving Contest at the Royal Aquarium, little Nellie Wick SHAVED FIVE MEN in 4 min. 42 sec. with the MAB RAZOR.

**Can be used entirely without stropping.**

*Many flattering notices from the Press and unsolicited Testimonials.*

H.M.S. "BEAGLE," RIO DE JANEIRO, Oct. 1, 1894.
DEAR SIRS,—I am pleased to say that the "Mab" Razors arrived all right and they proved excellent. I had hardly time to open the parcel before I had half the ship's company asking for them—in fact they are all in love with Mab. I enclose amount for two dozen more, which kindly send at once.
H. OVENDEN, Qualified Signalman.

Prices—Black handle, 2/6 ; Ivory, 3/6. Pair in case (Black), 7/6 ; Ivory, 9/6, post free.

**'MAB' Co., 94 Newhall St., BIRMINGHAM**

---

## Swan . .
## Fountain
## . . Pen.

**10/6, 16/6, 25/-**

Known the world over as absolutely reliable.

In the use of this famous pen, time and money are saved while handwriting is improved.

**CATALOGUE ON APPLICATION.**

**MABIE TODD & BARD,**
93, CHEAPSIDE, LONDON, E.C.

www.ingramcontent.com/pod-product-compliance
Lightning Source LLC
Chambersburg PA
CBHW021804230426
43669CB00008B/631